The School Mental Health Toolkit

The School Mental Health Toolkit

A practical guide to supporting the whole school community

Andrew Cowley

BLOOMSBURY EDUCATION
LONDON OXFORD NEW YORK NEW DELHI SYDNEY

BLOOMSBURY EDUCATION
Bloomsbury Publishing Plc
50 Bedford Square, London, WC1B 3DP, UK
Bloomsbury Publishing Ireland Limited
29 Earlsfort Terrace, Dublin 2, D02 AY28, Ireland

BLOOMSBURY, BLOOMSBURY EDUCATION and the Diana logo
are trademarks of Bloomsbury Publishing Plc

First published in the UK 2025 by Bloomsbury Publishing Plc

This edition published in the UK 2025 by Bloomsbury Publishing Plc

Text copyright © Andrew Cowley, 2025

Andrew Cowley has asserted their right under the Copyright, Designs and
Patents Act, 1988, to be identified as Author of this work.

Bloomsbury Publishing Plc does not have any control over, or responsibility for,
any third-party websites referred to or in this book. All internet addresses given
in this book were correct at the time of going to press. The author and publisher
regret any inconvenience caused if addresses have changed or sites have
ceased to exist, but can accept no responsibility for any such changes

All rights reserved. No part of this publication may be: i) reproduced or transmitted
in any form, electronic or mechanical, including photocopying, recording or by means
of any information storage or retrieval system without prior permission in writing from
the publishers; or ii) used or reproduced in any way for the training, development or
operation of artificial intelligence (AI) technologies, including generative AI technologies.
The rights holders expressly reserve this publication from the text and data mining
exception as per Article 4(3) of the Digital Single Market Directive (EU) 2019/790

A catalogue record for this book is available from the British Library

ISBN: PB: 978-1-8019-9515-3; ePDF: 978-1-8019-9516-0; ePub: 978-1-8019-9513-9

2 4 6 8 10 9 7 5 3 1 (paperback)

Typeset by Newgen KnowledgeWorks Pvt. Ltd., Chennai, India
Printed and bound in the UK by CPI Group Ltd, CR0 4YY

To find out more about our authors and books, visit www.bloomsbury.com
and sign up for our newsletters

For product safety related questions contact productsafety@bloomsbury.com

To Honey, who makes me smile, laugh and think.

Contents

Acknowledgements ix
Foreword by Dr Poppy Gibson xi

Introduction 1

1 **Creating a culture to support mental health in school** 9
 Case study: Growing a culture to grow a community, Meadowbank Primary School 24

2 **Leading and managing to promote positive mental health** 29
 Case study: Leading with values, Bramley Sunnyside Junior School 46

3 **Staff mental health and wellbeing** 51
 Interview with Gemma Scotcher of Education Support: Staff, statistics and support 66

4 **Identifying needs** 71
 Case study: An international perspective, Emmanuelle Brunet, latterly of Obersee Bilingual School 84

5 **Targeted support and appropriate provisions** 87
 Case study: Navigating the mental health journey, Stratford School Academy 102

6 **Staff professional development and training** 107
 Case study: The power of language and kindness, Hillborough Junior School 121

7 **Enabling the student voice** 125
 Case study: Hearing the voices of students, Altrincham Grammar School for Girls 143

8 Enabling parent voice and working with parents and carers 147
Interview with Ellie Costello of Square Pegs: Developing the relationship between schools and parents 159

9 Developing external provision 165

10 Developing the curriculum and learning experience 179

Conclusion 201

Appendix 1 207
Appendix 2 211
Appendix 3 212
References 213
Index 217

Acknowledgements

Writing is by its nature a solitary process, but in the experience of every writer there are a group of people who enable, support, encourage and critique the writing process, through their presence, their kindness and their love. My writing experience is no different and I would like to thank the following amazing people.

Firstly, the editorial team at Bloomsbury. Emily Evans, my commissioning editor, enabled this book to be written, and I would like to congratulate her on the birth of her daughter as I was completing my first draft. Lucy Vallance, for stepping in to support me when Emily was on parental leave, Lucy Tipton for giving me my first feedback and Amelia Mehra for coming back to me with thankfully very few edits on the manuscript.

Every interviewee for my case studies provided a wealth of information and shows that there are schools taking such a positive attitude to mental health and wellbeing in a range of settings. Nichola Hill, Laura Robson, Danielle Green, Emmanuelle Brunet, Rhianne Bond, Nadirah Khan, Liam O'Donnell, Penny Whelan, Morag Howes, Suzanne Bradshaw and Jack Stevens: thank you all for taking time out of your busy school commitments to talk to me. Ellie Costello of Square Pegs and Gemma Scotcher of Education Support both gave me a couple of hours of their wisdom and reflection, as readers will see from their interviews.

Of my social media community, I particularly wish to thank Lisa Fathers and John Magee for their support in enabling my case studies and encouraging my writing process. Adrian Bethune, Rae Snape, Maria O'Neill, Matt Young and Helen Dlamini have always been behind all my writing, as have Clare Erasmus, Samira Ashraf, Anoara Mughal, Cherryl Drabble, Patrick Ottley-O'Connor, Nicola Owen, Jessica Parker, Charlie Burley, Fiona Hims, Steve Waters, Kimberley Evans, Thérèse Hoyle and Frederika Roberts.

From the Carnegie Centre of Excellence for Mental Health in Schools at Leeds Beckett University, I would like to pass my sincere thanks to Rachel Bostwick for the opportunity to support coaching for both the Mental Health Award and the Senior Designated Mental Health Leaders programme. Thanks also to Martina Sanna, Louise Turner, Deborah Rose and Louise Clarke for their superb administration, and to Sue Webb, Liz Dawson and Andy Mellor for their support for the coaching network and the wider picture of mental health in schools.

Special thanks must be extended to Dr Poppy Gibson for her foreword for *The School Mental Health Toolkit* and support for all my writing. Sophie Smith-Tong has given her words of wisdom and experience in EYFS for the curriculum chapter, and Kelly Hannaghan, who has been a good friend since we met when I was writing *The Wellbeing Toolkit*, has added her thoughts about parental relationships and continued to publicise my work at every opportunity.

Unusually, I would like to thank my osteopath. Lolitaire Healey sorted out various ailments that made it tricky to sit at a computer or laptop, but also listened to my thoughts about my content and provided a couple of nuggets contained within the text.

Nothing, however, would be possible without the love and support of my family. Zoé, my wife, and our daughters, Evie and Lily, have become used to the sound of fingers on the keyboard and I would like to thank them for their patience.

Finally, I must acknowledge the role of my granddaughter Honey. She arrived on the same day as my author copies of *The Wellbeing Curriculum* and has brought light and joy to us all. The THINK acronym arose from one of our early morning walks, and although I thought this aloud to her at a time before she was talking, I felt her nodding in agreement. It is for her generation that our schools and educators need to think about how they support the mental health of our school communities in the future.

Foreword
Dr Poppy Gibson

Educators and leaders in our schools understand that we are now teaching in a landscape where conversations around mental health and wellbeing are essential. The Covid pandemic affected children and families in ways still not yet fully understood and, combined with contemporary pressures of the cost of living crisis and waiting times for mental health diagnoses, it is vital now more than ever that we invest time in deepening our understanding of how to support mental health in our classrooms.

The School Mental Health Toolkit by Andrew Cowley is an accessible and purposeful guide to supporting the mental health of our young people, and indeed the whole school community, in challenging times. Based on the World Health Organisation's concept that there is no health without mental health (2022), and building on the government's Green Paper (Department of Health and Department for Education, 2017) that details eight areas of learning for mental health leaders, this book provides practical advice on how to build on the good work that our teachers are already doing, in terms of daily support and referrals. *The School Mental Health Toolkit* provides advice that is relevant to all school staff, advising how we can facilitate meaningful discussions with the young people in our classrooms to help them to understand what mental health is, providing them with tangible strategies to take forward into adulthood and helping them to feel empowered to talk if they are overwhelmed.

The ten chapters in *The School Mental Health Toolkit* cover a wide range of areas for those concerned with supporting mental health in schools. There are chapters that discuss staff mental health and wellbeing and explore staff professional development; chapters that support leaders in managing mental health; chapters that look at the role of parents, families and carers and the need for partnership with external agencies; and chapters that look at practical ways to enhance our curriculum. Each chapter ends with a thoughtful exercise, encouraging the reader to reflect upon what they have learned through the simple acronym 'THINK': Time, Holistic, Inclusive, Non-judgemental and Knowledgeable. Using THINK, the reader can make key connections between theory and practice and consider how to take forward what they have read into their daily role.

Author Andrew Cowley, an experienced school leader and teacher since 1992, and a trusted coach for the designated mental health leaders training for the Carnegie Centre of Excellence, offers an insightful and often inspiring perspective on fresh ways to make space for mental health conversations, including a much-needed focus upon the positive sides of mental health for successful learning.

In terms of readership, while a core source for designated mental health leads in schools, *The School Mental Health Toolkit* by Andrew Cowley would also be highly valuable to all staff. This accessible text is recommended for senior leaders, pastoral staff, teachers, teaching assistants, early career teachers and trainee teachers. Mental health is everyone's responsibility, and this text is one way schools can help further equip their staff with tools to support the young people in their care. This book is the perfect next addition for any staffroom, opening channels to break down stigma around mental health and encouraging reflection and action to create a positive and supportive school culture.

Dr Poppy Gibson, Lecturer in Education, Open University

Introduction

'It is an odd paradox that a society, which can now speak openly and unabashedly about topics that were once unspeakable, still remains largely silent when it comes to mental illness.'

(Glenn Close, 2010)

Mental health is a difficult topic for many to discuss. Reasons are many and varied, relating in part to personal experience and in part to historical and cultural perspectives around the subject; *The Madness of George III* is presented as entertainment on both stage and screen, yet in the context of events, it was a time of great distress and anguish for the monarch and his family. It was a matter discussed by politicians of the time and hidden from a wider audience. Films such as *Psycho* or *The Shining* present mental illness in a misleading way and perhaps as something to fear, with the title of the former being one of those terms often used to describe certain unpredictable behaviours, and the latter spawning a generation of poor one-line impersonations of 'Here's Johnny!'

All of us have a heart; cardiac health is spoken of openly. We all have teeth, natural or otherwise, yet dental care is not a subject from which we shy away. Everyone is in possession of a brain, yet is there an openness or a willingness to discuss mental health without fear or favour? Is there a worry, a stigma, a fear of being uncomfortable or does a lack of comprehension and of empathy contribute to the lack of conversation? Or is it because there is confusion about what the term 'mental health' means?

Defining mental health

'Mental health is a state of mental well-being that enables people to cope with the stresses of life, realise their abilities, learn well and work well, and contribute to their community.'

(World Health Organisation, 2022)

The World Health Organisation goes on to state the role of mental health as being part of the holistic picture of health overall, describing how it is a fundamental human right and how it underpins both individual and collective wellbeing and supports the making of decisions and the building of relationships.

Mental health conditions include a variety of diagnoses and disorders, some requiring medical or therapeutic intervention. Some conditions can lead to difficulty and distress, with the impaired ability to function and lower levels of mental wellbeing in some but not all cases. Psychological and biological factors may make some people more vulnerable but, equally, socio-economic and geopolitical factors can impact negatively upon mental health. Bullying and physical chastisement, particularly during sensitive development stages, can have lifelong implications.

Mental health, though, is more than the absence of mental ill health. In considering physical health, it is generally considered that this is supported by diet, exercise, sleep and hydration. Positive physical health is seen as desirable and necessary as part of overall wellbeing. By extension, and through implication, with mental health being part of the all-embracing view of health, we should also be thinking about positive mental health – about being mentally well. In the same way as individuals and communities promote their physical health, they can surely do the same for their mental health. Promotion and prevention strategies are part of mental health care, including self-care. Not every person exposed to a risk factor will develop a recognised mental health condition, just as not all those subject to protective factors will be immune from a diagnosis requiring intervention. The interaction of risk and protective factors affects everyone differently, but the core knowledge is that mental health can be both undermined and/or enhanced by a range of circumstances. Mental health should be considered as a spectrum, with positive mental health at one end, ranging to mental ill health at the other, which can include more common conditions such as depression and anxiety, along with more complicated conditions such as schizophrenia or bipolar disorder.

Mental health and education

I trained as a teacher in 1992. There was nothing in my training about mental health and wellbeing, not my own, my potential future colleagues' nor that of the children I would subsequently teach. My training was very much about 'the whole child' yet seemingly omitted a key part of their development: growth and progress. Likewise, there was nothing in my induction as what was then called a newly qualified teacher or NQT (now known as early career teachers or ECTs – a longer and more exacting process), nor in any training days or staff development courses. We had a push on PSHE (personal, social and health education), which is still very much with us, and then SMSC (spiritual, moral, social and cultural development), an overarching umbrella reaching across personal development in the whole curriculum. We also had a document called 'Every Child Matters' (UK Government, 2003), with a focus on being safe and healthy, being economically aware and making a positive contribution to society, alongside enjoyment and achievement in learning. This document and its agenda faded from view after 2010 and the election of the coalition government. There was training out there, but schools had to look for it from organisations such as the Anna Freud Centre and Place2Be; this was often passed to the SENDCo or family worker to access, and little if any of the material, information or strategies made their way into the hands of teachers. The only whole-school training around mental health that I experienced was INSET days and other CPD sessions that I delivered, at around the same time that *The Wellbeing Toolkit* was coming together.

Go back further in time, to our own school days. Was there anything about emotions, feelings and worries in our primary and secondary experience? I can recall little if any in the way of support – just a very intense focus on examination results and top grades. It was not until my experience in sixth form that I felt any interest was shown in my learning process and personal development, with which I have credited Janet Lawley and Pauline and Chris Collier within my previous writing. Fortunately, I never experienced any issues around exam anxiety or had any issues around my mental health when I was at school; reflecting upon this now, I wouldn't have known whom to turn to in school if this had been the case, but I had friends who found the transition to university or the world of employment challenging because they hadn't been provided with a skill set to support their emotional wellbeing.

As young people, school was often a place where mental health would first be heard of in the playground, and not in a positive way either. Terms that would now be seen as inappropriate were used as playground banter or insults; references to the local mental health facility and to the unpredictable behaviours of various members of the local community demonstrate that, as young people, many of us who are now adult might have been exposed to ignorance, stigma and bigotry around mental health. In popular culture, Pink Floyd observed that 'The lunatic is on the grass' in 'Brain Damage', and latterly Fun Boy Three sang 'The Lunatics are Taking Over the Asylum', words repeated no doubt in a few bullying scenarios and which demonstrate that in the past when mental health has been discussed, it has been seen as something negative, bad, challenging and dangerous.

Statistics on the mental health of young people

Mainstream and social media sometimes make reference to 'the mental health crisis', but rather than use an emotive term, a look at the statistics from the most recent NHS report in England (NHS England, 2023) will demonstrate the need that our young people currently have.

The key statistic from the data in England shows that in 2023, about one in five children and young people aged eight to 25 years had a probable mental disorder. This was 20.3 per cent of eight- to 16-year-olds, 23.3 per cent of 17- to 19-year-olds and 21.7 per cent of 20- to 25-year-olds.

In 2021 this figure was one in six, and in 2017 it was one in nine. That this figure is now one in five shows why schools and society need to be acutely aware of the mental health and wellbeing of our young people, and equally aware of the need to support them.

The other important statistics from the NHS report are as follows:

- After a rise in prevalence between 2017 and 2020, rates of probable mental disorder remained stable in all age groups between 2022 and 2023.
- More than one in four children aged eight to 16 years (26.8 per cent) with a probable mental disorder had a parent who could not afford for their child to take part in activities outside school or college, compared with one in ten (10.3 per cent) of those unlikely to have a mental disorder.
- Children aged 11 to 16 years with a probable mental disorder were five times more likely than those unlikely to have a mental disorder to have been bullied in person (36.9 per cent, compared with 7.6 per cent). They were also more likely to have been bullied online (10.8 per cent, compared with 2.6 per cent).
- Seventeen- to 25-year-olds with a probable mental disorder were three times more likely to not be able to afford to take part in activities such as sports, days out or socialising with friends, compared with those unlikely to have a mental disorder (26.1 per cent, compared with 8.3 per cent).
- Just over half (54.8 per cent) of young people aged 17 to 25 years reported being worried about the impact of climate change.
- Young women aged 17 to 23 years were less likely to be optimistic than young men about having enough money (38.5 per cent, compared

with 60.5 per cent) and about their health (including mental health and wellbeing) (51.4 per cent, compared with 67.8 per cent).

- In 2023, eating disorders were identified in 12.5 per cent of 17- to 19-year-olds, with rates four times higher in young women (20.8 per cent) than young men (5.1 per cent).
- Of 11- to 16-year-olds, 2.6 per cent were identified with eating disorders, with rates four times higher in girls (4.3 per cent) than boys (1.0 per cent), while 5.9 per cent of 20- to 25-year-olds were identified with eating disorders, with no difference in rates evident between women and men.

Concerns are shared across the other constituent nations of the United Kingdom. In 2020, almost one quarter of young people in Scotland experienced two or more psychological problems in a single week and around one out of every ten children and young people between the ages of five and 16 had a mental illness that could be diagnosed clinically, but they lacked the services to support them (CYPCS, 2024). In Cymru/Wales in 2023, around one in every five children and young people aged eight to 25 had a mental health difficulty (20.3 per cent of eight- to 16-year-olds and 23.3 per cent of 17- to 19-year-olds) (Shafan-Azhar and Treloar, 2023). In Northern Ireland, the figure in 2023 was one in eight children who had a mental health difficulty, with 47.5 per cent of young people aged 11 to 19 years having experienced at least one adverse childhood experience (Mental Health Champion, 2023).

Issues around young people's mental health are global. The most recent report from the World Health Organisation (2021) recognises that, around the world, about one in seven ten- to 19-year-olds has experienced a mental disorder. The report goes on to state that depression, anxiety and behavioural disorders are among the leading causes of illness and disability in adolescents, and that suicide is the fourth leading cause of death among 15- to 29-year-olds. The consequences of failing to address the mental health needs of our children and young people extend to adulthood, impairing both physical and mental health and limiting opportunities to lead fulfilling lives as adults.

The reasons behind the statistics are multiple and complex. Poverty is one, the pandemic is another, with the changing nature of our national and global societies and our family structures also being a likely contributor. We need to consider problems, but our minds should turn also to solutions.

About this book

The School Mental Health Toolkit germinated from the seed of the 2017 government Green Paper (DoH and DfE, 2017) requiring schools in England to have a designated mental health lead by 2025. Of the other constituent parts of the UK, Scotland has had a mental health strategy since 2017 and Wales since March 2021, having issued a framework to embed emotional and mental wellbeing, while a similar structure was put into place in Northern Ireland in the same year. We don't undertake roles in school because our respective governments direct us, but because there is a need to support mental health in schools, as detailed in the aforementioned statistics. *The School Mental Health Toolkit* is seeded also in this need, and it is for the audience of this book to enable the seed to take root, to thrive and to flourish, to build positive mental health into everyday practice.

Mental health is the responsibility of everyone in the community, and although schools will have a designated lead, leadership always requires being part of a team and is impacted by how we work within that team. The book is aimed not only at our designated leads for mental health, but also at headteachers and other senior leaders, including governors, to consider mental health as a long-term strategy – especially if staff move on and a new face is brought into the role. I hope also that the book is shared by other members of support staff and teaching staff, including our ECTs and initial teacher trainees, as they grow in their understanding and support of mental health in schools.

I have tried to weave a few golden threads through this book. Culture, context, compassion and community run through each chapter; empathy and emotional intelligence feature too. Readers familiar with *The Wellbeing Toolkit* (2019) and *The Wellbeing Curriculum* (2021) may recognise these threads as part of a holistic view of the support for mental health and wellbeing that we can and should be embracing in our schools.

- Chapter 1 is about moral purpose, focusing upon the culture and ethos around mental health in schools, whether starting from scratch or working from an established position. I will discuss the 'why' around mental health strategies, alongside practical challenges to cultures.
- Chapter 2 is more practical, considering how to lead on mental health, including how we might gather data and use it to support our strategy.

- Chapter 3 will address staff wellbeing and mental health, particularly in the light of more recent areas of concern arising from the statistics raised by Education Support's annual Teacher Wellbeing Index (2023).
- Chapter 4 will address how staff may begin identifying mental health needs in school, considering the impact on attendance, behaviour and attainment of adverse childhood experiences.
- Chapter 5 will discuss the interventions at different levels across the school, from the support provided for all pupils to the specific programmes for identified needs, with particular reference to protective factors.
- Chapter 6 concerns continued professional development (CPD) and training for staff, including running training sessions and different roles in which staff can be trained to support the whole-school approach to mental health.
- Chapter 7 and Chapter 8 are aimed at enabling, hearing and gathering the voices of pupils and of parents and carers, and how these voices can be valued and used to inform our ongoing strategy.
- Chapter 9 is concerned with external provision, what might be out there and some of the challenges arising from local resourcing and funding issues.
- Chapter 10 rounds off the book with a discussion of practical and authentic ways of building mental health and wellbeing into the curriculum without being tokenistic.

Interspersed between the chapters are a number of case studies from six schools – a mix of primary and secondary, including one from overseas – giving a practical oversight of the actions and processes in place where schools have been prioritising mental health and wellbeing for some period of time. There are also two powerful interviews, one with Gemma Scotcher of Education Support, where we discuss the findings of the Teacher Wellbeing Index and the implications for schools, and the second with Ellie Costello of Square Pegs, giving an insight into respect for the voice of parents and carers.

Each chapter is rounded up by asking the reader to think about mental health and wellbeing within the context of the following themes of the acronym THINK: Time, Holistic, Inclusive, Non-judgemental and Knowledgeable.

- **Time:** We have become accustomed in schools to short time frames concerning results, progress and inspection. Time is a virtue – our most precious gift and one not to be wasted. Our strategy for mental health and wellbeing will take time and patience.

- **Holistic:** Please don't put mental health in one box, learning in another and progress, safeguarding and behaviour in others. On the contrary – consider each as part of the whole of the school, the whole child and the whole community.
- **Inclusive:** Mental health is for everyone – not just that 20 per cent of children with a diagnosed condition, but for all pupils, for their understanding and empathy, their resilience and their support. Inclusivity embraces the whole community, parents and carers and the whole staff, regardless of their role.
- **Non-judgemental:** The success of the role of mental health lead depends upon challenging any prejudice, stigma, fear or misinformation, facing up to amateur diagnosis and self-diagnosis, and recognising barriers that arise from the experience and opinions of others.
- **Knowledgeable:** Everything that this role entails must come from a base of knowledge, whether this arises from hard or soft data, from professional judgement or from the expert support of external agencies.

This book will not be an off-the-shelf solution, but I hope that it is part of the solution and a part that does make the reader THINK about making young people's mental health a priority in our schools in the years ahead.

1 Creating a culture to support mental health in school

> **Chapter overview**
>
> In this chapter, we will consider:
>
> - developing a sense of belonging
> - strategic thinking – knowing your 'why'
> - leading with values
> - defining mental health in the context of our school
> - building a 'culture of noticing'
> - developing positive behaviours for learning and for mental health
> - mental health and the holistic link with behaviour, safeguarding and attendance.

Developing a sense of belonging

I am sometimes asked, 'Why would I want to have a culture to support mental health and wellbeing in my school?' The simple answer is 'Well, why wouldn't you?', but the reasons run deeper than this sharp retort.

The culture around mental health is actually just part of the culture of the school; to have different cultures for other aspects of the school can be inconsistent and lead to challenges regarding boundaries and expectations. This is why a holistic approach is necessary. The culture of the school embraces the cultures around safeguarding, behaviour, assessment and learning, staff welfare, and relationships with parents and with students. Culture embraces every aspect of school life and the school day. The simple answer is now: 'Everything starts with culture.'

Social media as we know can be a bearpit of raw emotions, immediate and ill-considered responses, and education isn't immune from this, especially on X (formerly Twitter). When mental health training for schools is advertised, it can be met with 'Haven't teachers got enough to do without adding pupils' mental health to their workload?', and discussion of the post-pandemic mental health crisis among young people is often met with denials that it exists or with the 'sigh' emoji. Social media, however, doesn't run our schools, and neither do blue-tick influencers and 'loud' voices; school cultures are established by the leadership, the staff and the community, which form the seed from which the culture supporting positive mental health will grow.

Build or grow?

Are cultures built or grown? Anything that is built – your school building, for example – is solid and tangible, reasonably permanent and largely unchanging, aside from the occasional aesthetic improvement or mitigation if built with crumbling concrete. Something that is grown requires different care; it needs to be nurtured, developed, given the right conditions in which to thrive and survive. Any gardener will know that sweet peas, for example, need support to reach their height and full potential. If we take the Parable of the Sower from the New Testament as another metaphor, the seeds on the stony ground will be eaten and wasted, those on the poor soil germinate but cannot root, and those scattered among the thorns grow but are starved of light and cannot fully develop. The same too applies to any culture, which can thrive only in fertile environments, without the challenges that stop it growing in the first place or hamper it after germination. Building is also a linear process, while growth is cyclical; to make one further horticultural metaphor, we learn lessons about improving soil, providing support and protection, giving sustenance and knowing when to make changes. We can have a culture to support mental health in school, just as we might have a culture of learning, a culture of artistic appreciation or, less positively, a culture of bullying. The positive culture is there to benefit the children and the wider community of parents and carers, as well as the staff; all three points and sides of the triangle need to be equally valued and maintained.

Cultures also need to sit alongside relationships, and this is true of any workplace, as positive mental health is a societal concern, and not simply one for schools. Where relationships are sound, people feel supported and can be challenged to improve without feeling threatened; where relationships are toxic, workplaces become divided, unnecessarily stressful and unhappy places to be. Given current concerns about staff retention, with the 2023 Teacher Wellbeing Index from Education Support reporting that over half the teachers surveyed were considering leaving the profession, positive working relationships and a mutually supportive culture are essential to our profession. Culture and relationships: they are about systems and people and ensuring that the two fit seamlessly together.

Supporting mental health and wellbeing should actually be a simple concept, aiming for the minimisation of illness – the act of being healthy, both physically and mentally. As a school leader, despite the simplicity of this definition, promoting a healthy school isn't easy to get right, but it is ever so easy to get wrong, especially if the school culture doesn't support it. Things go wrong where attitudes are negative and cynical, where staff and children don't feel trusted or where they experience undue pressure and stress. While it could be argued that a certain amount of stress can be expected in any environment, as we face deadlines, unexpected events and external pressures, we cannot remain blasé about stress because, in the short term, stress can lead to low mood, fatigue, social withdrawal, irritability and angry outbursts. Stress can have devastating impacts upon long-term health, leading to burnout and insomnia, obesity and diabetes, blood pressure and cardiovascular disease. Any staff and pupil absence is a challenge, but if the absence is due to the stress arising from the institution and its practices, schools need to think about creating a positive culture; avoid the 'myths' about wellbeing, be strategic, act proactively rather than reactively, and lead with your values.

Mental health and wellbeing 'myths'

The greatest 'myth' about mental health and wellbeing is that it is somehow 'fluffy' and a soft option – that it can be addressed in school with the occasional session of meditation, 'Wellbeing Wednesday' as part of the pupils' wellbeing diet and, for staff, a few nice toiletries and the occasional box of cakes in the staffroom. These don't represent a positive culture; they are tokens – kind things to do, but still tokens. By examining each of these in turn, we can see why they aren't supportive of the culture we would like to see in our schools.

'Wellbeing Wednesday' for children is effective if the students have the opportunity to make a choice; for each child that appreciates mindful colouring, there will be one who would rather be in Forest School or gardening club, teaching games to younger children or simply having the chance to talk and listen. Similarly, with staff, hand creams and liquid soaps in the toilets might be appreciated, but if this is provided as an option only in the women's toilets, we are automatically excluding our male staff from the offer. In the same vein, if teachers are all guaranteed one paid 'golden' day off per term or per year, as many schools do, but teaching assistants are not, immediately we are saying that we value one group over the other, unfairly so. Likewise, if as school leaders we support staff who are finding their physical or mental health an issue – which we absolutely should be doing – are we also supporting those staff who are always present, who step up to help in a crisis and who always appear resilient? Some people are less open, more reserved and more private than others, but their right to wellness is of equal worth. **The lesson here is that mental health is for everyone.**

Meditation, mindfulness and massage are again often presented as the wellbeing offer in some schools – sometimes voluntary, while in other settings they are directed. For those people who appreciate and enjoy these practices, the provision of them in school can be beneficial. Many people find there is a positive impact from mindfulness, but it is not for everyone. It can make some people feel self-conscious and uncomfortable. Ultimately, these practices are about self-care, which is very much an individual choice. These are strategies for self-care that we can teach to our children, but they too need a choice – an option not to take part. Self-care cannot be forced; we are managing young people as well as adults, and each of these people is an individual able to express their own preferences and maybe their own emotions. **The lesson here is that mental health is not a tick-box exercise.**

Wellbeing days commonly pepper the INSET days in September or before a half term. They may consist of team-building activities, such as making a spaghetti and marshmallow tower, or they may be off site involving outdoor pursuits. Some even offer the mindfulness and meditation already discussed. These days may also offer discussion of time-management strategies, and many offer the opportunity to complete wellbeing surveys, plus – the highlight for many – the buffet lunch provided by SLT. The message of the day might be well intentioned, but if the strategies discussed are never used and the team-building breaks down as the year hits the stressful point of assessments, data submission and report-writing, the impact of the day will be questioned. If the day doesn't mention the mental health of our pupils, does it have a true purpose? The ends of term are always pinch points for stress; colds and flu seem to peak in November and February, and the weeks up to Christmas – particularly around the Nativity, which can be a highly anxious time for primary teachers – can make the heady days of the start of the year a distant memory. Children will also feel these stresses, particularly around testing and around other points that might make them anxious, such as speaking aloud before an audience. **The lesson here is that mental health is for every day.**

'Golden Time' for the children on a Friday afternoon and cake for the staff at the end of the week are both acts of kindness and appreciation, but do they support mental health effectively? The box of cakes on the staffroom table can be a mere token if those who have a food intolerance or medical condition may be effectively excluded from the offer; staff on break duty while their colleagues tuck in may miss out on the treats, should they have disappeared by lunch, as do those staff who never come to the staffroom. 'Golden Time' is a positive behaviour strategy but, in a similar vein to 'Wellbeing Wednesday', inconsistencies about how it operates and the exclusion of some children from that time for interventions or other reasons could make this an anxious time for some young children. **The lesson here is that mental health is about the 'bigger picture' in schools.**

Strategic thinking – knowing your 'why'

Readers familiar with Simon Sinek's *Start with Why* (2009) will appreciate his notion of starting with your 'why' and how it is communicated and understood through an institution. Although Sinek works from a business model, the clarity of communication and example of leadership that he advocates has a place in any school. If you take the question words – who, when, where, what and how – these are for school policies and protocols: who undertakes certain roles, when and where they take place, what resources are involved and how the impact is measured. 'Why' supersedes these, because 'why' is about intent and moral purpose.

If the offer for mental health and wellbeing in your school follows the model of the myths in the previous section, then it would indicate that it is considered an add-on or is not seriously thought through; there is no 'why', in that it appears tokenistic without any perceptible long-term benefit.

To be effective, your mental health offer requires a strategy and a commitment, served most effectively by the school leader, who will stand tall and say that mental health matters and that it will be supported. It needs the leadership of the school to stand squarely behind any initiative and to drive it. This does not necessarily require one of the senior team to be the mental health lead; in some schools, possibly depending on prior experience or the size of the school, this may not be appropriate. The mental health lead may come from middle leadership or from a recently qualified teacher seeking leadership experience. It may sometimes be led by a committee – a group consisting of staff from across the school, including support staff. Leadership means being part of the team, taking responsibility, being accountable and driving from the middle, in order to develop a sense of belonging.

James Kerr's book *Legacy* (2013) explores cultures and a sense of belonging in the context of the New Zealand All Blacks rugby union team, based upon some cultural shifts after an uncharacteristic run of poor results. The description of 'sweeping the sheds' explains that the role of cleaning the changing rooms of the mud and discarded kit after a training session often falls to the team management and senior players, rather than the apprentices, which might be the case in other sporting institutions. Nobody is too big for this task, and there is a responsibility shared among the group regardless of individual roles. A further illustration of belonging arises where a player was handed their black shirt on their debut for the side. Rather than pull the shirt on, the player spent several minutes caressing the shirt in his hands and burying his face in it, explaining to his team mates that he was the custodian of the shirt, its present holder, and that the intention was to pass it on in a better state. Although we wouldn't expect our children and staff to do the same to their sweatshirts (although I have heard of schools where staff wear school-branded kit like the children), the notion of passing the school on to successor staff and pupils in an improved state is one that embraces the notion of a positive culture. The culture – the whole structure and institution that rugby embraces – is consistent, respected and driven by national tradition and pride; for a small nation such as New Zealand to be such a consistently successful side for over a century, the culture has demonstrably grown and been consistently supported.

Communicating your sense of 'why' can take a number of forms. Any school leader will know that, however many forms of communication are employed, there will always be those who say that they don't know. We can email, tell colleagues in a meeting, reinforce and recap in a one-to-one session or in passing in the corridor, or place information on a noticeboard or the staff WhatsApp group if you have one.

Consider this, though: is it the amount of communication and the volume used in telling colleagues, or the authenticity used and the sense of belonging that is engaged? Communication is more than simply passing a message on; the importance lies in the ethos of it. Tone of voice, choice of language and body language, including eye contact, are equally valid forms of communication. Consistency of practice sends a strong message too. Inconsistency leads to confusion and uncertainty, particularly where the leader switches mood unpredictably or where there is an inconsistent manner and tone with staff and students alike.

Whatever the school has in place for mental health, it will work best where the whole staff backs the initiatives and actions of the mental health lead with substance, and where there are measurable impacts from any interventions and curriculum developments. Senior leaders can provide a strong role model here by demonstrating both self-care and empathetic leadership strategies around monitoring and accountability. This further communicates the sense of 'why' by emphasising the benefits of the approach. If monitoring leads to mistrust, if feedback is taken as a criticism and if suggestions are batted back in a defensive manner, the ethos isn't being embedded. A positive culture around mental health in the school is likely to lessen any perceived criticism and focus the attention instead on constructive means of moving forward.

School development plans that include a section on wellbeing and mental health, for both staff and children, demonstrate a start to strategic thinking. There are school leaders who don't include wellbeing and mental health as a part of their development plan, arguing that it is in place and doesn't require action. If it doesn't require action, has it been acted upon in the past? There is a constantly changing picture around mental health in our schools and society as we know, and the longer-term impacts of the pandemic on young people's use of digital devices, on their attendance and on their emotional resilience must be considered, as must the cost of living crisis, fuel and food poverty and concerns about the impact of environmental matters and climate change. If we are to be authentic in our sense of 'why', then including mental health and wellbeing in our action plans is essential.

Leading with values

Schools love a values statement, often painted large in the lobby, hall or library. Does everyone embrace it? Do children, parents and staff understand it? Values are more than decoration. We all have personal values, which determine our attitudes, beliefs and behaviours, and because we are individuals, these attitudes, beliefs and behaviours may differ from those of our colleagues and pupils. Each, of course, will come to the table with values forged in their family, their faith and their cultural heritage. We cannot impose our values upon someone to whom these are alien, but there are some core values that are universal, and which should be in the fabric of the school, lived and breathed by everyone. The very fact that people hold different values suggests that tolerance and respect should be two such commonly held values.

Leading with values, where these are authentic, means that strategic thinking and proactivity will be at the heart of the way in which you approach mental health and wellbeing in your school. For our colleagues, a reactive approach and an absence of strategy can effectively make their mental health a lottery or a seat-of-the-pants experience. We cannot take this chance; staff being off with stress impacts not only them, their colleagues and the children in the class, but it also impacts their families when that stress goes home. For children, values form part of their language diet and the positive behaviours that are modelled to them on a daily basis.

The school values will form part of the statement of curriculum intent. We will see, especially in Chapter 10, how the definition of curriculum can include the entire experience of a child in each school day and across their years in schools; give some consideration to a statement of intent for mental health, which encompasses school values, communicates the 'why' and demonstrates the sense of belonging for the broader school community.

Church of England and Catholic schools will already have their Christian values to include within any statements. Schools who are members of a multi-academy trust (MAT) may likewise share trust-wide values. Many values are common to all schools, regardless of size, status or demographic. For example:

- **courage:** to stand up to unacceptable behaviour, bad manners, bullying, peer pressure and to external pressures that will not benefit the individual or the school community
- **resilience and perseverance:** to model the ability to keep going and to develop healthy habits, but also to manage the pressures encountered by sensible decision-making, when to ask for help and when to offer it to others
- **celebration:** to know when and how to authentically reward pupils and colleagues for what they have done
- **empathy:** to understand that every work, action and even thought has an impact upon others, either negatively, neutrally or positively; to celebrate the positive, but own and act upon the negative, including how to give and mean a genuine apology
- **time**: admittedly, time isn't a value, but time is the most precious resource that we all have, pupils, parents and staff alike. Respect it, protect it, nurture it but never waste it, because if you do, there will be no time for the mental health of our community.

Defining mental health in the context of the school

Once a culture in which positive mental health can thrive is being established, then the school needs to clearly define what mental health means in its setting and context. There's an element of 'chicken and egg' here, but without working from a basis of a growing positive culture and before communicating the 'why', this piece of the sense of belonging won't fit the jigsaw. The definition that the school has must be mutually agreed, not imposed by a single person or school leadership, because what the school offers will be delivered by those adults in closest daily contact with the children. These adults will interact with pupils in different ways, because of the different relationships and circumstances of the school day; a child will have a different relationship with a midday supervisor, for example, than a class teacher.

Every member of staff, their opinion and their experience needs to be valued in reaching the shared definition. This requires a meeting of all minds, which is probably best organised for a training day when everyone can be present. Include any midday staff who are not already employed in other roles in the school, and pay them for their time; it is worthwhile in the long term.

Ask the big question, 'What does positive mental health look like in our school and in our context?', to drive the discussion. Present the World Health Organisation definition (2022) as a starting point; you may include the wording of this in your final definition, but it is vital to recognise there is no 'one size fits all' approach to mental health. Although many of the practices and principles we employ will be common to all schools, our context will determine our needs and what we can deliver. Knowing the context means having an understanding of the challenges that may arise in supporting mental health in our particular setting. Consider the contexts and challenges of this variety of schools:

- a small village school of a few dozen pupils, where everyone knows each other and there is a level of affluence and education ambition
- a similar village school with a catchment over a wider rural area, where children have little interaction with their peers outside of school
- a small urban school with two socially contrasting catchments, with local tensions that sometimes come into school

- a special school that takes children from a wide area, possibly across county boundaries, whose families do not know each other or interact
- an independent school with boarders, who are the responsibility of their house parent during term time
- a large mixed comprehensive in an area of higher than average social and economic deprivation
- a school where a vocal and active parental group has been publicly critical of staff, of behaviour rules or of aspects of the curriculum
- a large further education (FE) college spread over a number of sites, with student numbers of 10,000 or more.

There are, of course, many more examples of different contexts, with these being just some that I have encountered in recent years. In answering the core question, staff need to consider the challenges and circumstances, the environmental and economic factors, and the pressures and perceptions that affect mental health in the community the school serves. At the same time, there needs to be a recognition that these factors can change – imperceptibly over time, as the community changes, or suddenly, as the pandemic has taught us. An off-the-shelf definition is a starting point, but with context it has meaning and ownership.

Building a 'culture of noticing'

As class teachers, especially in primary, we are often told in our initial teacher training and in our first year or so of teaching to 'know your class' by understanding their strengths and weaknesses, their relationships in the class, their social skills and their family situations. As leaders, we should 'know our staff' in exactly the same way. Consider for one moment the conversations you have with your staff during the day. If those interactions are only around professional discourse, there remains little room for anything other than a stilted relationship to develop. Readers may have experienced their first interaction of the day with some colleagues beginning not with 'Good morning' or 'How are you?' but with 'Can I have…?' or 'Have you done…?', which are impersonal and stressful. While nobody would deny the importance of a professional approach, the relationships in a school will only develop well with a more human approach. My response to being asked to do something before I had even hung my coat up was to retort with 'Good morning. Yes, I am well, thank you. How are you?'

as a diversion device, but also to model the expectation that there should be a clear line between work-time and me-time.

This is why knowing and noticing your staff is important. The conversations we have can be the basis of our relationships in school. As leaders, do you know the names of your colleagues' partners or children? Do you know where they went on holiday or how they spend their spare time? Do you know how their parents are? Some people might dismiss this as small talk, but it is at the core of relationships, because it can build trust, especially if someone has a personal crisis. Having an open-door policy when conversations are only about work is near pointless; why would someone come for advice to someone who had only ever projected themselves as hard and soulless? Proactive thinking means giving consideration to the interactions we have. This theme will be developed in greater depth in the context of staff mental health and wellbeing in Chapter 3.

Knowing your staff is just one side of the culture of noticing; the other is how much and how well we notice our pupils and, to an extent, their parents and carers too. We will be aware of the impact of professional curiosity when it comes to matters of safeguarding, and we should be equally curious when it comes to the emotional health and wellbeing of our pupils. This doesn't necessarily require a change in practice, but a consideration of how that practice is pursued. Take something as simple as the primary school 'meet and greet' on the gate each morning. To families, this may appear to be the school presenting a polite and welcoming face to the community. While this is part of the essential public relations of the school, it can also form an active part of the mental health strategy of the school. This is the first point of contact of the day, presenting the opportunity to notice that child who normally comes bouncing through the gate but today appears less enthusiastic or a little upset. Equally, the child who always arrives looking a little morose because they haven't quite warmed up for the day might pass by with a little more agitation in their facial expression or body language, whereas the child who always greets the staff on duty with a smile might fail to make eye contact. This is also the opportunity for a parent to touch base if their child has experienced a poor night's sleep or if there has been a problem in the home or in the neighbourhood overnight that has affected their mood. This is one starting point for a conversation with the child or their family. In many cases, this may be something that just requires listening or a little reassurance; it is the consistent approach to these seemingly small concerns that demonstrates the culture of positive mental health in action. Noticing and acting upon the small things, especially if the whole staff is engaged, builds the consistency of culture.

Of course, something of greater concern could arise from this observation, which would require appropriate action, but a culture where concerns at any level are noticed and noted, be it on paper or on safeguarding software, enables the school to develop the bigger picture surrounding an individual child or a family. The child who is noted on the gate as not presenting their usual self by different staff on a number of occasions over a short time will require some professional discussion and a level of intervention or monitoring. Left unactioned, though, and where a child may need external agency support, the earlier events might represent a missed opportunity.

Developing positive behaviours for learning and for mental health

Positive behaviours develop best from positive language about mental health. In part, such language can challenge negative perceptions and prejudices, by normalising discussion of mental health. As a school, decisions will need to be reached as to what language is going to be used and how to ensure that it is used consistently. Using a script may form part of lessons in some schools, and it also has a place where restorative justice is in place. While I would not necessarily agree that a scripted conversation is the best way to discuss mental health with young people, some key words and phrases to use can be agreed upon and their use demonstrated in staff training.

Are you going to use the term 'mental health' in your daily interactions, displays and lessons? It would be desirable to do so, in order to establish the term in our pupils' vocabulary and to counter stigma. However, there may be a feeling that the excessive use of the term may result in a fatigued and jaded response, rather than the positive outcomes of increased resilience and talking openly. By all means, use the term 'mental health', but do so in a way that develops the vocabulary around the subject for students and staff alike, and shows that their mental health is both valued and valuable. The vocabulary around mental health in the curriculum is further discussed in Chapter 10, but while establishing the school culture and ethos, consider the following terms: emotional health, feelings, happiness, mental wellbeing, wellness, positivity, empathy and satisfaction. These are all words with specific meaning, but also with a place in promoting the culture of positive mental health.

Positive behaviour is also promoted through the recognition that the mental health and wellbeing of each member of the community will be respected, but in turn there has to be a respect for the feelings of others and all feelings are valid. A message that we can affect others positively or negatively through our words and actions needs to be actively promoted in every aspect of school life, as does how those hurting the feelings of others should respond in apology.

Mental health and the holistic link with behaviour, safeguarding and attendance

When schools recognise in their statements of intent that mental health impacts all aspects of school life, they will consider how behaviour, safeguarding and attendance have been affected, particularly in relation to the changing picture around mental health and the longer-term influence of the pandemic period. Schools that cross-reference their behaviour, safeguarding and attendance policies with their intent for mental health are on the way to embedding holistic links; schools that have this in their practice and culture will see the difference that empathetic and pragmatic approaches make.

Behaviour

Debates around behaviour often focus on the binary perspectives of restorative practices against a more sanctions-led approach. In reality, behaviour is more nuanced than this and approaches contain elements of both, but the key element is consistency of application and approach. All schools want to see 'good' behaviour, but is the behaviour good because of the expectations and ethos of the school, or is it compliant because of fear of consequences? The phrase 'all behaviour is communication' should not be considered simply in terms of poor behaviour either. The child who never breaks a rule and completes everything on time is also communicating something in their behaviour, be it respect for rules or trepidation of the sanctions for failure to follow them. The culture of noticing will spot the incidents where behaviour is poor, but equally it needs to notice when it is good. Likewise, there needs to be an awareness of the effect upon young people of detentions and other consequences of seemingly minor breaches of uniform or equipment codes. An undone top button can be solved by a polite reminder rather than a missed playtime; not having a sharpened pencil is an inconvenience and not a major disciplinary matter. A detention room with some children there for disruption or fighting and others for not having a ruler will generate a sense of injustice and imbalance. Schools should have rules, of course, but in a culture of positive mental health they should support order and calm in the 'why' of behaviour.

Safeguarding

Safeguarding is ultimately about working together to prevent and stop the risks and experiences of abuse and neglect. Schools will have to deal with incidents around grooming, sexual exploitation and substance abuse, among other traumatic concerns. Mental health also fits the safeguarding remit, and our positive culture will recognise that while a major trauma may lead to serious mental health consequences, other incidents that adults may regard as minor could be part of a bigger picture or a starting point for something that could develop into a more serious concern. A culture that says that everything should be recorded and nothing judged as insignificant sets the right tone.

Attendance

Attendance has been lower since the pandemic, with larger numbers of children regularly missing individual days or longer periods. There are a number of reasons for this, but there needs to be a recognition that the mental health of both children and parents has been a factor here. The school culture should be one that considers support and the reasons for poorer attendance ahead of warning letters and fines, which may simply result in a choice for home education and children being lost to the system.

Final thoughts

Growing a culture of positive mental health is not easy, and certainly not instant, but it is rewarding and valuable in the long term. Ignore the myths, be proactive and strategic, act on the negatives and the challenges and think ahead. Get it right, and those cakes on the staffroom table won't be a token; they will be an honest indication that you are getting it right.

So, why would you want to have a culture that supports positive mental health and wellbeing in your school? Well, why wouldn't you?

THINK about creating a culture to support mental health in school

Time

- Cultures don't develop overnight and cannot be enforced. A strong positive culture may take three to five years to be fully effective.
- Set realistic targets for progress.

Holistic

- Mental health doesn't sit in a box on its own. The culture around mental health is also the culture of every aspect of the school, from behaviour to safeguarding, and from learning to assessment.

Inclusive

- Every single voice needs to be heard, even though some stakeholders are more reticent and less confident. Voices can be expressed through the written word, facial expression and body language too.
- Cultures need to be led, but they also need to be embraced by everyone.

Non-judgemental

- There will be a range of opinions and experiences around mental health. Never dismiss them, always respect them and remember the 'why' of the school in trying to change them.

Knowledgeable

- Know your school context. Particularly when moving schools, you may find that a model that worked in one location may not succeed elsewhere.
- Beware of lines such as 'I have a tried and tested strategy for improvement' because it is likely to be generic, not necessarily suited to your setting and, crucially, not 'owned' by the school.

Case study: Growing a culture to grow a community, Meadowbank Primary School

Nichola Hill is the headteacher of Meadowbank Primary School in Atherton near Wigan in Greater Manchester. Her message on the school website emphasises from the outset the sense of family, warmth and belonging that supports the school vision of 'Together We Are Better', and inclusion and equality are at the heart of everything the school offers its community.

A sense of belonging: making school like home

Nichola has been headteacher since 2016, but served as deputy headteacher for the previous seven years. She feels that every child deserves to have a safe space, and her intention is very much to make the school feel like a home. The head's office is more like a lounge at home, with sofas and comfortable soft furnishings to sit upon when speaking with parents and children, rather than sitting behind a desk and laptop. This recognises the challenging experiences of school that some of the parents had as children, and is designed to put them at their ease. At Meadowbank, a one-form-entry school, 48 per cent of children are on the SEND (special educational needs and disabilities) register and 78 per cent qualify for free school meals; the school is in an area of poverty and socio-economic deprivation and challenge.

Meadowbank is 'big on wellbeing', and Nichola believes that if the school can get wellbeing correct, then everything else will fall into place. The Ofsted report specifically mentions a sense of belonging. This sense came from the children, who told inspectors that they felt they belonged, that school was a safe place and that they were loved and cared for.

Mapping the curriculum

Meadowbank does not abandon its curriculum in Year 6, nor does the school slim down the timetable to teach to the SATs. In some ways, the tests are seen as secondary to the needs of the children. They are undertaken because they are statutory, but for children in their final year, losing valuable curriculum was not deemed appropriate. The curriculum is mapped out holistically, not taking reading, writing and mathematics as a starting point, even though the children are deemed significantly behind the national average. What Meadowbank has done, though, is plan where the skills and knowledge base of literacy and numeracy fit into the broader curriculum – where reading supports work in history, or where writing gives genuine opportunity for further development in science and art. Nothing in the curriculum is shoe-horned in; every aspect is carefully considered. This is all part of the school's enrichment package.

The Favourite Five

Of particular interest to our discussion was 'Our Favourite Five', which is located within the English curriculum on the school website. This initiative very much encapsulates the holistic approach that Meadowbank takes towards mental health and wellbeing across the curriculum. Each half term, every class has five high-quality and age-appropriate texts, which are shared in some way with the class every day and are on prominent display.

- **Traditional tales:** These are read, reread and discussed so that the children have a sound knowledge not only of the stories but also of the structure of basic narrative – a core concept in any writing.
- **Poetry:** This was selected because the staff felt that children were not exposed to enough poems. Poetry was also chosen because it is supportive of wellbeing; nothing is ever wrong in writing poetry, especially in free verse, and it allows for expressive and emotive talk about emotions. It was used to powerful effect by children in exploring the emotional experience of Rosa Parks.
- **Diverse and inclusive texts:** These are in place to ensure that there is representation of all children in the books used in school. Nichola believes in the place of mirroring, reflecting the make-up of the families of the school. There are single parents, blended families, children with two mothers or two fathers, children of dual heritage. Six books a year in each cohort, from Nursery to Year 6, means exposure to 48 books with different kinds of representation. The school has yet to find a child or family that is not represented in some way in the chosen texts.
- **Teacher choice**: This acknowledges teachers sharing books that they have enjoyed from the past and books that have impacted them.
- **PSHE books:** These are chosen to enhance the teaching of PSHE themes through the school year. They include a range of texts that specifically address issues around emotional health.

The impact of lockdown on mental health

We discussed the impact of the pandemic on the school during the periods of lockdown. As we know, despite the narrative that schools closed, they did in fact remain open for the children deemed vulnerable in the guidance given in March 2020. In Meadowbank's case, in the first lockdown from 23 March 2020, some 50 per cent or more of the pupils were in school, at a time when much larger schools had just a handful of children on site. Nichola felt that these children are those who have coped best with this experience, with the knock-on effect of lockdown being felt most by children who were being educated at home. The impact noticed by school staff was on the children and parents' resilience, their ability to get back into routines and their attendance. It took some 12 to 18 months of work with children to return to pre-pandemic behaviour routines.

The school has seen children and families in a measure of mental health crisis. Some children with complex mental health needs were hindered in their development by the pandemic period, with some now having a special school placement that hadn't been considered beforehand. Some children have developed signs of ADHD (attention deficit hyperactivity disorder) and there have been concerns about self-harm and depression. One area of concern has been online exploitation, by both peers and strangers. The school has been proactive in asking families to share concerns. Issues that have arisen include abusive language, children staying up until the early hours on their phones, sending inappropriate photographs and misuse of apps such as WhatsApp, TikTok and Snapchat. There have been concerns about grooming, with gaming being the platform used by those with such intent, and even seemingly innocent-sounding games such as Huggy Wuggy being exploited.

Working with the parent community

The school has excellent relationships with parents, yet recognises that many have poor parenting skills. Some parents have been self-diagnosing their children with conditions, and this is indicative in some cases of poor parental mental health. The school very much wants to break this cycle for the children. The full-time pastoral manager works not so much in addressing behaviour, but more in terms of supporting parents. There has been a realisation that children have better digital connections than parents, having a newer generation of phones while their parents have older models. Again arising from the pandemic, the school has looked at how to communicate with parents who do not have Wi-Fi or have limited data.

Part of the way in which the school addresses the issue of communication is to have a large number of parent events – to invite them into school at every opportunity. Many of these events are themed around the school values of 'Be Ready, Be Respectful, Be Kind' and include events such as Eid, Diwali, Mother's Day and Father's Day. Meadowbank operates a fully inclusive assembly calendar, returning the agenda back to the theme of belonging and acceptance.

Embracing the cultural shift

The staff have been fully on board with the shift in culture that Nichola set in place. Nichola could not be more proud of her staff, and feels in many ways that the culture has fallen naturally into place, describing how staff 'got it' and were ready for positive change. The culture has become the norm, and everyone is now an effective role model for new staff. Visitors actively comment upon the welcoming atmosphere in school. Colleagues who may visit once a week feel like part of the team. Staff turnover is low, with promotion, retirement and relocation being the only reasons why staff move on. Teachers who began with Nichola as ECTs are now phase and project leaders and have grown into the leaders they are now. Staff express how they don't want to leave and feel that not moving on does not imply a lack of ambition. They work in a setting where PPA (planning, preparation and assessment time) and leadership time are protected and never lost. Staff needs around workload are considered, as are their needs around family, such as attending nativities, those precious moments that only happen once. Staff are granted a half-day off leading to Christmas for their own use, and have access to coaching support from one of three trained colleagues – and this is purely supportive and non-judgemental. The school values and culture at Meadowbank are truly embedded in all aspects of the community.

2 Leading and managing to promote positive mental health

> **Chapter overview**
>
> In this chapter, we will consider:
>
> - the benefits of a whole-school approach
> - leading for change
> - stigma around mental health – facing up to the challenge
> - developing appropriate language around mental health
> - the collation and use of data.

The benefits of a whole-school approach

A whole-school approach to mental health and wellbeing, as advocated in the document 'Promoting children and young people's mental health and wellbeing' (Public Health England, 2021), is necessary because of the statutory duty to promote the welfare of pupils and because Ofsted inspectors will be looking for our young people to know how to keep physically and mentally healthy. However, if we return to our sense of 'why' from the previous chapter, we don't do something merely because we have to but because we want to – our moral purpose driving our strategy as much as our legal purpose. Whereas Chapter 1 focused upon moral purpose, this chapter will be more strategic and concern some of the challenges that the mental health lead may face.

Nobody could argue against a whole-school approach on safeguarding, for plainly obvious reasons. Some aspects of school life do, however, generate discussion and dissent – the behaviour policy, for example. Such discussion may centre around the consistency of its application or the degree of support from senior leaders, or sometimes around a lack of understanding behind either the policy or its principles. When the behaviour policy is applied inconsistently, either in terms of rewards (too generous or too limited) or sanctions (some staff harsh, others lenient), then the structures around behaviour begin to break down, with consequences for staff and pupils alike. We can see similar patterns in other elements of the school where inconsistencies occur: in marking policies, the maths calculation policy or the attitude to children without PE kit.

Mental health needs the whole-school approach, not only for reasons of consistency and comprehensibility, but also because of the level of unfamiliarity that many colleagues will have around mental health, due to the absence of any training opportunities. It requires the whole staff team to be on board, because raising concerns around mental health is part of the safeguarding agenda in a school. Mental health is also going to be part of the broader curriculum of the school, through explicit teaching as part of the PSHE/RSE (relationships and sex education) programme, through other curriculum subjects and also through the wider pastoral support structure, which will include the behaviour policy and routines for moving around the school during the day. Staff will be supporting the children's mental health needs, just as they would support any specific need, with the longer-term view of all students being in the best position to learn and to succeed academically, socially and emotionally. Remember, too, that as a school you are one part in the process supporting a child through a challenging period; you may sit alongside professionals from other agencies, such as social care, NHS services and community and voluntary sector colleagues, taking a similar holistic approach. Your approach to mental health within the school community may impact positively on the pupils' attendance, conduct, confidence and resilience. The whole-school approach is the means with which to work to that goal.

Leading for change

Change is never easy. It can frighten some colleagues, particularly those who have experienced a range of leadership styles and ever-shifting priorities. Where a change is simply imposed, there is little if any sense of ownership, and chances of success may be limited. Especially in an area such as mental health, where colleagues' knowledge base may vary depending on their interest and experience, the practice of leading is one that requires working within the team rather than driving it from behind. If the role of mental health leader is taken on by someone outside the senior leadership team, there will be a level of challenge in building trust and confidence among colleagues in this new position. Whatever the level of seniority and experience of the appointed designated leader, for them to be truly successful in their role, they need to have the support of the whole leadership team and other colleagues, so that the role is not only fulfilled but is understood and recognised for its importance within the ways in which all children are supported.

Build a team

The designated mental health leader cannot possibly undertake this role single-handedly, and the support network that the leader has will depend not only upon the context of the school but upon the scale of it too. A small village school with a handful of staff may undertake a model where everyone takes joint responsibility in all areas of curriculum and pastoral care; but as numbers of staff and children increase, such a model would be unworkable. Whichever the option, the team working alongside the designated leader could be balanced as follows:

- **Representation from class teachers:** Teachers see the impact of poor pupil mental health in their classrooms every day, but will also see the benefits of a positive programme supporting mental health upon pupil engagement, behaviour, attendance and learning progress. They will be delivering the curriculum around mental health, so their place on the team is vital in this way. Secondary colleagues may want to ensure a balance of representation from departments; PSHE and PE should be a given, but departments where the impact of poor mental health has been recognised as impacting upon students should be present too.
- **Teaching assistants:** They often have a different relationship with our young people, with one-to-one or small-group work giving them more time with children than the class teacher might have. This may lead to different levels of trust and perhaps allow the child the confidence to say if something isn't right, knowing the message will be passed back to the teacher or elsewhere. Teaching assistants are also more likely to be from the neighbouring community, and hence more conversant with local concerns that might impact upon children and their families.
- **Midday supervisors:** These may be, of course, part of your teaching assistant team, especially in a small school. Again, their importance lies in the different relationship with the children, with the differences emphasised by change of location; out of class but in the dining hall and

playgrounds, students respond differently to the environment and what they may perceive as rules and expectations other than those they have in the classroom setting. A good midday supervisor is worth their weight in gold, often able to solve playground disputes and offer a listening ear.

- **Heads of year and tutors:** Having all the heads of year might be unwieldy, but certainly heads of Year 7 (for reasons of transition) and Years 10 and/or 11 (for reasons around exam stresses and pressure) could be part of the team. The tutor programme in secondary schools can vary, with some using time as an equipment check but others using it as an emotional check-in or as the space to cover PSHE; tutors will see a different relationship with their charges than a teaching or learning mentor might.

- **Family liaison staff and office staff:** They may have more daily contact with parents and carers than teaching staff do, and hence may be the first point of contact for parental concerns.

- **The SENDCo:** The SENDCo's methods of identification and tracking (or, at the very least, those of a member of their team) will be more than valuable in regard to this role.

- **A member of senior leadership:** Unless this is already the designated lead, this allows a dialogue with those responsible for strategic decision-making. This might then allow a member of the governing body to be engaged in the process too.

- **A selection of colleagues considered 'negative' or 'blockers' by others:** The quotation marks are deliberate, and this is certainly not language to encourage, but those who have been wary of change and have been vocal about it are the ones to win over, because often if *they* can be convinced of the benefits of the policy shift, they can help in the engagement of others who are wary of raising their concerns. A balance of those with a positive mindset, and those more willing to challenge, contributes to an atmosphere of healthy debate and discussion.

Also consider working with parents. This may be a little controversial, but the triangulation of pupils, parents and staff represents the community of the school. Schools may choose to include some parents in the meetings with staff or not, but at the very least they should be included in the consultation process of what the support for mental health is going to look like. Listening to parent voice is considered in more depth in Chapter 8.

How often the team meets depends upon the starting point and the existing culture in the school but, certainly in the early stages, meetings will be more frequent as the strategies and curriculum are rolled out. Attendance need not be compulsory, but try to ensure that there is a balance of representation at all times. To ensure that teaching assistants and midday staff remain engaged, some recompense for their commitment should be considered, either by time in lieu or through overtime payment.

The value of your team will come from the range of voices, the experience of the school and of the profession of education, the understanding of the context of the school and the recognition of need from a range of perspectives.

Develop a plan

The leader and the team will create the strategic plan for mental health and, rather than standing alone, it needs to fit the school development plan. In taking the holistic perspective, mental health feeds into and feeds off the other core aspects of school life. Working with the template used by the school or trust is an obvious starting point, as it is in the format shared with staff and governors and presents an overview of the long-term priorities and desired outcomes, whether the long-term view employed by the school is a one-, two- or three-year development plan model.

The plan needs to include aims and objectives, and these need to be wider than 'to put a programme to support mental health in place', as the matter is not this simple – nor will it be instant. Aims need to be SMART – Specific, Manageable, Achievable, Realistic and Time-specific, for those unfamiliar with the acronym.

Aims could include these areas:

- to audit the current provision for mental health support in school
- to survey staff attitudes and experience with mental health in school
- to survey staff, parents and children's wellbeing through an established measure or one devised by the school
- to review existing policies for their reference to mental health
- to identify protective and preventive factors in the school and wider community
- to consider intent, implementation and impact of the plan.

Within the records of the group, this longer-term plan would need to be broken down into medium- and shorter-term aims. Surveys are delivered within the short term, but actions arising from them will be a medium-term provision and impact within the longer-term evaluation of the plan. For example, a parental survey might suggest that they do not feel listened to; actions could include delving deeper into how they could feel heard and respected, as well as setting up practices and procedures, be they meetings, workshops or mentoring, with this support needing evaluation and feedback as to the value and effectiveness of this – or any – intervention.

In developing a plan that will lead to change of practice and attitude, these three questions should be considered:

- **Are the suggested actions reasonable?** Proposed actions need to make sense and be delivered in a logical order. The conditions, attitudes and resources need to be right to enable long-term outcomes to be fulfilled and impact felt. Potential gaps in what is planned need to be identified too.
- **Is this plan practical?** Any initiative needs to be realistic, in terms of the manner of delivery and the capacity of the staff involved to deliver it. If a member of staff is already overwhelmed by workload, adding to the workload is impractical. New practices need the review and removal of some old procedures.
- **Is what we plan verifiable?** What constitutes 'measurable' data for our mental health provision is discussed later in this chapter, but evidence in whichever form it takes to show positive impacts of interventions will justify the validity of the actions put in place, as well as persuade any sceptical persons – staff, governors or parents – of the value of the programme to support the pupils' mental health and wellbeing.

Develop a safe space

A psychological safe space for a team to operate in allows for the taking of risks and for speaking up and sharing opinions and experiences. It allows for participants to question, to challenge and to admit to mistakes, all without any fear of the consequences or feeling judged. This will be a theme we will return to throughout the book, but the starting point for it lies in the team leading for change, particularly in embracing some challenging voices, because we can respectfully disagree but still have supportive and trusting professional relationships. The modelling of such a safe space should roll out through the whole staff body and be exemplified by school leaders. The headteacher who announces, 'My door is always open' should consider whether it is a metaphorical as well as a literal open door; some conversations will have to take place in a private environment, but it is the safety of that space that allows for the appropriate level of trust to be appreciated.

What is in place already?

There will be few, if any, schools that have no mental health provision in place, even if they believe they are starting from scratch. There will be pockets of good practice, likely centred around the work of the SENDCo or family liaison staff, who may already have set up interventions on their own initiative or based around training they have accessed. The school may already have arranged to train emotional literacy support assistants (ELSAs) but not yet shared the purpose and benefits of the role with colleagues.

It is the role of the mental health lead and the team to evaluate what is in place across the whole school or used in individual practice, why some initiatives were put in place, the impact they have had and whether they have continued simply out of habit. Many schools are further along their journey of mental health than they thought, but should consider what can be grown and developed and what can be put aside.

These are examples of practice and provision that I have encountered in my own experience and through discussion with colleagues. Consider these with a 'what went well?' and 'even better if' approach. Would you continue, expand, amend or discard?

- 'Worry boxes' have been set up by year group partners in a primary school but not used elsewhere. The class teachers report that children began using the boxes for their confidentiality and have become more confident in talking about their concerns openly as a result.
- A 'buddy bench' has been set up as a response to children having nobody to play with on the playground. It was successful initially, but recently parents have complained that their child has been sitting alone on the bench for entire playtimes.
- In a secondary school, the PE department has demonstrated a positive model of building trust with young people, leading to a number of referrals for mental health, noticeably more than other departments.
- A member of support staff has a reputation as being able to lead positive restorative conversations. Their patience, empathy and support has been

noted by students and parents and they are regarded as a trusted adult. However, the workload has become overwhelming at times.

Stigma around mental health – facing up to the challenge

One of the greatest challenges the leader for mental health in a school will face is any stigma around the subject that may exist among the staff. Left unchallenged or not spoken of, it could easily disrupt or derail the mental health strategy that the school wishes to put in place.

Stigma is not a word that often appears in our day-to-day vocabulary. A typical dictionary definition of the word describes it as 'a mark of disgrace associated with a particular circumstance, quality or person', so it is very much a term with negative associations. When 'stigma' appears in the written word, it is often used as part of the verb 'to stigmatise' – for example, the action of treating someone unfairly through public disapproval. This can take a number of forms: targeting an individual because of race, gender, sexuality, disability or neurodiversity. People may find themselves stigmatised for being in a single-parent family or being on state benefits. It can manifest itself in offensive language, social exclusion, comments on social media posts and sometimes in physical violence.

In short, stigma is when a person – or group of people – is viewed in a negative way because of a characteristic or trait that is thought of as – or sometimes is – a disadvantage. It is prejudiced and a negative stereotype. Sadly, negative attitudes towards mental health in general, and to those who have a diagnosed mental health condition in particular, are common.

How stigma around mental health presents itself

Verbal insults around mental health, sometimes a feature of school playground bullying but also used in the workplace, can be offensive and upsetting. There is no need to go into some of these words, just as racist terms would not be used even in an academic or analytical piece of writing. However, even terms such as 'snowflake' are offensive, as the implication is that there is a lack of resilience on the part of the recipient. Phrases such as 'keep taking the tablets' are not only callous but also ignorant; some people with a mental health diagnosis do take medication, but others are in receipt of other kinds of treatment. Use of such language is insulting, but it emerges from a lack of knowledge as much as from prejudice.

In a wider definition of 'stigma', other aspects of individual and societal attitudes bear consideration, particularly in discussing mental health with children and young people.

There are sometimes fears around saying the wrong thing, inadvertently causing offence or making a mistake that might worsen a situation. This might be particularly true in school settings where staff are trained to identify when there is a specific educational need, particularly around neurodiversity, but may be wary when discussing or signposting mental health support for a young person. The lack of training or discussion around mental health needs stands out here. Some colleagues may express that mental health isn't their responsibility – that they have enough to deal with in teaching and assessment.

Others might feel uncomfortable discussing mental health because of their own experience. If a person has in the past received counselling or some form of therapy, or been diagnosed with depression or anxiety, this may make them reluctant to discuss mental health with others. Similarly, if a loved one has been diagnosed in the past, discussion of mental health might again cross boundaries of personal confidentiality. In schools, some teachers might feel comfortable being open about aspects of their mental health, while others would not wish to talk so openly.

There are also cultural and societal barriers to discussing mental health. Some faith groups in particular might not support discussion of mental health, preferring instead to keep it within their own group boundaries or within the family. There are some cultures where there might not be an acceptance that a mental health issue exists in the definition that a mental health professional might give. While such belief and practice might not be agreed with, it is important to respect and understand why such a position is held.

These broader considerations around stigma go beyond the basic dictionary definition. If a narrow definition of stigma as one that concerns prejudice and discrimination is taken, there may not be an acknowledgement that, in talking about mental health, there is sometimes fear of the unknown, of making a mistake, of saying the wrong thing – all of which are barriers to debate around mental health as much as negative stereotyping can be.

A proactive approach to challenging stigma

Let us just remind ourselves of the World Health Organisation definition of mental health (2022) as 'a state of mental well-being that enables people to cope with the stresses of life, realise their abilities, learn well and work well, and contribute to their community'. They very much recognise that everyone has mental health and that it is a basic human right, crucial to personal, community and societal development. The social and economic circumstances in which our young people and families find themselves can also increase the risk of experiencing mental health conditions. This is where taking a proactive approach to the challenge of stigma in our schools and workplaces can have a positive impact.

Firstly, a positive and responsive leadership can determine the culture in an organisation and direct a cultural shift. Those schools, that are actively pursuing the designated mental health lead training, place a premium on the leadership being determined to develop positive practices. This will take time, and often involves overcoming and dismantling existing barriers, especially where negative attitudes and poor relationships have existed beforehand. By setting up structures that actively identify and measure mental health – considering ways to support the needs of the young people identified, having trained mental health first aiders on site and being committed to training staff and making this part of their performance management – leaders can drive change in a positive, empathetic and understanding manner. This is far more effective than leading through fear and forcing change. The same principles could be applied to any workplace in taking care of colleagues and clients.

Responsive practices in a group or organisation can set the tone for a positive mindset and be a powerful tool in working with those who perhaps have concerns about discussing mental health. If the leadership is seen to be taking a proactive lead, this sets an example for others to follow – a model or a scaffold of conduct that is far more effective to follow than a memo, directive or email instruction. If this is nurtured and reflected upon, it becomes part of workplace habit and routine. Where inappropriate language, inadvertent or otherwise, is challenged and accompanied with an explanation of why it shouldn't be used, the mindset will continue to grow.

Finally, there needs to be an open attitude towards discussing understanding, knowledge and unconscious bias. Unconscious bias is, as the term suggests, something people are not always aware of. An open attitude will allow members of the group or organisation to talk about their own mental health and ask questions to clarify their understanding, and may possibly lead those who have been reluctant to discuss their own struggles to seek professional support. Taking time to talk and having a listening ear can have a positive impact on mental health but also on attitudes towards it.

Overcoming stigma and embedded attitudes is no easy matter. However, whatever the organisation, be it a school, college, workplace or voluntary group, the desire to promote a positive culture, and to grow and nurture it, is surely at the root of a positive culture around mental health in these challenging times.

Developing appropriate language around mental health

The designated lead and the senior leadership team need to make a proactive decision about the kind of language that is going to be used by the adults in the school as a model to each other and to the pupils and their families. Are you going to use the words 'mental health' or are you going to use other terminology? The use of the term 'mental health' will certainly challenge stigma, because it normalises its use in everyday language rather than being more guarded in its use. However, there also needs to be a sensitivity to the community, as certain faiths and cultures may prefer to keep mental health concerns within the family while others will seek solace in the words and guidance of their faith leaders; again, we are returning to the understanding of our context.

In some schools, although the children feel appreciative of the support they receive, there may be a feeling of fatigue related to possible overuse of the term 'mental health', with few other alternative expressions. Having a choice of vocabulary is good for our language variety, and decisions need to be made about using the terminology 'emotional health' or 'wellbeing', as well as 'feelings', in a meaningful way, so that there is a level of understanding of when children feel that something is wrong, but also when their mental health is in a positive place.

Negative and inappropriate language

Care needs to be taken in the use of some words. While 'anxious' and 'anxiety' are commonly used words, there is a huge difference between being anxious about remembering your spellings for a test or whether you have remembered your towel for swimming, and medically diagnosed anxiety. Anxiety can lead to stress, panic or fear and affects physical and psychological health on a daily basis. Generalised anxiety disorder can lead to persistent and excessive worry about daily activities or events. Panic disorder consists of panic attacks and a fear of having more attacks. Social anxiety disorder is manifested as high levels of fear and worry about social situations that might make the person feel humiliated, embarrassed or rejected. Other kinds of anxiety disorders include agoraphobia, separation anxiety disorder, selective mutism and specific phobias, shown by intense and irrational fears of objects or situations, which can lead to distress and avoidance tactics (World Health Organization, 2023a).

Depression, suffered by an estimated five per cent of the global population (World Health Organization, 2023b), is not characterised by somebody looking upset or crying at one specific incident, because these can be specific in their duration and resolution. Rather, it is a feeling of persistent sadness and a lack of interest in pursuing previously enjoyed and rewarding social and leisure activities. Sleep can be affected, appetite can be diminished, and tiredness and poor levels of concentration may result too. Depression may be long lasting or may be recurrent; either way it can impact on the ability of a person to enjoy a functioning and rewarding life. Causes can be social, biological, psychological or a combination of any or all of these three. Childhood adversity, bereavement and financial pressures can all contribute to or trigger depressive episodes.

We would not ask a child, 'Are you anxious?' or 'Are you feeling depressed?', because to do so would be to ask leading questions. With schools reporting in some cases that children and parents are almost self-diagnosing, such a line of questioning would only inflame a sensitive situation. A more positive use of language, in a setting where children feel able to talk, might be 'Can you tell me what is worrying you?' or something similar, to win their confidence and to share their concerns.

There are other terms, some with particular relevance to mental health, that can be used in a pejorative tone:

- **Aggressive:** We might hear this in reference to the conduct of an adult or a child in a meeting, but someone being forthright or passionate about their cause does not make them aggressive. Consider also that when someone is neurodivergent, disagreement isn't aggressive but a way of making sense of a situation.

- **Naughty:** Often used in frustration about behaviour, it is neither a helpful nor accurate term, just as 'Why can't they just behave?' is also pejorative. A far better term in understanding a behaviour related to a child's mental health is 'dysregulated behaviour', for which the school may be using zones of regulation within its universal behaviour offer.

- **Difficult:** This is often used in reference to parents. Is the parent being difficult or are they standing up for their child? Has the parent got mental health needs of their own that the school doesn't realise? Has the parent had cause to be disaffected by their previous dealings with the school?

- **School refusal:** This is an emotive term and the word 'refusal' has implications around truancy or an act of defiance from a child. Emotional-based school avoidance (EBSA) is a far less judgemental term and acknowledges the emotional, psychological and social factors making attending school a challenge for a child. It moves the narrative from one of blame to one of support.
- **Trauma:** Having a bad day isn't a trauma; it is simply a day when things haven't gone right. As a teacher, having an IT failure, forgetting your PIN on your bank card or forgetting to mark a few books – these are just unfortunate and, while upsetting, aren't life-changing. Trauma has a very specific meaning (see Chapter 4 on adverse childhood experiences) relating to a deeply distressing or disturbing incident, leading to severe and lasting emotional shock. This is another word to use carefully and specifically in our mental health vocabulary.
- **Other inappropriate vocabulary:** 'Drama queen', 'attention-seeking', 'kicking off', 'they're on one'... you can probably add more to this list, all of which are judgemental and show misunderstanding of emotions and a lack of knowledge of trigger points.

The school needs to determine the kind of language that it considers negative and inappropriate. I wouldn't advocate a list of banned vocabulary, because this will constantly be added to. Rather, there should be a consideration of tone and whether something may be considered unsuitable. Scripts to use to address inappropriate language could be developed, much as exist for restorative practice. The scripts could be used for adult-to-child discussions and, as the children's role and confidence develops, for pupil-to-pupil interaction too. Staff training will allow the opportunity to highlight examples of language that may cause offence, which is discussed in Chapter 6, and part of this training could include an adult-to-adult script and how adults can respond to inappropriate comments about mental health from colleagues.

Positive language

Positive language around mental health should be visibly and audibly present in the school environment. Vocabulary, though, isn't absorbed by osmosis; it needs to be taught and practised, modelled and praised. When working with our own children or grandchildren, we use the word, repeat the word, demonstrate the word and praise the word when it is used well and becomes a habit. Take 'kindness' as an example, which is discussed in depth in *The Wellbeing Curriculum* (2021). There is little point in asking a child to 'be kind' if they have no understanding of what kindness is. By demonstrating kind acts, encouraging kind behaviour and recognising it with suitable praise, this enables it to become a habit. Politeness can also be taught as a habit: opening doors to an adult or peer, greeting someone in passing or making an authentic apology.

Are kindness and politeness about mental health? They are, because they can help to create positive emotions, as can many of the values that the school will typically have. Especially where a school has regular assemblies supporting its values, the language used can be drip-fed through follow-up discussions in class or in tutor group time in secondary settings. Corridor and classroom displays are another way of sharing vocabulary, as too are age-appropriate knowledge organisers. Whether your school values include respect, equality or independence, for example, you will already have started to develop the language to support the children in living these values.

Positivity, though, is not a utopian ideal, nor should it promote a vision of a world where nothing goes wrong. Be wary of toxic positivity, which is the belief that, however dire or difficult a situation is, we should always maintain a positive mindset. Negative emotions are part of life, and over-sweetened positivity might lead to the suppression of such emotions, which could be damaging in the longer term. Part of Carol Dweck's work on growth mindset (2017) acknowledges that failure is there to be learned from and thus is part of life's lessons; failure happens but we learn from it. The positive language that we would look to use should be solutions-focused. Things can only get better? Well, they might not, without knowledgeable action to put them right.

In considering our positive language, we can also look at developing resilience, which many schools, in both primary and secondary sectors, report has been in decline since the pandemic. Resilience involves recovery from setbacks and having the skill set and strategies to face challenges that place us in stressful positions. These can include helping children to solve problems by breaking them down into manageable steps and realising that parts of the solution are within their own control. It can also incorporate management – rather than avoidance – of emotions, by encouraging the sharing of emotions through talk or writing or even crying, to avoid bottling up an issue. Part of resilience also includes having the ability to seek help, and the positive language here comes from the practitioners who are able to demonstrate that they are prepared to listen and to do so actively and empathetically. A judgemental voice might say, 'You're too old to be behaving like this' but a more curious one might say, 'What are you trying to tell me? How can I offer support?'

The positive language will develop over the course of time, and is discussed further in the chapters of staff training, pupil voice and developing the curriculum. Language is powerful; it helps us to determine our vision of the world as adults. It is our role to equip our young people with the tools to enable them to comprehend their vision.

The collation and use of data

Data-gathering, input and interpretation are part of the teacher's professional life. We are all used to identifying areas of strength, aspects for development and individuals, groups or classes needing a change in focus to ensure that they are keeping pace with expectations. These form part of our dialogue in pupil progress meetings. Are these meetings, however, purely focused on academic attainment or do they go further? Are you being holistic in your approach, thinking of the whole child, or is everything about results?

To be at their most effective, pupil progress meetings need to include knowledge of what enables a child to thrive and of any circumstances that hinder their learning. This will include any identified learning needs, but should also cover their mental health and general wellbeing. The data or evidence to be considered can be quantitative or qualitative. Are you going to use one exclusively or a combination of both?

Quantitative data

Quantitative data is what is presented for academic progress, usually from populated spreadsheets and presented into tables, and will be familiar to staff, leaders and governors. Academic data will usually show upward trends, but the very nature of mental health and wellbeing means that there will be peaks and troughs in any data collected. Many readers may logically ask how we might represent mental health in a spreadsheet. There are commercially available products, such as Thrive, which involves termly online surveys of whole classes and then populates a spreadsheet, identifying issues that can be addressed as a whole class, but also indicating children who may require a particular level of support. In this case, the software does the work for the teacher. Boxall Profiling is also now available as a spreadsheet, but this requires input of data by an adult which, if completed with a class of 30 children, presents a workload issue, even before the data is interpreted. Possible issues here are teacher fatigue in entering their own data or children misinterpreting a question and giving an answer leading to receipt of support when someone else may need it more, or not having an intervention when there is a need.

Other quantitative data can come from entry and exit profiles (before or after any intervention), strengths and difficulties questionnaires (SDQs) and surveys with parents. Each of these can indicate whether the intervention or support programme has had an impact and the level of effectiveness that it has had.

Qualitative data

Qualitative data might be regarded as 'soft data' but it is no less valid than information produced from surveys, calling as it does upon professional judgement and curiosity, both vital components of our culture of strong safeguarding. Your qualitative data is going to be more subjective than the numerical information raised under whichever quantitative method the school chooses to employ, but it is going to draw upon the rich vein of knowledge about the children, their families and their social and economic circumstances.

By returning to the 'culture of noticing' from Chapter 1, and recording these observations on the chosen safeguarding software, it is possible to build a narrative about a pupil's experience from the perspective of a number of colleagues. Three to four notifications over the course of a week or two, which on their own may not have represented a cause for action, could be the beginning of a pattern and worthy of further investigation.

Trusting and trustworthy staff relationships also enable the same 'culture of noticing', where colleagues feel comfortable to raise a concern face to face with the mental health lead or senior leaders. These 'micro-conversations' form part of the picture around the whole child.

Is your school dominated by a qualitative or quantitative approach? It is more likely that schools operate on a mixture of the two. It is the balance between hard and soft data, and the way in which it is used, that will reflect the context and the culture of leadership for mental health in school.

Final thoughts

Once the school is establishing its culture around mental health, it can at the same time develop the leadership structure that will support the culture. Both the culture and the leadership need to be in alignment, and where they are, staff wellbeing and mental health can be prioritised, as the following chapter will discuss.

THINK about leading and managing to promote positive mental health

Time

- Allow your team plentiful and scheduled times to meet.
- The positive language that you wish to develop will take time to establish and embed. Habits take time and patience, but are worth the wait.

Holistic

- A support team, balanced with responsibilities in the school, should value each role and enable feedback to be cascaded at an appropriate scale.
- A holistic approach is more likely to lead to whole-staff buy-in to support the mental health of the school community.

Inclusive

- Respect all opinions from staff, even where they express doubts and opposition.
- Debate is healthy and is more likely to enable colleagues to embrace the practice and position that you wish to see.

Non-judgemental

- Negativity may mean opposition, but equally it may mean fear. An assumption that negativity represents an attempt to block change may be counterproductive.
- Stigma may arise from experience around mental health as much as from lack of knowledge and understanding.

Knowledgeable

- Knowing where your colleagues are coming from on their personal mental health journey will engage their commitment. If they feel understood and listened to, their acceptance of change will be greater enabled.
- Data is knowledge, but value the soft data as much as what the spreadsheets and surveys show.

Case study: Leading with values, Bramley Sunnyside Junior School

Bramley Sunnyside Junior School in Rotherham prides itself on its values of creativity, confidence and collaboration, values that embrace everything that happens in the school, as the headteacher Laura Robson and PSHE lead Danielle Green told me as they guided me through life in school.

Art at the heart

The school's most recent inspection was undertaken in January 2020, and the report captured much of what is so positive about the school. The report particularly highlighted the school's commitment to art and design, a commitment that goes beyond subject provision and that ties to the value of creativity in particular. The school is fortunate to have, among many talented staff, an art specialist in Sue Davis, one of the higher-level teaching assistants (HLTAs). Sue teaches art across the school, giving each class in the three-form-entry school two timetabled art lessons each week. Working in a separate modular unit that operates as the art classroom, the children have the opportunity to work outside their own classroom and become used to the culture of a specialised subject space, almost giving them an experience of secondary readiness. Art features prominently in display around the school, especially in the murals created collaboratively by the children. Sue is also an accredited art therapist and runs art therapy sessions on a Monday morning for identified groups in upper and lower Key Stage 2, a deliberate decision for when children have been away from the school over a weekend or holiday, forming an additional check-in going deeper than 'Are you OK?'. She also runs a club for a group of children, Nurture Nook, which also takes place in the same space. Parents drop children at the club, where sensory activities have been set up and soft music plays, easing the children into the start of their day. The children's work is further valued through the 'Picture This' project, linked to the National Gallery, enabling the children to exhibit their work for parents and a wider audience, not only in school but at other locations across Rotherham. Some children have the opportunity to take a foundation level GCSE in art, recognising those with a particular talent or creative passion for the arts. There is a recognition that some of these children may not reach the national standard in English and mathematics, but they can develop their understanding of art as something to take forward into later life. This is an excellent example of the curriculum being used to support mental health and wellbeing, a theme explored further in Chapter 10.

The package of additional activities, a known protective factor in mental health, includes street dance, run by a former pupil of the school. Unusually, the school offers floristry as an activity, drawing upon the skill set of another member of the team. Laura likes to engage former pupils as a means of raising aspirations beyond wanting to be a social media influencer. This has included clubs such as photography, music and animation. Bramley Sunnyside thinks more broadly about the curriculum to include core life skills within the children's learning experience.

A culture of kindness

One area of improvement mentioned in the report was the exposure of some children to derogatory language, and this not always being reported to adults. The school took this as a positive opportunity, actually working on this in the term before the inspection. This is where they linked not only to John Magee and the Kindness Matters project, but also to development of the PSHE curriculum and embedding this within the digital safety aspect of computing lessons. Four years on, the impact is seen in a much greater appreciation for children's differences and in celebrating that appreciation. In the school, the support staff are highly valued, with all HLTAs having 'specialist' on their job titles and other support staff known as 'learning coaches', which has been part of the culture shift in the school. Children know who their trusted adults are and readily turn to them for support, being more open about their worries, rather than hanging onto a concern and keeping it inside.

Part of the culture shift has seen children challenging other children if they know something not to be right. In a Year 6 class, somebody had said something to a child with autism and the class very quickly became those to stand up and challenge that comment before the teacher did. This was an excellent example of the value of confidence: being able to speak up and stand up against derogatory remarks.

Making positive language count

We discussed whether there had been any issues with boys, given some of the concerns that primary schools have expressed about misogynistic behaviour being demonstrated by some boys. This is a subject that the school has discussed, especially asking all the pupils whether boys behaved differently towards girls. Student voice here was strong in saying that the only differences they noticed was that there are separate toilets and a girls-only football club in addition to a mixed football group. The school has worked hard on the positive language to be used around the protected characteristics enshrined in the Equality Act 2010. This work includes workshops with parents around contextual safeguarding and digital safety, particularly over what grooming looks like (a particular issue in Rotherham) and sexualised behaviour. Some examples of behaviour in school have come from what they have seen at football clubs outside of school, some run by parents. The school has addressed issues around children using social media, with children using WhatsApp in ways that might be deemed examples of bullying.

Growing relationships

Laura's welcoming statement on the school website emphasises that nothing they do would be possible without the relationships that the school has with its families and friends. This is something that happens from the outset with parents and children. Being a junior school with a larger intake than the neighbouring infant school means children coming from a wider catchment and new children coming into relationships already established through EYFS (Early Years Foundation Stage) and Key Stage 1. As part of the transition plan, rather than make a presentation to 90 sets of parents in the hall, which feels impersonal, Laura takes parents around the school in groups of eight, enabling them to see the school in action and to ask questions in a smaller group, which they might be less inclined to do in a larger group. Her door is always open to those parents who wish to ask anything further. These starting points with parents let them know that the school works with them and wants to get the very best out of them.

The transition process with the children from Year 2 includes staff visiting the infant school to observe and fact-find, as well as to share a story or two with the children, but also having four to five transition days in the later part of the summer term. Come September, the children are familiar with which door to come to, and where to put their coats and bags – small things but things that are important in the minds of seven-year-olds making a crucial transition, enabling them to feel safe from the outset.

PSHE at the core of everything

The school PSHE curriculum is a mixture of material from the PSHE Association and elements more bespoke to the needs of the school. This has enabled staff to be more confident in a subject they may not be familiar with and to access resources readily, especially in areas such as puberty and body changes. Danielle ensures that the PSHE lessons are delivered by the class teacher, the person with the strongest established relationship with the class, rather than leaving it to the PPA cover. The curriculum includes quizzes, knowledge organisers and very clear golden threads, returning to key concepts each year in a spiral curriculum reflecting the growing maturity of the children.

A positive culture for staff

The planning of the PSHE curriculum, alongside the art curriculum, forms part of staff wellbeing. The art lessons allow staff to have leadership time alongside guaranteed PPA. Wellbeing for all staff includes a staff wellbeing charter, part of which promises each member of staff a day in lieu to take at any point in the year. They also have an entitlement to an afternoon off site in December – nominally a Christmas shopping afternoon, but staff can use it for any purpose. Staff feel listened to. Previously given a whole day for report-writing, with a half-day added to their PPA time, teachers asked whether they could have a whole day for reports in addition to their PPA, which has been acted upon. Relationships between staff are important, a factor in the stability of the staff body. Staff only leave for promotion, relocation or retirement. Staff wellbeing is firmly embedded in the school culture.

Sunny by name and by nature

The school name, Bramley Sunnyside, is one of the most positive-sounding school names I have heard. The school has embraced its name in the logo on the school website and in the names of its support spaces, the Sunshine, Sunbeam and Rainbow rooms. I left my meeting with Laura and Danielle with a definite sunny outlook.

3 Staff mental health and wellbeing

> **Chapter overview**
>
> In this chapter, we will consider:
>
> - the Teacher Wellbeing Index
> - negative impacts on staff mental health
> - the staff mental health and wellbeing survey
> - sociograms
> - staff prioritising their own mental health and wellbeing
> - wider issues around staff mental and physical health.

There is no more valuable resource in a workplace than the staff, more so in schools because the interactions between staff and pupils, accumulated over each day, each week and each school year, determine the nature of the young people who emerge at each transition in their education and into the rounded characters that they become at the end of their formal schooling. In short, we need happy staff to make happy children, and happy children make happy learners. Any discussion of staff includes everyone who works in school, cleaners and caterers, teaching assistants and site managers, office staff and midday supervisors, as well as our teachers and leaders, because our teams need to be truly inclusive. For this reason, any discussion about supporting mental health in your school community must begin with that of your staff.

The Teacher Wellbeing Index

However, if we look at the statistics from Education Support's annual Teacher Wellbeing Index (2023) and the current retention figures from the Department for Education (DfE, 2023a), we can see that our school staff are not always happy and that staff mental health should be a priority in any school. The 2023 Wellbeing Index reported that 78 per cent of staff are stressed, with this figure being 89 per cent for senior leaders.

This is nearly four out of every five of your colleagues, and close to nine out of every ten school leaders.

Other statistics that individual schools may wish to consider include:

- 55 per cent of staff feel that their organisation's culture has a negative impact upon their wellbeing.
- 46 per cent of all staff say that their organisation does not support staff with mental health and wellbeing problems particularly well.
- 81 per cent of staff experienced symptoms because of their work.
- 39 per cent of staff had a mental health issue in the year up to the point of the survey.
- 45 per cent of staff thought the symptoms experienced were a sign of anxiety and 28 per cent thought them a sign of depression.
- 35 per cent of staff thought that symptoms were a sign of burnout.

The mental health lead and senior leadership should also consider the reported statistics relating to loneliness in school. Twenty-six per cent of staff overall feel either isolated, left out or lacking companionship at school, with 22 per cent of staff from a global majority background feeling this way. Seventeen per cent feel isolated and 17 per cent feel left out in the workplace. Support staff feel the most left out and teachers feel the most lonely. Fourteen per cent of staff always or often feel lonely at work; this is twice the national figure. Some 9.5 per cent of education staff who contacted the Education Support helpline in 2022–23 – some 4,178 colleagues – were clinically assessed to be at risk of suicide.

How are we in this position? Why are staff feeling isolated and left out? We are in a profession that relies on teamwork and togetherness to be successful as a school. In the pages that follow, we will consider some of the issues and possible strategies to put into place.

Negative impacts on staff mental health

The pandemic and its after-effects

The outbreak of the Covid-19 pandemic was frightening, fuelled by the sense of the unknown and by the stark warning to stay at home. However, teachers and other school staff didn't stay at home, providing support for vulnerable pupils and children of key workers and online learning for those pupils not in school. In the second and third lockdowns, staff were very much in the school building throughout this period, yet we had press and politicians that fed a narrative about 'lazy teachers', which some of the public sadly believed.

The real impact of the pandemic on school staff was not so much the virus itself but the impact on the way in which schools worked. Returning to school in September 2020, they worked in 'bubbles', which meant the staffroom being out of bounds and none of the social interaction that is part of wellbeing, leaving staff isolated in many ways. Meetings held on Zoom or other platforms, while addressing the need to communicate, lacked the nuances and subtleties of discussing a matter face to face. This remained the case through 2021 and into the subsequent year, as new variants of the virus emerged and restrictions remained in place.

Likewise, staff were also put under pressure by the notion of 'lost learning' and the need to 'catch up' with funding provided for tutoring, some of which had to be provided by teachers in addition to their full timetables. Both 'lost learning' and 'catch up' are emotive terms, especially when dropped into professional dialogue with staff already under pressure with getting the children back into learning and behavioural routines back in the classroom. Secondary staff, especially those with responsibility for GCSE and A level assessments, faced two years with no exams and of teacher-assessed grades, with inconsistent advice from local and central authority and the additional burden of pressure from parents, especially with university spaces at stake. Once formal examinations returned in 2022 and 2023, the subject of grade inflation entered the conversation, with young people who had never sat a formal public examination since their Key Stage 2 SATs requiring a different level of support through the revision, testing and results phases.

We know about the pandemic and its impact on the global community, so why raise it as an issue in relation to staff mental health? The reason: it is a stark reminder of environmental factors affecting mental health, a factor that none of us probably imagined when we first planned the role of the mental health lead.

Inspection

There is no getting away from inspection. In December 2021, schools that had been inspected reported words along the lines of 'we don't want to hear about the pandemic' during their inspection, at a point when another variant of concern was spreading and where the associated issues of attendance and moving back to the cycle of formal examinations were at the forefront of teachers' minds.

Ofsted was on newspaper front pages early in 2023, with the tragic death of Ruth Perry and many headteachers sharing the impact that inspection had upon them. As I was reviewing this chapter, the inquest verdict was delivered by coroner Heidi O'Connor. The inspection 'lacked fairness, respect and sensitivity' and was at times 'rude and intimidating', in the words of the coroner (Martin, 2023), adding that there was clear evidence that the deterioration in her mental health and her death were contributed to by the Ofsted inspection.

Many other headteachers will have been affected by the actions of inspectors in the past, but inspection has an effect on the entire staff. Despite the words of the then Chief Inspector Amanda Spielman in April 2023 on the Laura Kuenssberg programme (Political TV, 2023), inspection does impact teachers, as anyone who has had to face a 'deep dive' into their subject will tell you. The Teacher Wellbeing Index found that 73 per cent of respondents felt that inspection wasn't fit for purpose, with 71 per cent believing that inspection impacted their mental health (Education Support, 2023).

However, it is not just the days of inspection, but the weeks, months and years leading up to it that cause stress. For leaders with the school in the inspection window, to get to the middle of the week without 'the call' is a relief – until the following Monday rolls around. Trial-run or mock inspections (known colloquially as 'Mocksteds') carried out by school leaders or local advisers can be a harsh and harmful experience, particularly if they set doubts into the minds of staff who previously have had no concerns about their teaching standards. Dropping the 'O-word' into staff briefings only heightens anxieties, and language such as 'Ofsted are in the area' isn't helpful to the emotional health of our colleagues. Ofsted *are* in the area; so is the Amazon van, but there's no guarantee it will call.

Budget restraint

The reality of recent years of deficit budgets and the rising costs of heating and of school resources, accompanied by unfunded pay rises and top-slicing of school finances, has meant doing more with less. Small schools have the tightest budgets and may feel these pressures more than larger institutions, but nobody is immune. Very often, this has led to colleagues moving on through staff restructuring, which may affect support staff and teaching assistants, but also the staff who have the higher salaries. It may be more cost-effective to replace a teacher on UPS (the upper pay scale) with an inexperienced ECT, but is there consideration for the mental health impact on staff having to leave a job that they love, or on the school community losing the experience and wisdom of long-standing members of staff?

Who, though, is taking on this additional responsibility? Teachers, who are used to working with their teaching assistant as a classroom support, may now be seeing that colleague redeployed to specific interventions only, or be having no additional support at all. HLTAs might find themselves removed from their specific interventions to cover teachers' PPA time or teacher absences. Teachers, particularly in a small school, may find themselves taking on subject leadership very early in their careers, or sometimes managing several subjects at a time when inspection is demanding the same standards and knowledge across all subjects. On a different level, fewer adult bodies means more playground, lunchtime and gate duties that need covering, eating into valuable time. There are issues here around capacity and cognitive load to consider, whether this additional load is shared evenly or whether it is shouldered by a small number of staff. Even those who appear the most resilient have a point at which their health is impacted and where burnout may occur. A hard-headed economic approach may say that this is what business has to deal with, but in education, we are in the business of people; empathy should trump economics every time.

Staff absence and staff shortages

Staff are absent for a range of reasons: for health, parental leave, jury services and attending courses – this is part of school life. How the absences are managed can affect the stress levels of other staff, particularly if it results in additional workload or inroads into their time.

Tight budgets, as referenced above, may make the engagement of supply staff a challenge, resulting in colleagues covering absence. Although some union advice is not to provide such cover, teachers and support staff will generally do so because they put the children first. If such cover cannot be avoided, it must be done fairly and equitably, so as not to trigger any work-related stress through extra responsibilities. A simple way to answer queries about the fairness of cover is to have a chart of favours asked and favours returned in the office of the person organising cover, as a visible demonstration of fairness. A balanced chart demonstrates a fair-minded approach; an imbalanced one shows a less empathetic approach.

Managing short-term absence is just that: a management issue. Repeated and longer-term absence requires a more strategic approach, one with preventive and protective considerations for both the absent colleague and those present in school. Such actions could include:

- **Dealing with resentment:** Staff who have frequent or regular absences can be the subject of complaints from others, especially teachers who miss out on their valued release time. It is best to shut down conversations of this kind that start in the staffroom, as discussing a colleague in absentia is both unprofessional and can lead to false impressions. Equally, do not permit the resentment to fester, by ensuring that staff aren't missing out because of the long-term absence of another.
- **Rumour, gossip and speculation:** A regular pattern of absence could be due to medical or other personal issues. Again, this is nobody else's business, but we know that staffroom gossip about relationship problems, health issues or teachers attending interviews can be hurtful and have the effect of making a member of staff feel isolated.
- **Accusations of favouritism:** This manifests itself in a number of ways; from time away from school for family events or other leave while others have requests denied, to snow days where some staff can work from home while others are expected to attend school. In this latter case, it is more often than not our support staff who live in the local area.

Behaviour

Being challenged by, managing and then facing the consequences of poor classroom behaviour is a reason for stress in school, causing some teachers to leave the school or exit the profession altogether. Discussions around behaviour don't fall into a simple binary formula. There are teachers who promote restorative conversations; there are others who promote a stricter model. Even in a school where the behaviour policy is applied consistently and to the letter, differences between the behaviours in some classes will be observed because one teacher will have a different relationship with the class than the next teacher; that is not a judgement on teacher professionalism, but is how humans react differently to other people. To utter the phrase 'They behave for me' is not the best way of supporting a colleague, but experience will tell us that there are teachers who can maintain the attention of the class with a glance or a gesture, a carefully chosen word or a raised eyebrow, whereas others may feel that all their strategies fall flat.

The way staff are supported by senior leadership around behaviour can also affect staff mental health if it isn't dealt with effectively. Where children are sent to a senior leader for a behaviour issue and then return with what is interpreted as 'ten minutes calming down and no sanction', has behaviour been addressed or not? Was the behaviour policy followed by the teacher and the senior leader?

Was there communication between both adults? Is there a confusion between the behaviour policy and behaviour strategies, because these are not the same? Where consistency and communication are present, staff will feel more secure in the support that they have from senior colleagues.

Behaviour can also include the conduct of parents, which is discussed in Chapter 8.

Toxic cultures

A toxic workplace in any setting will affect the mental health and wellbeing of the staff. For schools, reliant on positive relationships in order to function effectively, toxicity can undermine years of relationship-building very quickly. As readers of *The Wellbeing Toolkit* (2019) will know, toxicity can originate from anywhere in the staff: from leadership, from elsewhere in the staff and in the school community. Each year, the Teacher Wellbeing Index asks about workplace culture; in 2022, a staggering 42 per cent of respondents reported that their organisational culture had a negative impact on their mental health and wellbeing, while only 24 per cent felt that there was a positive impact (Education Support, 2023).

Some staff feel that toxicity comes from leadership, and if leaders are those driving the culture of the school, it is easy to understand this perception. Toxic leadership habits can vary on a spectrum, from workplace bullying to excessive micromanagement, from social exclusion of some and favouritism of others, to encouraging cliques and tale-telling. From teachers called into the headteacher's office after school to explain what they had allegedly said in the staffroom at lunchtime, to teachers receiving an email rebuke because the staples on their displays were diagonal and not horizontal, there are practices and habits that trigger anxiety for staff and which demonstrate not a culture of care but one of fear. If your school is one where staff are regularly leaving the headteacher's office in tears or where senior leaders are measuring displays for the consistency of border widths or background colours and using this on action plans, the toxic culture will be undermining the mental health of your colleagues. Schools have a duty of care to their staff; a toxic culture does not embody a duty of care.

All toxicity does not, however, originate from leadership, and indeed many leaders have been at the sharp end of rudeness, bullying, cliques and gossip. Such habits can undermine the positive steps that the school leadership is trying to put in place. In part, this goes back to explaining your 'why', as we discussed in Chapter 1, but it can also be explained by the fact that some people do not like change or understand the reasons for this. Be wary of the member of staff who takes a new and inexperienced colleague under their wing. This could, of course, be a genuinely kind act, but many readers will recognise when this is used to gossip or be malicious about colleagues. Be aware also of the new staff being befriended and those who are not. This will be explored later in the chapter, with the use of sociograms. Another habit that will be familiar is that of staff coming to leadership or gossiping to colleagues about what staff may have posted on their social media. Making a disparaging remark about the school may be a concern, but speculation about a colleague's social life, relationship status or holiday photographs should not be. This is an intrusive behaviour, and staff who feel that they are being spied upon will be made to feel anxious by such actions. It is important to address toxicity among the staff because in our shared culture, everyone takes responsibility.

Constant review, embedding an ethos and raising challenging questions are essential to ensure that this does not remain a mere paper exercise, because if this is the case, the paper might be papering over the cracks. The cracks appear with staff absence linked to stress in the workplace, which could in itself be linked to workload. Workload around planning, marking, reporting and assessment should be considered in relation not only to the needs of the school, but also to what is feasible and what is needed. Are teachers required to email their plans on a Saturday to senior leaders for 'feedback and improvement' by Sunday evening? Are marking policies requiring teachers to mark in a plethora of highlighters with different-coloured pens and codes? The question to ask here is 'why?', because often these are unsustainable and are issues that can impact staff with stress and burnout. The lesson here is that wellbeing needs to be considered proactively, anticipating any negative impact.

The staff mental health and wellbeing survey

The staff survey should be carried out at least annually, although some schools will send these to staff termly and others will have some form of emotional check-in on a weekly basis. The purpose of gathering this data, as much as with the pupils, is to gauge the emotional temperature of the staff, identify concerns and put mitigations into place. Schools that make the survey part of the positive routine and culture of the life of the staff and are seen to act upon it are going to be knowledgeable and understanding of the needs of the staff.

When I have spoken to school leaders about the conduct of such surveys, some express reservations about it. Some are of the opinion that it is used as a tool to be critical of the headteacher and their policies and initiatives. Others have noticed a remarkable similarity in responses and feel that staff have discussed and colluded with answers. Further reaction has been that unreasonable and impossible demands are made, particularly of new or less experienced leaders. A number of headteachers have felt that their stress levels have increased after reading and collating responses, either because they have taken comments personally or because respondents have used the anonymity of the survey to be directly critical of others, naming them in the process. Such a scenario would suggest that there is something amiss with the culture of the school in such a situation where colleagues can raise their concerns online but not face to face.

The greatest issue for staff was over the question of anonymity. Handwritten surveys can identify people through their handwriting, but digital surveys can include questions such as 'what is your role in the school?' or leave space for written answers where grammatical style and choice of vocabulary indicate who has made a particular response. Surveys with space to enter name or email address or require the completed survey to be sent by email have no anonymity at all. It is the matter of anonymity that leads to a reluctance to be honest for fear of consequences. Some staff have felt pressured, either by leaders or by their colleagues, to answer in a certain way or to avoid certain responses. Either scenario fundamentally changes the accuracy of the survey and raises questions about its validity.

The strongest impression I gathered from my research into staff was that the survey was either a waste of time or a tick-box exercise – read, filed and not acted upon. The overwhelming issue for leaders was that it gave vent to the more negative members of staff and that the silent and more passive colleagues didn't find themselves recognised. Such polar-opposite views risk key concerns being overlooked or missed with regard to the mental health of teachers, support staff and leaders.

The staff survey needs to be a seed for growth of positive mental health, and not a battleground for sniping and mud-slinging. Many schools will undertake their surveys in a professional manner, and those that do it best have a high degree of trust and respect between colleagues, as well as a proven ability to listen. The most productive surveys have these supporting factors:

- The survey is a regular part of the school diary and is delivered at the same time each school year or term.
- Questions are consistent from one survey to the next, so that patterns can be identified and there is familiarity from all participants.
- Questions asking about the respondent's role in school are avoided, not only because of possible breach of anonymity, but also because the emphasis is on the benefits for the whole team.

- Questions are in two parts. The first part is perhaps on a 1–5 numerical scale, rather using terms such as 'fairly satisfied' or 'very unsatisfied', which can be limiting. The second part, in a free-text box, asks what could be done to change the answer given in the first part. This gives greater meaning and relevance to the survey.
- Leadership accepts that a level of constructive criticism will arise from the survey. They take the criticism, but act upon it.
- Findings are shared with staff and planned actions agreed, but the actions are 'done with' and not 'done to', so that concerns are resolved from all sides.
- Feedback from the survey is delivered promptly and shared with all staff, ideally in a face-to-face meeting rather than an impersonal email.

Sociograms

A sociogram is a simple but effective way of understanding the foundations of the relationships within any group, be it your staff group or a class of children. The use of sociograms as a basis of class intervention is discussed elsewhere in Chapters 4 and 7.

An internet search will bring up a number of examples of sociograms. Explained in its simplest terms, a sociogram consists of a circle representing each member of the group, and arrows or lines between the circles that show the relationships between the members of the group. The lines and arrows are at the heart of understanding and, crucially, knowing the ways in which group members interact with each other. The lines show who interacts with whom, but the arrows are the informative feature of the sociogram: arrows at both ends of the line show that there is a balance to the relationship, while an arrow at one end only could show that one party is more dominant and the other more passive. This, however, is where context is key and also where we should not be judgemental based on our first impressions. There will be colleagues who are louder than others; does this make them a workplace bully or are they confident and knowledgeable? Those who are quieter – are they being targeted or maybe they are reflective, shy or reticent? The sociogram is a valuable part of our toolkit, particularly when it comes to identifying those colleagues who may be feeling lonely and isolated, as the Teacher Wellbeing Index findings (Education Support, 2023) have outlined.

Particularly when new to a school, the process of completing the sociogram isn't an instant exercise. The sociogram is a paper or whiteboard exercise and, as it is being developed, should be kept confidential until the point at which actions arising from it can be determined. The opportunity to take time and return to the task as we have more knowledge of those with whom we work allows for a higher level of sophistication to be introduced. Thicker lines and arrows could be introduced, which might indicate the frequency and /or quality of the interactions. A wider line in one direction but a narrow one in the other may be one feature of the relationship between any two people. Equally, one colleague may have many lines linking to other members of staff, while some will have fewer.

The next stage of sophistication is to colour-code or RAG-rate the interactions with red, amber (or likely yellow or orange) and green, used in addition to the width of the lines. Green lines represent positive relationships, amber are professional but largely neutral interactions and red represent the situations that may be directly impacting upon the mental health of the staff and affecting levels of confidence, resilience, job satisfaction and also absence, through work-related stress. At this point, the sociogram becomes part of the staff mental health and wellbeing action plan and possibly part of performance management.

The person completing the sociogram and using it to develop strategies to support mental health in the workplace needs first to ensure that they have a level of emotional intelligence and empathy with their colleagues. The starting point for this exercise might lie with one person, but before any actions are rolled out, consultation with at least one colleague who may have a different perspective is essential, to avoid being judgemental in any way.

In any team, organisation or community, whatever the best intentions of the leadership, it takes just one person and their attitude and toxicity to shatter the balance of wellbeing in the group. Likewise, the person who describes themselves as kind or an empath should not make that judgement themselves. It is for those interacting with that person, who feel their warmth or otherwise, to decide.

Staff prioritising their own mental health and wellbeing

Our individual wellbeing differs from that of our colleague in the room next door, and from that of the school business manager and the teaching assistant who has seen several generations of children – and teachers – through the school. It differs because we are individuals and what we choose to do with our own time is down to choice. The school may have 'staff prioritising their own mental health and wellbeing' as an aim in the action plan, but it needs to be a reality and not something to tick off a list.

The aim will only be achieved if staff are enabled to do so. Your colleagues' wellbeing might be served by Friday evening swimming, a weekend climbing, running a half-marathon or an afternoon following their favourite spectator sport. Some may want to stay after 4.00 pm on a Friday so that they feel prepared for the week ahead. They may prefer an evening out with friends, time with family or simply their own company. What prevents the enabling of staff to give themselves priority is excessive workload, unreasonable demands that eat into weekends (such as uploading or emailing plans and being ready for feedback) and email contact out of working hours.

Another effective strategy is to encourage the concept of 'quiet quitting', which is not giving up an employment position but rather a statement of fulfilling the demands of the role and nothing more. We know as teachers that there is always something more to do, but quiet quitting allows boundaries to be set and is a firm but professional way to say 'no', especially to short-term and unexpected demands. Rather than let this be seen as an act of defiance, it can be built into effective leadership of staff mental health. Eliminating weekend emails and work is a start, but so too is not holding meetings for meetings' sake, setting an agenda and keeping to time. So-called 'fun' activities and team-building sessions can also be cast aside, as the after-school yoga session probably isn't for everyone. These are quite simple steps but are more effective and meaningful than 'Everyone out by 4.00 pm on a Friday' directives.

Wider issues around staff mental and physical health

Mental health is affected by physical health. We can feel emotionally drained, particularly if recovery is slow or symptoms return. There should also be consideration of feelings of guilt for being away from school; pressure increases if colleagues gossip or leaders apply pressure to return.

Menopause awareness

In a profession where women are in the majority in teaching, and even more so among support staff, it may be surprising that this is an issue. Schools with an excellent programme supporting staff mental health include menopause awareness within it, understanding that there are physical and emotional characteristics involved in the menopause. Such a programme would include ventilation and temperature control within classrooms and communal spaces, cover at short notice to use the toilet and washing facilities and ready access to cold drinking water. Most important is that all staff are menopause-aware and women are not made to feel uncomfortable in discussing symptoms. For this reason, if the school has a menopause group, it should include male staff so that they are informed and enabled to offer empathetic support. A school that makes reasonable adjustments, embraces flexible working patterns and encourages women to seek support will be more likely to retain experienced and committed staff.

Menstrual and reproductive health

A school with a culture of care for staff will have an ethos of period dignity for staff and pupils, one designed to avoid embarrassment or self-consciousness and one that educates male staff and boys. Menstrual health can be subject to a mix of misinformation and offensive comments, which can be upsetting, particularly for women suffering with painful periods or a heavy flow. An approach focused on dignity will include the opportunity to take necessary breaks, with cover provided without question. Some schools also provide the option of a day at home each month to manage period pain; these schools also address any judgemental comments or colleagues who believe this to be unfair.

An emotionally intelligent approach will also consider the needs of staff in all stages of pregnancy, but also those who have difficulty in conceiving. It is heartbreaking for some colleagues who have to hear the news of impending arrivals from elsewhere on the staff, when they are still waiting to share the same. Fertility treatment is an emotionally draining procedure, especially when there have been unsuccessful attempts. These colleagues need support in school but also protection of their privacy if they choose to keep this to themselves.

Life events

Life happens and the changes in the lives of our staff can impact their mental wellbeing but also affect the ways in which they relate to colleagues. Grief may be faced with resilience or a retreat into a shell; either scenario needs recognition and support offering. Likewise, with separation and relationship breakdown, your colleague may become withdrawn or put on a brave face.

Relationship breakdown can also alter professional conduct, with behaviour considered intimidating by others. In this case, support needs to be available to those on the receiving end of a change in behaviour.

Final thoughts

Staff mental health and wellbeing has been very much at the forefront of the thinking of empathetic school leaders. Others have realised that they may have forsaken this aspect of their mental health and wellbeing programme while readjusting to 'normal' post-Covid. There are also schools where it hasn't been a priority. How does this latter scenario sit with supporting our children, our parents and the broader community? The following chapters discuss this in further depth.

THINK about staff mental health and wellbeing

Time

- If staff are our most valuable resource, time is their most valuable resource. Staff need the time to do what they have to. Their PPA time needs to be protected, guaranteed and paid back within the same week if lost. They do not need their time wasted by unnecessary meetings and meaningless tasks.
- If time is wasted and lost, it adds to staff's cognitive load, which, if overloaded, can lead to stress and anxiety.
- Hard work should never be rewarded with more hard work.

Holistic

- Mental health and wellbeing is just one part of staff development, and one to take seriously, particularly given the statistics reported by Education Support (2023) and the concerns about teacher recruitment.
- Mental health needs to feature as part of the appraisal process – not linked to targets, but as part of professional development and job satisfaction.

Inclusive

- Does the practice in the school consider the needs of neurodiverse staff? Or of those who have a global majority background?
- The school should have a policy and strategy around menopause awareness and reproductive health, one that includes and informs male staff and challenges any stigma.
- Does your practice consider the needs of those staff who do not have a diagnosed condition or do not take time off with work-related stress? Their mental health still needs consideration in authentically inclusive practice.

Non-judgemental

- Stigma, speculation and gossip should be challenged professionally.
- A colleague taking time off with work-related stress means that they require support, both in their absence and on their return. They do not need to face any criticism for their time away and any additional workload caused to others.

Knowledgeable

- Do you know your staff or are they mere numbers on a spreadsheet? Knowing their strengths and weaknesses, their vulnerabilities and potential, is part of leadership responsibility – to develop and promote academic and pastoral excellence.
- The knowledge of staff needs also to include their personalities and their abilities to work in a team. The importance of this will become paramount when you have periods of increased stress – knowing whom to support, whom to keep an eye on and who might be best to counsel their colleague at a challenging time.
- The key strategy for staff mental health and wellbeing is to put in place protective and preventive measures, which applies to the mental health of our young people in school too.

Interview with Gemma Scotcher of Education Support: Staff, statistics and support

Gemma Scotcher is Director of Communications and Public Affairs at Education Support. Since 2017, the Teacher Wellbeing Index, or TWIX as it is known on social media, has provided statistics about the mental health of staff in schools and some of the factors impacting this. The TWIX formed the basis of our discussion.

Why should schools pay attention to the Teacher Wellbeing Index?

We've got seven years' worth of an evidence base, looking at the experiences of everyone working in schools and FE, and a broad cohort of educators, published at a regular point in the year. This is what individuals working in the sector are saying and experiencing and feeling; increasingly, the results provide an insight into the cultures that exist in schools. Much of what the evidence proves is what staff on the ground know and experience already in their own setting. I think what lands for them, and has value, is a feeling of being seen and a sense that we are being an independent voice for their experiences to the government.

Some of the answers that come out of the data are enlightening educators, particularly the different experiences among different cohorts. School leaders are the most at risk of chronic stress, insomnia and symptoms of poor mental health problems; this has been consistent over time. What we've seen over more recent years is a real deterioration in the experiences of support staff. There are few surprises in the headlines for educators, but the value is being seen and heard. There are nuances that are important for them to see, such as questions about the culture of the school having a negative impact and the question about whether you are actively seeking to leave. What does that mean for a leader's school if half of the staff told them they were miserable? Do they really have a sense of who is happy and who isn't? I use that statistic when talking with leaders. It is not a measure of them doing a bad job, but is indicative of systemic issues and what the culture they wish to create in the school will look like.

I think a simple way of thinking about cultures and relationships between staff is to consider who is more introverted and who is extrovert. There is an assumption by some that everybody in education should be gregarious and confident and this comes naturally to them. What we don't think about is what this takes from them and how much they might need to recover, nor do we think about giving space to allow for the more introverted colleagues. We need to be aware of neurodivergent members of staff.

How does intensity of working affect moral purpose?

There is also a place for thinking about intensity of different half terms in the year. A five-week half term before Easter can be as intense as the first seven or eight weeks up to the October break. There is pressure to get just as much done in these very different time periods, and this intensity has costs on the body, plus the rhythm of working at such a level means that you are working on fumes before collapsing into the holiday. These fumes, though, are cortisol, the stress hormone, and we risk teacher burnout. Teachers need to see the importance of sneaking regular moments for themselves, moments of connection to themselves, to sources of joy and to seek rest and rejuvenation. Teachers need to recover and remember that they are not machines, that they have limited reserves of energy. My invitation to educators would be as part of your moral purpose and as part of the passion for the job. Remember that you're not a machine; don't let your moral purpose sit between you and your human wellbeing needs. Every human body needs to rest, needs to rejuvenate, needs to be hydrated, needs to move, needs to connect with other human beings in a way that is meaningful. Moral purpose is amazing for creating meaning, but it's important to be aware of the dark side of that too.

There's a lot going on within schools because of the wider context. We've been through Covid and the cost of living crisis. The amount of social, emotional and mental health needs that are showing up in schools is at an all-time high, and on top of that, public services are under resourced and schools are the first port of call on the frontline of public services. They are squeezed from every direction. So many responsibilities are placed on teachers' shoulders, but they can't solve all of these, much of which are beyond their control and down to systemic issues. The education sector is a public service but not funded like one. As a society, we've let down our leaders and teachers by not giving them enough to work with and not investing in them. These are people who make miracles happen with very little but at high personal cost.

Why have you asked in the Teacher Wellbeing Index about loneliness?

The loneliness question came off the back of the heartbreaking case of Ruth Perry. We decided that we wanted to look at suicide risk, of which isolation is one risk factor. Ruth had to keep that judgement confidential over an eight-week period, including Christmas, and her experience of isolation must have been just awful.

We hear anecdotal things from staff who may have gone all day without speaking to another adult. I spoke to a leader who was recruiting some teachers recently, and the teachers said, 'I can't believe you have a staffroom.' We know that good cultures are made with positive connections and interpersonal relationships. Connecting with humans, even if you are introverted, is a vital part of your wellbeing, so it just felt important to ask about isolation, and on top of that we carried out some research into the experiences of global majority staff. One theme that came through strongly was that global majority staff very much wanted connection with other people who shared their identity and their cultural experience and background, so we are looking to develop our evidence base to build a clearer picture around this group.

The sense of loneliness and isolation is higher than the average for the general population. There is work to be done here. Staff need conversations with their colleagues, not isolation. Isolation adds to stress and heightened levels of cortisol and adrenaline. Staff need to replace these with oxytocin. Stress is the big headline statistic each year in the TWIX. Chronic stress and loneliness combined put people at a very real risk of suicide. In addition, chronic stress has long-term health risks through higher blood pressure, risk of cardiovascular diseases, risk to sleep patterns, the immune system, muscular and skeletal health. In our webinars with education staff, we talk of practical ways of bringing stress down because of the long-term health benefits. Teachers don't need to be constantly thinking and firefighting, becoming disconnected from themselves or limping over the line at the end of term. Even the simple task of sitting in the staffroom on a Friday after school, sharing a cup of tea and a packet of biscuits, can build connections, very much like sitting around a campfire and sharing stories built communities in the past, creating safe spaces and allowing people to decompress.

Has there been a change in the numbers of staff accessing the 24-hour helpline?

Numbers have kept quite steady, but what we have noticed is that staff who rely on our services are more likely to call multiple times, and that they are calling with more complex and a wider range of issues than ever before. We are a four nations charity, so anyone can call us; it is important that the number is up in every staffroom across the UK. We know that mental health waiting lists are long and not everybody can afford to pay for a therapist privately, so it can be incredibly hard to get access to mental health support – but when you call up, you speak to a qualified counsellor, trained to understand the nuances of working in education.

From talking to people that have used the service, they tell me of the difference that it makes and how helpful it is. Even those who are a little wary or sceptical about mental health services and talking support come away completely surprised at how much of an impact it has. I feel very confident that our professional supervision has kept people in the profession, and our helpline has at times kept people back from the brink of a crisis. We support staff in a variety of roles: leaders, teachers, college lecturers, support and administrative staff, as well as retired teachers.

In the last three years, we've really upped the amount of digital content and interactive content that we're producing, so if staff want to go and read about a mental health subject that has been specifically drafted and written and designed for a school setting, or engage in education webinars, the material is there for them. We have increased the content for teaching assistants, who have been underrepresented, as well as for middle leaders. There have been webinars on menopause, which have been well attended and have seen a number of male staff attend. We know that men are more represented at leadership level in schools, so as culture-setters and role models, their attendance on such training is important.

What do you hope the Teacher Wellbeing Index will be telling us in the future?

Change will be slow, whether there is a change of government or not. My hopes are that when change happens, it is meaningful and impacts staff retention. If we get retention right, then recruitment should look after itself. Much of what is happening on the recruitment side is dependent upon the breakdown of the reputation of teaching as a profession. I want to see that as a real focus from the government, to ensure that the statistics in the report start coming down, with more staff saying they want to stay. I would like to see the cultures in school change and that everything that feeds into this is invested in. We need to invest in and support leaders to be able to create the cultures needed to keep staff well, engaged and fulfilled. I obviously want to see the stress that teachers experience come down. We need staff to prioritise their own mental health and for schools to recognise that the bodies in front of the children for a long time each day are human beings first. We are pleased that Ofsted are undertaking 'The Big Listen', but very much hope that it leads to meaningful and lasting change. Change needs to be deep and a quick fix will never be enough.

Teachers, support staff and leaders need to be living and leading their lives, but need to know of the ways we can support and assist them at Education Support. We just need to keep banging the drum.

Education Support

Education Support is the only UK charity dedicated to supporting the mental health and wellbeing of teachers and education staff in schools, colleges and universities. It supports a 24-hour helpline on 08000 562561 for immediate and confidential emotional support.

4 Identifying needs

> **Chapter overview**
>
> In this chapter, we will consider:
>
> - the link between mental health and attendance
> - the link between mental health and behaviour
> - the link between mental health and attainment
> - the impact of life experiences – adverse childhood experiences
> - processes of identification and referral
> - review, evaluation and using feedback.

Mentally healthy pupils are in the best position to learn and achieve: they will be happy, resilient, focused on their learning, and able to work to deadlines, complete assessments and work academically and socially with their peers.

This is very much an idealistic position, although few of us would disagree with its sentiments. We know that, for all our pupils, all the above criteria fall on a spectrum and that their position on that spectrum isn't fixed but can vary according to a range of circumstances. Mental health concerns can affect many areas of children's experience, including their quality of life, academic achievement, physical health and satisfaction with life in school, and negatively impacting relationships with teachers, classmates and friends, as well as with their family members. These issues can also have long-term consequences for young people, affecting their future academic and career prospects, earning potential and lifelong health.

In identifying emerging issues, the school needs to act in a timely fashion, but also in a way that draws upon the knowledge of the children and of their families, and the relationships that the children have with school and schooling. The school will draw upon every aspect of the pupils' experience in school, including how they attend, how they behave and how they attain.

The link between mental health and attendance

School attendance has been lower than expected since the pandemic, and has been a concern for ministers and school leaders. Good attendance supports academic attainment; the act of being in class means that the pupils have the experience of learning. Attendance also supports social development, self-esteem, relationships with peers and teachers, and in providing stability and consistency. Missing out on social and academic interaction can trigger anxieties around lost learning but also around classroom dynamics, which can change noticeably even over a day or two.

Covid times and the fear generated by the tide of information and misinformed opinions have amplified the worries many of our children already had and added more. Lockdown was a traumatic period; towns like Blackburn and Bolton had high levels of infection and mortality, with many children losing parents or grandparents. Loss and grief impact mental health, but so too does the fear of the possibility of the passing of a loved one. Children were reluctant to come to school, particularly after the return to education in September 2020 just as infections began to rise again. Clearly, issues around attachment were exacerbated during this period.

Taking registration on school information management systems allows for patterns of absences to be analysed for individuals and families, for year groups and for individual classes. Some of these patterns could be indicators of an underlying mental health condition:

- Are there similar patterns with siblings within the same school or in the primary or secondary setting where other family members attend? If there are, what reasons are given? Are there consistent explanations and how can these families be supported?

- Are there regular days taken – typically Monday or Friday? A judgemental attitude would be, as I often heard in my career, 'They're at the caravan again!', which normalises a stereotype. More often than not, such patterns could involve issues as diverse as avoiding homework or family dynamics, both of which could be followed up and supported with a different mindset.

- Is low or sporadic attendance historic or is this unusual for the individual or family? Is this an indicator of underlying patterns of physical or mental ill health that the school was not previously aware of? How can the school be of support?

Although education welfare officers (EWOs) and school attendance staff have a specific role to fulfil, some parents can regard their work as heavy handed or intrusive. Which approach is better: an 'authoritarian' one, backed by talk of legal action, fines and custodial sanction, or an empathetic one, which emphasises the benefits of consistent attendance alongside the legal requirements, but which also promotes a supportive culture for families that are struggling? As we discussed in Chapter 2, the way we use language is important, and any notion of 'truancy' or 'school refusal' is best now seen through the lens of emotional-based school avoidance (EBSA), which acknowledges the root of the issue. EBSA is a broader issue than not attending the school site, and includes not entering the classroom or staying in class, not attending certain lessons and the avoidance of certain spaces and people, both peers and adults in school. The risk factors for EBSA could lie within the child (anxiety, trauma, self-esteem or attachment), may originate from the family (family stress, home environment, family history of EBSA), may come from the school (bullying, difficult subjects, difficult relationships with some staff) or may, of course, be affected by a combination of any or all three.

A word to the wise about attendance awards: although set up with good intent, to reward those with high or 100 per cent attendance, there are children who will catch every virus or bacteria because they are still developing their medical immunity. We also have children who are medically vulnerable and those who require regular treatment, meaning that they have time away from school. These children and their parents often feel excluded from the reward process. In nearly 30 years in schools, I have only ever known of one child with 100 per cent attendance through primary school; although Dame Rachel de Souza, who since 2021 has served as Children's Commissioner, has said that she would like to see 100 per cent attendance from all children (de Souza, 2023), we know that regular seasonal infections and waves of chicken pox will make this a challenging goal to achieve.

The link between mental health and behaviour

Behaviour in school includes all aspects of the term: good or poor conduct, social interactions, factors impacting upon children's confidence and emotional development. Behaviour is also an expression of the student voice, and in Chapter 7 we will consider a little more about how behaviour is also an expression of communication.

Poor behaviour is a risk factor to the mental health of other children, whether they are on the receiving end of it or have witnessed it. Bullying in school and cyberbullying out of school can have a devastating impact, one that can be lifelong, leading to fear, lack of trust, depression in later life and increased risk of suicide. Peer-on-peer abuse (which can also include sexual abuse and any form of discrimination) and peer pressure leading to disruptive or unlawful conduct both require the school to be aware that this can happen, as well as to know where and how this can occur. Our spaces in school need to be safe: toilets and bathrooms, changing rooms and outside spaces out of sight of duty staff or CCTV. Creating a position of psychological safety by placing an emphasis on physical safety in the school is a powerful protective factor.

The quality of relationships between pupils and staff need to be explored in understanding risk and protective factors. A poor student–teacher relationship can negatively affect self-esteem and self-confidence, which can undermine how the pupil performs academically. The student may feel that they are being constantly criticised or ignored; this could be their interpretation of the relationship, one that may not be shared by others. Questioning isn't criticism, but the feeling of being bombarded with questions – especially if the answers given aren't correct – can affect the resilience of a young person. Pastoral observation of the practice in class may give rise to support for the child in this aspect of resilience. Positive stuff–pupil relationships are demonstrated through a low level or absence of conflict and a high degree of support, which will promote academic performance, resilience and social interaction.

Nobody would ever wish to excuse poor conduct in a school, but we do need to have an understanding of the reasons behind some behaviours, particularly around behaviour disorders. These disorders can only be diagnosed by a professional, and we need to avoid conversations that use such terms inaccurately and without a secure knowledge or evidence base. We also need to avoid taking one or two typical behaviours and making assumptions from them, particularly if this is repeated among staff and a child earns an unfair reputation. We need to be aware of these and other behaviours as a possible early sign of a mental health disorder requiring external support.

Oppositional defiant disorder (ODD)

Some of the typical behaviours of a child with ODD include:

- being easily angered, annoyed, frustrated or irritated, often resulting in tantrums
- arguing frequently with their most familiar adults, such as parents or teachers
- apparent refusal to obey rules
- annoyance or aggravation of others
- low self-esteem
- seeking to blame others for their own conduct.

Conduct disorder (CD)

Often associated with the term 'anti-social behaviour', typical behaviours of a child with CD may include:

- frequent refusal to obey parents or other authority figures
- poor school attendance
- risky behaviour with drugs, cigarettes and/or alcohol at an early age
- lack of empathy for others
- being aggressive to animals and other people or showing sadistic behaviours, including bullying and physical or sexual abuse
- aggressive behaviour to random individuals, possibly with weapons
- petty and more serious criminal behaviours
- a tendency to run away from home.

Attention deficit hyperactivity disorder (ADHD)

The characteristics of ADHD can include:

- inattention – difficulty concentrating, forgetting instructions, moving from one task to another without completing anything

- impulsivity – talking over the top of others, having a 'short fuse', being accident-prone
- overactivity – constant restlessness and fidgeting.

Children diagnosed with CD and ODD may also be diagnosed with ADHD.

Although the causes of ODD, CD and ADHD are unknown, there are common risk factors for the school to consider in its plan for managing mental health associated with behaviour:

- **Gender:** Boys are more likely than girls to be diagnosed with behavioural disorders. This could be linked to experience of socialisation. There is no clear evidence of genetic links.
- **Gestation and birth:** Difficult pregnancies, premature birth and low birth weight may contribute to later difficulties.
- **Family life:** Exposure to domestic violence, poverty or substance abuse are potential risk factors.
- **Learning difficulties and brain development:** These can also be contributory factors.

The link between mental health and attainment

Pupils with better mental and physical health and wellbeing are likely to achieve better academically. If we support children in their social and emotional literacy, they are likely to develop a growth mindset and be able to set and achieve goals. Learning that is enjoyable and which offers engagement, challenge and progression can provide motivation, especially to children with lower expectations than their peers.

Poor mental health can affect engagement in lessons and can be demonstrated in a reluctance to ask or answer questions or to complete set tasks. Concentration can also be affected by poor mental health; a culture of noticing will recognise this change in a young person's learning behaviour. High expectations and pressures to achieve affect some children, with this pressure originating from family and from school. The shift back to fully examined GCSE and A level examination since the full return from the pandemic has exacerbated this. Likewise, progress through the academic year can also be an indicator of poorer mental health; pupil progress meetings can be used to highlight such concerns, while at the same time remembering that a 'plateauing' of progress is quite a normal aspect of learning and growing.

Thinking holistically, although social relationships aren't measured in terms of academic progress, a child becoming withdrawn from their usual social groupings and demonstrating a reluctance to engage in their usual school activities will be requiring a level of support so that this does not impact on their learning experience. Likewise, a change in levels of energy and enthusiasm can highlight that a pupil is under pressure in some way and needs support in their emotional resilience.

The impact of life experiences – adverse childhood experiences

We have all faced challenging situations in our childhoods: making and breaking of friendships, finding a test in school difficult, losing a much-cherished possession. These are simply part of growing up, and we have coping strategies and a degree of resilience to enable us to move on. As an adult, we recognise when we might have had a bad day, but the strategies that we have learned growing up enable us to face day-to-day challenges.

Some children face experiences and environments that they cannot manage or cope with, which can have lifelong effects upon emotional development, learning, physical and mental health, and the ability to form lasting relationships as adults. Adverse childhood experiences (ACEs) are highly stressful and potentially traumatic events and situations faced during childhood and adolescence. An ACE might be a single event, such as a fatal accident or act of violence, or prolonged risk to safety, security or bodily integrity.

In my time as a classroom teacher, I was aware of these examples of ACEs:

- abuse or neglect by parents, carers, siblings and other family members
- violence and coercive behaviours, including domestic violence and gang membership
- any form of prejudice, including racism, sexism and misogyny, LGBTQIA+ prejudice and discrimination around disability and neurodiversity

- taking on adult responsibility – being a young carer
- suffering inhuman treatment, such as torture, human trafficking, female genital mutilation (FGM), modern slavery or enforced child labour
- bereavement and grief, particularly if the death is one of a parent or sibling
- family history of substance misuse
- family breakdown and unstable relationships
- financial deprivation, especially during the cost of living crisis
- trauma around warfare, oppressive regimes, migration and refugee/asylum status.

Around half of children in England have not experienced an ACE, but of the remainder, 23 per cent have experienced one, 16 per cent have experienced two or three, and nine per cent have experienced four or more (YoungMinds, n.d.). Around half of all adults have experienced ACEs as children or adolescents. Children who have experienced ACEs are more at risk of undertaking risky behaviours, including binge drinking, experimentation with illicit drugs, unprotected and underage sexual intercourse, and involvement in violence. They are also more likely to have low levels of wellbeing and life satisfaction.

Not all children who face adversity will go on to develop a mental health problem. There are a number of protective factors, environmental and domestic, that can be employed. Schools are likely to be working with external agencies in supporting some of these children, but there are strategies to put into place which can protect against adverse outcomes and will also benefit every child in school:

- Be ready – have a structure in place, including policies and referral pathways.
- Be prepared to intervene early, as access to appropriate services may avoid repeated trauma.
- Have a positive, compassionate and supportive pastoral structure.
- Enable safe relationships with peers.
- Involve young people in the decision-making process.
- Teach problem-solving skills, strategies for resilience and conflict de-escalation.
- Model regulation of emotions and teach self-regulation.
- Ensure that staff are trauma-aware, recognise need and avoid labelling children and any stigma around ACEs.

Processes of identification and referral

Awareness and knowledge

The starting point for identification of concern needs to lie in the awareness of all staff in school of their responsibilities and what to look out for. In Chapter 1, we discussed having a culture of noticing, one where staff are vigilant and professionally curious to the early signs and symptoms that can alert the school of difficulties. This encourages a holistic approach, one that supports secondary settings particularly well, as the movement of a student between five lessons a day in addition to tutor time could quite easily lead to them passing under the radar of one or more teachers and key signs being missed. Never make assumptions either; we may think that everyone knows each other in a small school or village school, but do they? There is a huge difference between knowing a child and their family by sight and by name and actually *knowing* them – what motivates them, challenges them, inspires them or worries them.

Knowledge through sociograms

If we want our teaching staff to be knowledgeable, we can return to the use of sociograms, the mechanisms of which were discussed in Chapter 3. In the same way as with staff, the sociogram with pupils shows who interacts with whom, the groupings within a class and who is more isolated, either by the actions of others or through their choice or needs. In a primary school setting, the sociogram can be a joint venture between class teacher, teaching assistants and PPA teachers – in other words, those that know the dynamics of the class. It needs to remain as a living, organic document, one to return to as the children grow and change. Your EYFS classes will see this in particular, as children become more confident and forge new relationships. For our secondary colleagues, if the students move from lesson to lesson as a form group, then this is a document into which subject teachers can feed. Where there is ability setting and when options are chosen, the dynamics of the group will change, maybe leading to these subject teachers considering a sociogram of their own. A core sociogram document could be kept at tutor level, where students may remain with the same tutor from Year 7 to Year 11, based on the deep knowledge of the group members that the tutor ought to have.

The benefits of using a sociogram to support positive mental health in schools include the following:

- They show which groups or individuals may be stronger and more influential in a class. The influence could be positive, in terms of acting as role models, or negative, if there is bullying or disruptive behaviour.
- They indicate children who are outsiders, lonely or isolated for a number of reasons: new to the school, victims of bullying or social exclusion, or difficulties with communication and social skills.
- The sociogram may indicate if a child is neurodiverse, which may not at this stage have been diagnosed or even raised as a concern by parents or staff.

Going under the radar

If you have children who may pass notice on your teacher's radar, who do not stand out in exceptional ability or struggle academically, who are quiet and well behaved but don't stand out in class, these are the children on whom to focus in your sociogram. The 'invisible children', as James Pye (1988) described them, offer little challenge or difficulty to their teachers, meaning that the adults in school don't really know them at all. This theme has arisen in recent conversations, especially where schools are unaware of an emerging mental health crisis, sometimes resulting in self-harm or attempted suicide. Children who are 'loud' in either positive or challenging ways are noticed by a wider audience; it is the quiet ones that we need to notice – to engage and develop their emotional literacy to enable them to be supported as positively as the rest. As trainee teachers, we were encouraged to 'know your pupils' and to look beyond their academic attainment. Consider this in depth: knowing your pupils means not just what their abilities are but what makes them tick, what challenges them, what barriers they have to learning, communication and socialisation and what their home lives are like; the experience of education is about the whole child.

The referral pathway and process

For teachers and support staff, the starting points for the referral process are always going to be from our knowledge of the pupil, from observation, and from noticing changes in behaviour and language. The children may seek help themselves, perhaps directly if the culture of the school has given the children the capacity and confidence to ask, or more indirectly through a change in the way they question or in their body language and facial expression. Referrals can also begin from the parents and carers or from the pupil's friends. Schools that have developed a strong culture around mental health will have a very clear referral process. In the first instance, new referrals could go to the class teacher or form tutor, who may find that an initial conversation with the pupil can allay any concerns. The 'could' here is qualified: as a matter of early help, this is a logical and organisational first step. If, however, the concern has been raised only after previous opportunities to intervene have been missed, then an acceleration to another level of support may be required sooner. Having the class teacher or tutor taking this initial step works in a similar way to finding that a new child has some difficulties in learning; the first step isn't to refer straight to the SENDCo but to consider other strategies for learning in class, and only when these have not proved successful, to seek the advice of the special needs department.

The schools that have the best referral pathways often set this out in diagram form, as a flow chart employing text boxes and colour-coding. These pathways might also be called intervention maps, because mapping the potential pathways of support forms a key part of an efficient process. The initial point is the class teacher or form tutor; in order for them to fulfil this level of responsibility, they need to be equipped with skills and strategies to provide an appropriate level of support, which is covered in the following chapter.

A good referral pathway will show the responsibilities at each stage of the process. Typically, the first level of a pathway will go from the initial concern to the class teacher/form tutor, who may conduct daily check-ins and parental liaison and initiate a pastoral support plan (PSP) if necessary. The documentation and practice will also clarify who informs the child, parents and colleagues and what happens when, a given time frame providing a level of reassurance. The next step will be heads of year or key stage leads, dependent upon the size of the school or whether primary or secondary, who may take on more of a mentoring role and take the PSP further, again with parental involvement. In some schools, this may be taken on by the SENDCo or family liaison staff, depending upon the responsibilities and organisation within the school.

This level of support on an initial level may be sufficient for pupils who do not require a further level of intervention, but the second level will be more specifically directed to supporting those with an identified need, which can emerge from a triage system of assessment. Triage, if you have spent any time in an A&E department, is about prioritising and seeking the most appropriate intervention on the pathway. As much knowledge and data – soft or hard – as can be accumulated needs to feed into the decision-making process. The decision may be to continue support in school, such as with interventions around anxiety, anger or body image, for which the school may have the capacity. It is possible that the school has an in-house counsellor or the financial capacity to buy in support. Costs can be high or prohibitive, but sharing a counsellor among a MAT or a group of local schools may be a viable option. There may be other services that can be accessed on site, including bereavement support or dedicated time with a pastoral mentor. All this would precede the next level, which will involve external services; this will be covered in Chapter 9.

Review, evaluation and using feedback

The referral pathway and intervention map will consist of a cycle of assessment of initial need, planning appropriate support, delivering the interventions and review of the interventions. Review doesn't mark the end of the process but provides the chance to evaluate the impact and effect that the intervention has had: to decide whether a greater or lesser degree of support is required and whether support continues internally or more expert external provision is called for. We need to decide whether the difficulties that a child has had are persisting and to what degree they are continuing.

Teachers and support staff are time-poor, and evaluation of any support programme – and perhaps the delivery of the intervention in the first place – can be impacted by the paucity of time. This is one reason for mental health and wellbeing having a priority place in the school development plan, and for budget, staffing and resourcing to be considered carefully. If the school is going to invest in commercially available screening tools or devise its own, such as strength and difficulties questionnaires, then budgeting and workload responsibility will dictate whether these can be used effectively. The evaluation and review process for mental health intervention will require time and reflection, the opportunity to talk with the child, parents and colleagues involved in the process and, for the sake of consistency, the same questioning at the outset as at the end of the intervention. There should be a further review, a half term or full term after the end of the intervention, to evaluate whether the intervention has had a lasting impact or whether further support may be required.

Final thoughts

Identification of the needs and concerns demonstrated by our young people is part of our professional responsibility, just as much as safeguarding and managing behaviour is. We may not be experts in the field of mental health but, as educators, we are adept at recognising barriers to learning, and possible interventions we can deliver in house or which require the support of external agencies. The following chapter will discuss the targeting of support.

> **THINK about identifying needs**
>
> Time
>
> - Identification should be timely and evidence-based, rather than hurried and drawn from an incomplete picture.
> - Quality time allows for quality control to evaluate intervention most effectively.
> - Allow time in timetabling for colleagues to discuss their concerns and observations and for pupils to do so too.
>
> Holistic
>
> - Consider how mental health impacts on learning, attendance, behaviour and attainment, and in turn how they affect mental health and each other.
> - Need concerns the whole child, and your bigger picture features every child in your school, regardless of their level of need.
>
> Inclusive
>
> - Although there may be a stereotype that areas of higher deprivation have a greater risk of mental disorders being diagnosed, remember that mental health affects everyone, regardless of socio-economic background, race, gender or academic ability.
> - Policies and practices should address specific needs but also provide a universal standard of care.
>
> Non-judgemental
>
> - The 'Keeping children safe in education' document (DfE, 2023b) reminds us not to attempt to diagnose mental health; to do so can be harmful and have impacts more widely across the school.

- We need to recognise when something may be wrong and require the intervention of an expert, who is better qualified and more able to support than the school can provide from its own resources.

Knowledgeable

- 'Know your pupils' is an old adage from our trainee days, but it holds true.
- Building a picture of connections, relationships, backgrounds and interests gives a deeper understanding of the lives of our young people and of the pressures they face at school, at home and in the community.

Case study: An international perspective, Emmanuelle Brunet, latterly of Obersee Bilingual School

Obersee Bilingual School is situated in Wollerau, Switzerland, on the shores of Lake Zurich, having recently relocated from St Gallen. The school has some 450 pupils, from Early Years up to International Baccalaureate level, with one third coming from over 40 countries. The school is student-centred, with a pedagogical approach focused upon open and positive collaboration rather than the application of unnecessary pressure. The school promotes self-efficacy and positive relationships, strengthening wellbeing and listening to learners, alongside the positive use of digital technology and contemporary educational skills.

Emmanuelle Brunet was, until 2024, the Head of Wellbeing at Obersee, teaching PSHE, French and Italian, and was also a team and personal coach. Emmanuelle believes that it is a happy child who will flourish the most. It is only through developing soft skills, and coaching children to understand themselves and others around them, that they will grow into confident adults. Emmanuelle is a passionate teacher who believes that the teaching of languages, cultures and wellbeing is key to a brighter future, and a very empowering one. She feels truly blessed to have worked with children and adults who both inspire and help everyone to grow, by learning from each other and by preparing them to embrace the challenges of the future.

To address any concerns that arise in relation to children's mental health in the school, the PSHE curriculum serves as a platform to help the children to manage their emotions; this includes teaching them from an early age to name and to know their emotions. Encouraging the children to talk about how they are feeling is a priority – an important tool for young people to have when they reach the teenage years and their emotional and hormone-led changes need them to be monitored closely. Emmanuelle's major concern was originally that young people did not possess the tools to deal with emotions and social conflicts, because of the interference of adults, and because of the interactions that occur on social media.

To support the needs of the children, the school put in place a strong wellbeing curriculum, from Early Years to upper school. Wellbeing workshops, PSHE days and lessons where students learn to self-reflect serve to support the emphasis on their own mental health. Each child also now has a personal coach and a team coach, enabling them to be supported on an individual level but also to be aware of relationships between themselves and peers. The school appointed 'Peace Keepers' – young student leaders who help staff to keep an eye out for children experiencing some difficulties.

Wellbeing questionnaires provide a degree of measure for the personal coaches to refer to, identifying young people in need of additional support. The school counsellor offers support or advises external agency intervention if appropriate. The school works closely with families, keeping a tight and supportive network in place.

Switzerland took a different approach to Covid lockdowns from the UK, introducing mitigations at an earlier stage and not having as rigid a lockdown in the spring of 2020, enabling earlier reopening of services, although the second wave led to much tighter restrictions. The impact on young people in the school, similar to the UK, was on the social and emotional skills of the children, spending time learning online and missing out on the interactions with their peers. Certain year groups did show more heightened levels of anxiety, but the coaching structure in the school enabled these identified needs to be supported appropriately.

Emmanuelle prides herself on the wellbeing structures she was able to put in place and, just like the UK schools in *The School Mental Health Toolkit*, she took a holistic, non-judgemental and knowledgeable approach to supporting the mental health needs of the school community, promoting healthy habits alongside supporting the development of emotional intelligence.

5 Targeted support and appropriate provisions

Chapter overview

In this chapter, we will consider:

- universal provision
- risk factors and protective factors in the school environment
- support that the school can offer to all pupils
- selective provision
- intensive provision.

Your school will be looking to promote an informed discussion about the mental health and wellbeing of the members of its community. In addition to promoting good mental health, you will also be looking at prevention within the school setting, the starting point of which is the culture, ethos and leadership of mental health in school. Prevention might be concerned with changes in environment, with the context and social conditions of the school, with academic and pastoral factors, with what happens in lessons, and with transitions between lessons and between year groups and key stages. The provisions and interventions that the school makes available to all stakeholders will project how serious school leaders are about promoting positive mental health. An approach that is proactive and responsive to anticipated situations will trump one that is reactive and which seems a constant fire-fighting exercise. In evaluating the provisions that the school has in place, gaps will inevitably be noted, but by considering the three levels within the context of the school, priority can be given to the most pressing areas of need.

Universal provision

The universal offer, to which every child has access, includes the curriculum around mental health and emotional wellbeing, which is discussed in depth in Chapter 10. It also includes the entitlement to support, which every child and family has, regardless of their level of need. It includes all the schemes of learning and the measures of support that are available to the whole school community. The universal offer acknowledges the risk factors that may lie in the context of the community, and the protective (or preventive) measures that are in the policies and practices of the school. The importance of this part of the offer around mental health and wellbeing is in its universality – in the acknowledgement that mental health is for everyone, that it affects each and every one of us and that our conversation promotes a judgement-free awareness of what mental health is.

Risk factors and protective factors in the school environment

Risk factors – those factors making individuals and groups more at risk of developing mental health problems – are cumulative, as the section about ACEs in Chapter 4 discussed. Risk factors can relate to the characteristics of the child – their learning and communication difficulties, developmental delay or perception of academic failure. They can lie in the family – parental conflict, relationship breakdown, inconsistent discipline, physical, sexual and/or emotional abuse, neglect or a family history of psychiatric illness. Equally, they may lie in the community, if there is exposure to discrimination or exploitation, gang culture and/or online abuse. As a school, these risk factors need to be on our knowledge radar, as we may be called to support other agencies in a wider team supporting a child or a family. The risk factors in school include bullying, discrimination, lack of positive relationships, peer pressure, peer abuse and poor relationships with adults in school.

Protective factors are there to help children to develop their resilience and to try to prevent mental health concerns from emerging or becoming more serious. The more a child is exposed to risk factors, the greater the need for them to have protective factors. Schools therefore have a place in providing the safety and security of having a trusted person to speak to and to talk openly with. Protective factors already covered in previous chapters include the whole-school approach to mental health and the ethos embedded across the school, effective safeguarding, a consistent behaviour policy and the school's actions around attendance.

Bullying

The single most effective preventive strategy that a school can adopt is its approach to bullying. This approach needs to be more than policy, because if the policy is not followed, does not work or is not effective, its aims and objectives will lie empty. Bullying is a barrier to learning and also has lifelong mental health impacts, including upon domestic and social behaviours, and it can also lead to suicide ideation in young people and in later life. Bullying needs to be identified and addressed at an early stage in a child's school career, to minimise the opportunity to repeat the actions and to minimise the chance of being bullied. Bullying isn't part of growing up or a test of resilience, but a challenge to the mental health of the bullied and the bully alike.

Staff behaviour

Staff behaviour should be a given, although the evidence discussed in Chapter 3 shows that negative conduct and attitude have an effect upon colleagues. Likewise, the conduct of staff needs to make our children feel safe, and the code of conduct should include reference to how children are spoken to and spoken about. There may be a 'no shouting' protocol, because shouting can be upsetting or triggering and also implies a loss of control or authority in a situation. The way pupils are talked about can influence the way other colleagues think about them, whether it is stereotyping a group by beginning a sentence with 'The problem with these children…' or something similar or describing individuals in less than complimentary terms. While it is true that teachers may need to sound off about frustrations, there needs to be an appropriate outlet – the 'open door' from Chapter 2 – to do so professionally and with a solution-focused attitude.

Staff raising concerns and complaints

Such an 'open door' can support our positive culture of mental health, both so that staff can discuss their concerns for an individual child or a wider group, and also to raise concerns that they may have about policies and procedures. This is an important part of the ongoing review and evaluation process and should be welcomed as a means of constant improvement, and not taken as a criticism. It is possible that gaps in the referral pathway may be noted, but it may also be a conduit for concern about colleagues not following procedure and opportunities being missed. This is a chance to develop the CPD around mental health, and not a route to a support plan.

Positive staff relationships with pupils

The negative aspects of poor staff–student relationships was detailed in the previous chapter. Good staff relationships convey respect, allow the young people to know which adults they can trust and encourage them to seek support when they need it. Children will naturally have different adults to whom they might turn first: the deputy head, a long-serving teaching assistant, a family liaison officer, their teacher or form tutor. Always pay heed if certain staff or departments don't have this positive relationship. It only takes one negative experience to undermine the work of others and for the young person to feel unsupported.

Open door for pupils

Although some colleagues may recoil in protest at children being allowed to leave the classroom on a whim, if a child suddenly needs to talk to an adult, they should be able to do so without fear of consequences, because timely support may be necessary. Successful schools, with an established ethos around mental health and where staff may recognise trigger points, will allow a child to speak to a key person when required. This isn't performed on an ad hoc basis but with a clarity of communication – maybe a visual signal or showing a card that the teacher will accept without drawing attention to the pupil or interrupting the flow of the lesson.

Positive classroom management

Positive classroom management is all about creating a supportive and respectful learning environment where students feel valued and engaged. It focuses on preventing problems through proactive strategies rather than relying on reactive discipline. High expectations can be reinforced by positive and constructive criticism. Linking closely with the behaviour and rewards strategy of the school, the strategies need to be consistent between classes, which needs the 'why' of the school to be clearly outlined in guidance and in training.

Sense of belonging

A sense of belonging is about connection, acceptance and being valued, and about the class, year group and whole school being a safe and secure network of support. The school as a community can show that pupils are part of something bigger than themselves but which recognises their individual role in the success of the community. A strong sense of belonging can boost self-esteem and resilience and add to a sense of purpose. This can be boosted by a house system in school, enabling every child to contribute to their team by earning rewards for all aspects of school life – academic, sporting, cultural or behavioural. No child should ever be left feeling that they contribute little or nothing; a strong sense of belonging can help to overcome this.

Positive peer influences and friendships

Lessons and assemblies can reflect upon how friendships form, but also draw attention to the fact that children may not always get on or may be influenced to do something that they shouldn't. There are ways to demonstrate children acting as positive role models, which can include the confident children – unafraid to share their opinions – but can equally include the quiet, reflective and more introverted young people. Demonstrating that we can be positively influenced by a range of different people is good for challenging stereotypes, particularly around certain behaviours, such as sexism or ableism.

Range of activities

Schools can offer activities beyond the classroom that offer enrichment and enjoyment to our young people. These could be in the form of after-school clubs, often sports- or arts-based, but can also include activities in other parts of the school day. Any opportunity to be outdoors and active is good for wellbeing, and offering gardening or Forest School opportunities at lunchtime gives those children who find a noisy playground overwhelming a chance to use their time productively. There is a place too for traditional and, to an extent, lost playground games, which keep children active but also help with cooperation and developing socialisation skills.

Valued social and leadership roles

In *The Wellbeing Curriculum* (2021), I dedicate a chapter to developing leadership roles in primary school. The emphasis there is not on the roles often perceived to be the place of the more confident children, such as running the school council or having the responsibility of showing visitors around and sharing their thoughts about the setting. In the school where I am a governor, this latter responsibility is shared among the whole of the Year 6 group, enabling me to meet and converse with every pupil in that year group across an academic year. They thrive in this environment and are confident in talking about their learning and the support that they receive, as well as showing the confidence that they need in this transitional phase of their education. There are other roles that give the children responsibility but also allow those more reserved in their character to perform an important task and have adult and peer validation for their role.

High morale

Morale can take time to establish and can be hard to define, but you know it when you see it. A school that immediately feels calm, safe and respectful, with enriched learning opportunities throughout, is a school with high morale. Children are engaged, have a high level of autonomy and know how to behave. High levels of morale tend to be associated with strong but emotionally intelligent leadership.

Communication skills

If we can't communicate, we cannot say how we are feeling, what we are feeling and how this is affecting us. Colleagues in Early Years settings, in the period following the reopening of schools after the pandemic, very much noticed that children were coming to them in nursery and Reception classes with poorer communication skills than previously. Social and independent skills, such as toileting, were also affected. The reason for this was largely due to missing pre-school provision during lockdown and the slow return to full service afterwards. Poor communication skills pre-date 2020, but the reduction of face-to-face interaction and the increased reliance on digital communication, which lacks the nuances of verbal communication, may need us as schools to give priority to how and why we negotiate, discuss, alert, question and socialise through the power of speech.

Positive attitude

Toxic positivity was discussed earlier. Positivity is not a rose-tinted spectacles approach, but rather one that embraces optimism, hope and resilience. It also involves expressing gratitude and developing positive relationships with peers and adults. Arguably, a positive attitude may need to be modelled and taught in order for it to be normalised and expected.

Experience of success and coping with failure

Growth mindset, developed by Carol Dweck (2017), concerns the belief that abilities and intelligence can develop through dedication, effort and practice. A growth mindset sees life challenges as an opportunity to learn and grow, whereas a fixed mindset has a fear of failure and the avoidance of difficulties and of taking measured risk. With a link to positive attitude, a growth mindset acknowledges 'failure' as part of the learning process; after all, it is more important to know how and why something went wrong than to not understand how something went right.

Reflection and evaluation

Reflection and evaluation are both life skills, skills that require modelling in a world so geared – in part through access to social media – to instant solutions and gratification. Life concerns encountering, overcoming and solving problems, and this is why resilience is of such importance. The ability to reflect encompasses respect for self and others, taking responsibility for the consequences of our actions and the ability to be independent in thoughts and words. Children with a greater ability to be reflective will be those less likely to develop mental health difficulties.

Support that the school can offer to all pupils

The school is a safe, secure and welcoming place for everyone

Safety is a fundamental right and need, and in schools this facilitates the capacity of every pupil to flourish and to learn. School may be the only safe place for some of our children, so the importance of consistency in the ways in which the protective factors are embraced, promoted and communicated is paramount. This is fed and sustained by the culture around mental health in the school; a thriving culture that all staff buy into is one that offers the highest level of safety and continuity around learning, safeguarding, behaviour and all matters pastoral.

Trusted support

Children do not walk into a new school and immediately trust the adults around them. It takes time and skill, something that our EYFS colleagues have in abundance. The preparatory work that they do, from home visits to win the confidence of our very youngest learners to the welcoming manner in the nursery and Reception classrooms, gives many of our children the secure start that teachers and parents wish them to have. Some of our children enter formal schooling with insecure attachments, with a background of trauma and ACEs and with parents who have found the first years of raising children a challenge for any number of reasons, and for these children the transition can be overwhelming. Gaining trust isn't a given, but a process that takes time and patience and an understanding from adults of their background and needs.

You may be familiar with children identifying their five key adults in school, sometimes represented by drawing around a hand and adding a name to each finger. This is a simple strategy for children to know whom they can talk to if they have a worry that overwhelms them so that they cannot wait. The five may not include the class teacher, but this should not be regarded as a lack of respect but a question of attachment; if a child has built secure relationships in the past, maintaining these for moments of worry are reassuring. If one of these adults moves on from the school, it is possible for the child to feel a degree of loss. This is often seen if a child has had one-to-one support from the same adult for a long time; the attachment being broken needs to be acknowledged and planned for to protect the child. The child may choose not to have a male figure in their trusted list, because of trust issues with males outside the school or in previous settings. Equally, they may seek out a man to show trust in, recognising a lack of a stable male role model in their lives to date. It is important too to consider the diversity of your staff reflecting the diversity of your school, so that children can also identify with adults of their cultural heritage.

Secondary settings offer far greater challenges in building trusting relationships, in part because of the sheer scale of numbers, arriving from very diverse primary school backgrounds, and the movement of pupils around the site. The schools with the most effective cultures have a tutor system that, if possible, keeps the same tutor with the group from age 11 upwards, combined with heads of year focused on the pastoral aspects within their holistic thinking. How the tutor time is organised and how much actual time is spent with young people determine the effectiveness of any support given. The shortest time that I have been aware of is ten to 15 minutes, allowing time for registration and an equipment check – is this evidence of pastoral support or one of rules and expectations? Let us not dismiss the importance of rules being there to help self-regulation, but is there more that can be offered? This may be when PSHE is covered, but it can also be the opportunity for a daily check-in with every pupil, not just those seen as vulnerable, because this offers the opportunity to pick up on the small differences, the obscure worries, the lack of usual engagement that could be an indicator of something else in the child's experience that may warrant additional action. This is the conduit to trusted and trusting relationships.

The mental health lead needs to make themselves aware of departments and individual staff who have poor relationships with students and who demonstrate a less supportive attitude to the place of mental health in the school. This may be from departments where examination pressure is the greatest – more likely English and maths departments. Heads of department are the key personnel here and are those who should be the most aware of the holistic nature of learning. This could be a focal point for training staff in the reasons why effective relationships play a role in supporting the development of the whole child.

How to talk to and talk with pupils

A school may display posters proclaiming itself a talking school, but these words will be hollow if the children don't know whom to talk to or how to access an adult to talk to, and if the adult doesn't know how to speak to them. This last point may come as little surprise; some teachers and other adults in school don't know how to speak to children, pitching their language choices – particularly in situations of disruption and other behaviour – above the capabilities of the child and not at the appropriate emotional volume or in a suitable tone of voice either. Examples of poor language choices include:

- 'What is wrong with you?'
- 'Why can't you just behave?'

- 'I'm the adult; you're the child.'
- 'Would you do that at home?'
- 'You've got an attitude problem!'
- 'You're going to have problems in secondary school/Year 11/sixth form/college with that attitude.'

There will be similar and further examples in your experience too. All are examples of confrontational language, lacking emotional intelligence, which can produce an answer that may be interpreted as rude. They may trigger an emotional response, either one of upset or one of anger, neither of which promote an attitude of positive mental health.

The simplest step in speaking in a reassuring manner is to get down to the children's level. Being at our full height can be physically intimidating. Sitting or kneeling at the level of the child, ideally to enable eye contact, is more likely to enable the child to feel at ease. Our body language too can convey positive or negative impressions; folded arms, closed fists or pointed fingers – even if done inadvertently – can send out the wrong signal, implying that you may not be listening fully or taking what the child has to say seriously.

Always listen to the child without interruption, because otherwise this shuts down conversation. Only respond once the child has finished speaking. When asking questions, keep them open rather than closed, which will only produce yes/no answers. Being an active listener, repeating back what a child has said and asking how they feel provides validation and assurance. Sometimes a child just wants to feel listened to. Leading questions, asking why something happened, aren't helpful, but ones that establish facts are.

Managing transitions

When we think of transition in education, we might think principally about the movement from primary to secondary settings. Children also transfer from infant to junior schools and, in the areas where they still exist, into and out of middle schools, with their particular contexts and challenges. We also have in-year transfers to consider, with families moving for a plethora of reasons, some of which may impact their mental wellbeing. Think deeper, though; if transitions can affect the emotional health of our young people, have we considered the effect of transition between years and, on a smaller timescale, between lessons and breaks?

Transitions between schools

Having seen a class of Year 6 transfer to as many as 14 secondary schools, I know that transition arrangements can be variable and inconsistent. The best practice sees a visit from the transition tutor, face-to-face meetings with pupils and teachers in the primary setting, and a genuine professional dialogue about the whole child: learning and pastoral, behaviour and attendance, family and wellbeing. The least effective, especially when only a single pupil was involved, may have been a phone call to the school or an impersonal and lengthy transition form. The immediate post-lockdown years saw transition between schools change considerably, with Year 7s being reported as showing less maturity and more inclination to be involved in friendship and aggression issues than had previously been expected. Good transitional arrangements would ensure effective communication of pupils likely to demonstrate such concerns.

In-year transitions

There are a number of reasons why children transfer in-year, some of which could indicate a traumatic response. Children who move because of bullying, exclusion or other issues with the school, such as a poor school–family relationship, will require support, as may their family. There may be families fleeing homelessness, domestic violence or gang-related crime involving a sibling. Such transitions often involve a move to an unfamiliar area, which means rebuilding friendships in the school and the community. In class, one new child can impact the balance of relationships within a short period of time, with issues often around behaviour and bullying most commonly associated with this situation. New children may feel welcomed, but equally the dynamics of the class may leave them feeling isolated and having difficulty in striking up relationships; the sociogram is a useful tool here to identify supportive peers.

Transitions between lessons

Primary colleagues will be familiar with the use of a visual timetable to indicate the patterns of the school day, often recommended for children with a diagnosis of ASD (autism spectrum disorder) to help them with organisation, but also suitable for others who may have anxieties around certain lessons – writing, mathematics and PE being the most likely – where avoidance strategies might be witnessed. A useful strategy for children with learning anxieties – some but not all of whom may be children with additional needs – is the notion of pre-teaching and pre-learning. This involves an adult working with one or more children on a concept that will be covered in the subsequent lesson, perhaps using manipulable materials or word mats and sentence-makers, to give the pupils a head start on the whole-class learning to come and to give a boost to their assurance and resilience about their abilities. Anxieties around PE lessons may be in relation to not feeling particularly skilled, but can also be triggered by concerns about changing, particularly when children become more body-conscious or some body-shaming language is being used in class. The language issue can be addressed through appropriate PSHE lessons; the issues around changing by allowing this to be done in a more private space that supports the dignity of our young people.

Breaktime and inter-classroom transitions

For some children, playtimes are the most stressful parts of the day: a time when they may feel socially isolated or frightened of the movement around them, away from the routine of the classroom that may be their safety blanket. Children do not want to be jostled, verbally harassed or physically hurt in corridors. Rules and routines are part of the way to address this, but so too is school ethos. We hear much about some schools with 'silent corridors' and orderly walking around the building, and of others that acknowledge that children are sociable creatures who may chatter on the way to their next class but know how to move safely between rooms. Are these behaviours taught with a 'why' or with an expectation of compliance, and which scenario supports the emotional wellbeing of the school population best? We return again to the context of the school and what works well for your young people, having listened first to their voices.

Selective provision

The selective level of provision is more focused upon the needs of individuals and of groups of pupils more at risk of developing a mental health condition, who may have been identified early because of specific risk factors and vulnerabilities. It is these children who will be on the next step along in the referral process and who may be supported in building skills around their resilience, and whose families may also be in receipt of early help. Delivered effectively, selective interventions have the greatest and most positive impact upon children with poorer levels of emotional wellbeing.

How much of this level of intervention can be offered by the school depends upon budget and staffing capacity as much as how the need has been identified and the qualifications of staff to deliver such intervention. As has already been discussed, the school is a place to promote positive mental health, and not to deal with mental ill health. Our schools are not clinical settings and we do not have the expertise and qualifications that mental health professionals possess. Schools may have staff trained as emotional literacy support assistants (ELSAs) or in a commercial level of training, such as being a Thrive practitioner or qualified in LEGO® Therapy. You may be fortunate enough to have a counsellor on site, or one shared with other schools or across a MAT, or have a member of staff such as a teaching assistant who has undertaken the appropriate training. Qualification is important but wider reading, although professionally useful, does not represent qualification in a subject; being a mental health first-aider or a cognitive behavioural therapy practitioner requires an accredited course and, in the latter case, a recognition of whether it is appropriate. A badly delivered, ill-advised or inappropriate intervention can be damaging, and it is essential that the mental health leader, alongside the SENDCo, knows what support is being offered and how it is being evaluated.

Central to the success of any selective intervention is how useful the qualitative and quantitative data is. The use of screening tools, such as strengths and difficulties questionnaires (SDQs) or an online survey, can be variable within a school and across a trust; some staff may draw upon their experience and professional judgement, but less-experienced colleagues may have only the screening results to draw upon. Surveys completed on the computer, for example, especially if it is the first time that the children have completed them, can produce variable and unreliable results if the children do not understand the question, feel rushed or are distracted. Equally, over-supporting a child by reading each question to them but not providing the same support to others risks a level of inaccuracy. Another risk is over-identification of some pupils' needs and non-identification of other concerns, which might be masked or missed.

The types of selective intervention that might be offered in school may include:

- one-to-one mentoring
- behaviour support
- attendance mentoring
- school counsellor
- nurture sessions.

Some of these are discussed in further depth in Chapter 6, under the remit of staff professional development. Other selective provision could fall under the remit of external agency support if it is brought in from outside the resources of the school or trust. Chapter 9 covers these in further detail.

Intensive provision

Intensive or targeted provision is aimed at those children experiencing early symptoms of a disorder, one that may result in a clinical diagnosis at some point during time in school or later in life. It requires expert-level support and needs to access the knowledge and skills of multiple professionals, at CAMHS (children and adolescent mental health services) level, through other external agencies and possibly through the school, if appropriately qualified staff are employed or engaged through service-level agreements (SLAs).

The need for intensive intervention should, in an ideal world, not come out of the blue. A strong culture of noticing should be a major protective factor in highlighting need and concern at an early stage. Careful observation, recording changes in behaviour, tracking of patterns through data, a child seeking support from a trusted adult – these should all build a growing picture of a child. This picture should then inform the need for selective intervention, the results of which, if improvement is needed, may lead to further intervention. There will be traumatic occurrences necessitating intensive intervention – unexpected and sudden bereavement, impact of war or terrorism, a major incident (such as the Grenfell fire or the 2024 Southport stabbing attack) – but the school should have a network of local services to refer to in its referral map in such circumstances.

The greatest concern schools have with intensive interventions relates in part to funding and staffing but also to a discrepancy in identified need across the country. CAMHS is also not the magic and instant solution that some schools imagine it to be; indeed, we need to consider not only joined-up thinking but also joined-up working with all the agencies that might be involved with a young person if, when and arguably before such levels of need arise.

Final thoughts

Targeted support is very much about being responsive, being ready, setting in place the seeds of conversations about good mental health through the universal offer and having the capacity to support the next level of intervention in whichever form it materialises. The following chapter considers some of the ways we can provide training to our staff to support possible intervention strategies.

> **THINK about targeted support and appropriate provisions**
>
> Time
>
> - Although any intervention should be timely, any emotional or wellbeing support needs a longer period of delivery and evaluation than might be given to an academic intervention.
> - Any degree of measure should include the thoughts of the child, the parents and any professionals involved.
>
> Holistic
>
> - A holistic approach recognises the individual beyond the concern or disorder that they have; this shouldn't define them. The support that is offered doesn't tick a box, but is part of the larger picture of overall health.
> - A holistic view looks at underlying causes – the risk factors.
> - Talk and communication are tools with which to build the bigger picture around a child.
>
> Inclusive
>
> - An inclusive perspective means taking unbiased approaches that appreciate diversity.
> - Raising awareness of the mental health provision on offer and having conversations about mental health can be empowering for all stakeholders.
>
> Non-judgemental
>
> - Addressing a concern through a specific intervention is supportive of the needs of an individual. Everyone has a need, but for some, the universal offer does not suffice and further interventions are required to try to rebuild resilience and other self-help strategies.

Knowledgeable

- Knowledge is key. To what risk factors are our young people exposed? What trauma have they experienced? What protective factors will be of the most support to their level of need?

Case study: Navigating the mental health journey, Stratford School Academy

Stratford School Academy, in the London Borough of Newham, serves a diverse and vibrant community. It is a co-educational comprehensive school on two nearby sites, which converted to academy status in 2012. The school has some 1,500 pupils, aged 11 to 16. Nadirah Khan is an assistant headteacher and head of year, and she guided me through how mental health and wellbeing are supported at Stratford School Academy.

Holistic thinking

Under headteacher Craig Hewitt, there has been a shift in the culture around mental health, with the previous head having seen it as a separate issue from academic progress. This change in attitude was important because of the impact of the pandemic on the surrounding area, with Newham being one of the worst hit of the London boroughs in terms of rate of infections and fatalities. Because of the wider impact upon the mental health of the young people in the school, the decision was made to buy into the services of Place2Be, with the school being in the fortunate position of having the funds to afford this provision.

The general picture of mental health in the school when we spoke early in 2024 was that Year 11s were readily self-referring for help because of their anxiety about forthcoming examinations, which had been a trend stemming from the pandemic years when examinations were based on teacher assessments; when GCSEs returned, there was no school benchmark against which for the children to challenge themselves. The school has noticed that behaviour, like the national picture, could have changed due to a number of factors, such as increased youth violence, given the local context and levels of domestic violence.

The impact of lockdowns on the mental health strategy

The position around mental health needs in 2024 was regarded as 'amber', as opposed to the 'red' in the immediate aftermath of lockdowns and extended absence. Aside from Year 11 and exam anxiety and Year 7s, who, after a term of settling in, were beginning to test boundaries but had the lowest level of mental health concerns, the largest concerns were with Year 9. This was a year group who, as Year 7s arriving in September 2021, had a transition out of primary school that was impacted by Covid restrictions, meaning less face-to-face communication and working under restricted circumstances, both at primary school and after their move into their secondary setting. With this year group, the main issue with girls is around self-esteem and with boys around their behaviour.

As part of the strategy for pandemic recovery, emphasis has been placed upon the value of citizenship lessons to cover the curriculum content around mental health, acknowledging the huge chunk of time and opportunity that was lost across nearly two years of restrictions. Tutor time has also been utilised, as a means of checking in on the more vulnerable students and to encourage the idea that it is 'OK not to be OK' and that being open about this is a positive step in self-awareness around mental health. Tutors work in a preventive manner, promoting the use of a one-to-ten scale for how the students are feeling and encouraging them to explain the score that they have given themselves. Mindfulness and breathing techniques are covered in these sessions. Mindfulness journals are also used, and the school is looking to develop a bespoke journal for this purpose.

The school has made the decision to have signposted services listed in the students' diaries and planners rather than listed on posters, feeling that this encourages more students to seek access to support. The pictures of the staff students can turn to for support – of whom Nadirah is one – are also included in the diaries, enabling clarity around which adult to turn to when needed. These staff also include mental health first-aiders (MHFA), and the school is embarking on MHFA training for the leadership team. A lack of space means that there is no official safe room, but the listings in the diary indicate the designated points where students can call in if they need time to talk. Mindful that lunchtimes are often stressful periods for some young people, the school offers a calm club and craft activities.

Many of these decisions were made in the light of the experience of the pandemic, and of the change in the leadership culture. Staff have been given guidance in having supportive conversations with children. Some staff were initially uncomfortable with this, but with senior leadership having an attitude that they are humans first and leaders second, this has somewhat eased. The next task that Nadirah has is to train the governors in a similar way.

A positive perspective on boys and young men

We discussed concerns with boys, particularly around the issue of Andrew Tate. The decision was made not to raise the issue of Tate in lessons, as it was felt that this may give him positive attention and draw pupils into seeking out his online content. In general, though, Nadirah has observed little in the way of misogynist attitudes. What the school has done for male mental health, seizing on the Movember initiative, was to film male members of staff reading selected poetry on a mental health theme. The male staff have also started a football team, in part to demonstrate the importance of looking after themselves physically. Statistics around male mental health are shared, alongside discussion of what masculinity is in a modern society.

Understanding the community

One of the barriers around mental health that the school faces is that of the cultures that the children are from, with the greater challenge being the stigma around mental health. The term does not exist in the vocabulary of some of the first languages of the school's families, some 80 per cent of whom are of South Asian heritage, with Bengali and Urdu two of the most commonly spoken languages at home. One of the biggest successes that the school has had is in communication, owing to coffee mornings enabling parents to meet with teachers and other staff from their culture or community. The school is working to educate the parents to educate their children; this is still a work in progress, but conversations are being had with parents about the importance of confidentiality and of mental health safety, not just around low mood but around CAMHS Tier 4 concerns, so that they have a contextual understanding of their children's mental health. One local move that has been made is to change the name of the mental health support team to the Wellbeing Team, to encourage engagement with the service.

There have been some issues around self-harm, one of which is that some students don't want their parents informed. They are, however, encouraged to look at a safety plan and to identify what their possible triggers might be. Again, the school has taken the approach that talking about this subject may be a trigger for more occurrences, preferring to identify trusted adults to turn to.

More practically, the school does not permit compasses and pencil sharpeners to be brought to school; instead, these are provided in lessons and are counted out and back as a safety measure.

Managing mobile phone use

In dealing with issues around phones and social media, one strategy has been to talk to parents about the effect of blue light on sleep patterns. The girls in school discuss apps such as Instagram and its influence on body image and fashion. Teachers have discussed airbrushing and filtering with pupils and how this creates a false image. The school personal development curriculum is continuously evolving to identify gaps for both students and parents.

Phone use was banned in June 2022. Students in the past were given the Wi-Fi password for the school, but this caused problems in a variety of ways. The rule is that if a phone is seen or heard, it is confiscated and not returned until the end of the week. Any devices found on a Friday are not returned until the following Friday. The decision wasn't a blanket ban overnight; although not up for consultation with the student and parent body, it was recognised that the first step was to inform and then to trial the policy, before finally having it fully in place. It was also recognised that phones were being used as a means of social communication and so, to develop more appropriate social skills, lunchtime games and activities have been provided. Alongside this has been education for parents about locking phones, isolating home Wi-Fi from certain devices and talking to children about not glorifying fights by filming and posting them.

A work in progress

Nadirah recognises that Stratford School Academy's mental health journey is a work in progress, but in truth it is for every school. The school is lucky to have the budget to afford the support of Place2Be and to have access to other services that being a London-based authority offers, but it is equally keen to develop its own resources for free, such as scripted conversations for staff to use as starting points with young people. The school took great pride in achieving the Optimus Wellbeing Award, which provided the structure that was needed. Stratford School Academy celebrates its good work, and the shift in culture and moral compass of taking all the stakeholders in the school on its mental health journey.

6 Staff professional development and training

> **Chapter overview**
>
> In this chapter, we will consider:
>
> - running a staff training day around mental health
> - evidence-based strategies
> - other training opportunities for staff.

Running a staff training day around mental health

Undertaking a training day on any new initiative can be daunting, whether arising from a decision related to school development, one driven by local and national priorities or one coming from a MAT leadership direction. If the school is just beginning the journey into being a mentally healthy school and there has been little in the way of policy, strategy or knowledge, in many ways it will be starting with a blank slate.

However, is the slate really blank? Every participant in every meeting brings something to the table, but in the case of mental health they could be bringing their own experiences, which may have left them with negative feelings; likewise, they may come to the session with a level of stigma or unconscious bias. Equally, especially with experienced staff who have lived through times of much professional change and challenge, some may feel jaded and overwhelmed by what they may regard as something else in the workload basket. On the other hand, there will be some colleagues who will approach the meeting with an open mind and be prepared to make the changes because they have recognised the need in the school. In addition, there will be staff – typically but not exclusively the SENDCo and staff involved in parent and family support – who will already be using strategies and interventions successfully about which other staff know little. A combination of positivity and challenge is helpful, because it can generate debate and discussion as well as help all participants to have an understanding of the context in which they all work.

The traditional attendance at a training day might be teaching staff plus leaders, with teaching assistants sometimes invited but often left with administrative or classroom tasks. Is this the best use of their time? For a mental health training day, especially when launching the initiative from a baseline, each member of staff should be asked to attend: every member of caretaking, catering, lunchtime and office staff, every job-share and part-timer. Invite governors too, especially the chair and the wellbeing governor. Before the excuses start, turn on the answerphone, put 'out of office' on all emails and reschedule deliveries. Offer payment or time in lieu for those working outside their days or hours and arrange for childcare facilities if necessary. Those 'essential' meetings can wait; nobody appreciates the absence of a school leader from essential CPD. As the agenda unfolds, the value of including the whole staff community will become apparent.

The agenda for the day will depend upon whether the session is delivered by an external speaker or by a member of staff, perhaps one already trained as a designated senior mental health leader. Whichever the case, the agenda and timings for the day should be set out and shared beforehand so that valuable time is not wasted; this time does need, however, to allow for breaks and reflection time, in groups, pairs or individually. The agenda should also set out the fact that the day does not stand in isolation, and there will be opportunities to evaluate, feed back and reflect in the weeks and months that follow.

It is important that the session begins by establishing a space of psychological safety for all participants. This means that there should be no fear of speaking up and challenging, of raising ideas and opinions or of any negative repercussions for what may be said. This should be established as part of good working practice anyway, but mental health is by its nature an emotive topic, which may generate some honest, raw and impulsive responses. There also needs to be a clear understanding that colleagues can raise their concerns and any discomfort at any point of discussion, which includes their right to step outside the workspace if they feel upset or triggered by any part of the agenda.

The language of mental health

Begin this section by asking colleagues to share some of the language and terminology they have heard or used in their lifetimes: as children at school and in the community, or as adults in the workplace; what they may have heard on television and other media – things they have heard that make them feel uncomfortable or which they have challenged. Sticky notes and flipchart paper are ideal tools for this activity.

Language when discussing mental health is important, because offensive, inappropriate and even misplaced language can cause offence or upset. For a moment, let us just consider the language used in other aspects of life. I would anticipate that most, if not all of you, reading this would never use an obviously racist term and would challenge it if heard in school, whether from a child, parent or colleague. Similarly, with sexist language, some is quite obvious, but other terms are more subtle in the way the user employs them. What seems innocuous to some people may be considered banter by others. One person's throw-away language could be an example of misogyny or harassment to another. Language use changes over time too, with terms used almost without a second thought 20 or more years ago now deemed unsuitable.

With mental health, you will find that this activity will generate some obviously inappropriate terms, but others that will not have been considered so. One example is the term 'snowflake', thrown around with some abandon by certain politicians and television personalities. It is not good language to use in a reasoned argument, because it suggests emotional weakness and a lack of resilience in regard to mental health. You may wish to raise terms that you have heard in your professional practice. 'Keep taking the tablets' or 'the men in white coats' are examples of language where I have had a quiet word with colleagues about language choice. An example that I used when I ran this session was an incident where an ambulance was called for a neighbour having a mental health episode. Police attended too and I had remained with the neighbour to keep him safe until professional support arrived. 'Is he a nutter?' asked one officer, to which I politely but firmly replied that he had a diagnosed mental health condition for which he was taking medication, and that such a word wasn't helpful in this situation.

The point of this exercise is not to generate a banned list of words, but to identify when our choice of words – and those our children and parents might be exposed to out of school – may not be appropriate. This can also help us to understand what stigma around mental health looks like. Here lies an opportunity to discuss stigma and attitude towards mental health and the strategies and language that we may use to challenge it.

The value of talk and the value of listening

Ask colleagues to reflect on what they have just been doing. How did they communicate? How well did they engage? Were they active or passive? Did they challenge or accept what they heard? Did they tolerate or refute the opinions of others?

Use this as an opportunity to dive deeper into the way we talk with children – and each other – using the content that we discuss in Chapters 5 and 7. Ask everyone to pair up with someone that they don't know particularly well and use questioning to find out three things that they didn't know about them. Ask the pairs to give feedback to another pair or a larger group about what the discussion has uncovered.

An extension or addition to the above activity is to suggest a list of random topics to discuss. These could be education-based or themed around current affairs or some aspect of popular culture, such as television or fashion – the choice is yours, but the point of this exercise is to generate discussion and value other opinions. The only caveat is that after each person has finished what they have to say, they must ask, 'And what do you think?' as a means of continuing the discussion.

A third activity, and one emphasising listening skills, is again to pair up and for one partner to talk on a subject of their choice or one from a suggested list for a given time of one to two minutes. Some people can talk for much longer, but be aware of time limitations and the pressure of being put on the spot. The other person is the listener, who may not make notes or ask any questions but may nod, smile, raise their eyebrows or make any other facial expression in acknowledgement or encouragement. Their task, to show how well they have listened, is to repeat back the gist of what they have been told to their partner, another pair or the whole group.

The purpose – the 'why' of this section – is to emphasise the value and importance of the way we talk to, talk with and listen to our young people. While it has the most vital place in supporting children where they seek our support for their emotional health or where they may be disclosing a matter of safeguarding concern, it also has a place more broadly in supporting learning health and specifically in subjects that children find more of a challenge.

Identifying training needs: A shift in culture

Building a whole-school approach to mental health will represent a major cultural shift for some schools and colleges. In Chapter 1, we discussed how leaders can grow a positive culture, and the training day allows the opportunity for the staff to consider what the culture of the school looks like and feels like from their own and others' perspectives. Remember, the culture cannot be imposed; it is led and shaped by school leaders but grown and supported by the whole team. Whole-staff training is the ideal opportunity for this approach to be outlined and its benefits promoted, acknowledging that it will take time to embed and that further training may be required as knowledge and experience grow.

The following are some aspects that can be covered on the day or in subsequent training opportunities, which can feed and nurture the whole-school culture.

What does mental health mean to you?

The point at which you introduce this question into the training day depends on how well you know your staff. After acknowledging the psychological safe space, this might work if you have staff that are open-minded to discussion, but otherwise this could wait until after the language activity, which could stimulate further debate. This section may lead to some open and frank expressions of opinion and of experience, but will be an important indicator to the attitudes of colleagues, where challenges lie and where strengths already exist.

Developing the 'why' and growing the statement of intent

The sense of 'why' is explored in Chapter 1. A whole-school training session represents the ideal opportunity to share this with everyone. Be prepared for questions and challenges, anticipating that there will be colleagues who may not understand the ways that good mental health supports learning and attainment, attendance and behaviour. Take a positive mindset towards questioning; it isn't criticism but an indication perhaps of a knowledge gap or lack of understanding, and where further opportunities for training may be identified.

Stigma

Discussed in Chapter 2, stigma concerns negative beliefs about a subject or a group of people. Again, here, knowing your staff is a vital starting point, as some may demonstrate a stigma around mental health. This part of the agenda could be used to discuss what stigma is and how it might be demonstrated overtly through negative language, or inadvertently through unconscious bias. An important part of this session is to identify where stigma may exist within the school community among students and parents, and then to consider means of approaching stigma sensitively and without conflict. Role play and group discussion are possible means of developing strategies such as small steps, positive interactions, modelling of appropriate behaviours, correcting misinformation or signposting to helpful reading or social media that can develop mental health literacy.

Stress

It is likely that if you asked your colleagues whether they were stressed, there would be a 100 per cent answer in the affirmative. The consideration with stress is the effect that it has on the body and the mind, especially with prolonged periods of stress, which education professionals experience. A discussion of stress also needs to acknowledge how stress can be added to by the actions of others, by their words and actions, by missing deadlines or not completing tasks. Prejudicial attitudes can also add to stress; racist, sexist, transphobic, homophobic or biphobic comments can add to a sense of isolation and loneliness. This part of the session needs to recognise the barriers to resilience that our pupils face in learning and in life – that their home circumstances offer a range of challenges and that peer pressure and the impact of phones and social media are real and something that we need to understand and empathise with. This session can include strategies for managing stress that can benefit colleagues and pupils; the term 'strategies' should be emphasised, rather than 'tips and techniques', because it supports the positive culture rather than the token and tick-box approach that the latter term implies.

Empathy

Empathy is an important social and life skill. It can build bridges, resolve conflicts and develop interpersonal relationships. Empathy is about understanding the impact of what we do or don't do. We tend to notice the lack of empathy more than its presence, particularly during periods of heightened stress or challenge. Empathy is best modelled and practised in school and college settings, with compassionate and attentive behaviour actively demonstrated. On a training day, empathy can be addressed through active listening, as outlined earlier in the chapter; through role play, allowing the opportunity to tune into the feelings of others; or by sharing the wisdom of Brené Brown, who speaks eloquently on the subject (Brown, 2013).

Evidence-based strategies

If, as a school, the decision has been made to employ evidence-based strategies in support of mental health interventions and training, colleagues will be engaging with strategies supported by scientific research and data that demonstrates their effectiveness in achieving specific goals or addressing particular challenges. Such strategies are used and applied in education and healthcare but also in the fields of psychology and social work. Evidence-based strategies are subject to rigorous testing in randomised controlled trials, with results replicated in different studies and settings. Outcomes are measured and subject to continual review, to reflect the changing picture of the subject matter, which in the case of mental health in schools has very much changed, in part due to the impact of societal pressures, some of which are linked to the effects of the pandemic.

In education, we may see evidence to support the use of explicit or direct instruction, cooperative or group learning and metacognition. A look at the more combative discussions on social media around the merits of group work against direct instruction might suggest that there is a place for one strategy but not the other, but colleagues – especially in the primary sector – will recognise that a combination of methods will be employed during the teaching day to suit the subject matter and the children's access to the intended learning.

Similarly, in the fields of healthcare and psychology, cognitive behaviour therapy (CBT) and other therapies are subject to a rigour in their testing, as too are medications, for effectiveness and safety. Mindfulness, which will be familiar to many readers as something either that they practise out of choice or that may have been introduced as a strategy for the pupils in school to focus and improve self-awareness, has also been subject to testing and analysis.

Evidence-based strategies are not one-size-fits-all solutions, nor should they be employed as a box-ticking exercise. The effectiveness of any strategy depends on specific context, individual needs and implementation, as well as the commitment of the practitioner to it, hence the need for appropriate training. Recognising that some strategies can be dismissed as pseudoscience in some quarters should form part of action planning. Mindfulness can be dismissed unfairly as pseudoscientific, but activities such as Brain Gym have less basis in hard evidence. Such planning goes some way to further reinforcing the sense of 'why' around training and intervention. Cost-effectiveness should be considered too in these times of budgetary restraint; will it be used, who will deliver it and what impact will it have?

Other training opportunities for staff

Some colleagues will express an interest in taking their training further, while others will be in a position to use a level of qualification in their daily responsibilities.

Mental health first aid

Mental health first aid (MHFA) is designed to equip individuals with the skills and knowledge to identify, understand and assist someone experiencing a mental health crisis. Whereas physical first-aid training in schools largely focuses on first-aid treatment for everyone, with the exception being paediatric first-aid training, MHFA has two specific qualifications. MHFA for adults will enable schools to support their staff and parents, while the youth qualification is for supporting our children and young people. MHFA training empowers people to offer initial support for mental health concerns. Each of the four nations of the United Kingdom has their own dedicated MHFA-licensed and evidence-based provider.

Mental health first-aid training covers the following:

- common mental health issues, such as anxiety, depression, psychosis and substance use disorders
- how to recognise early warning signs and symptoms, to enable an understanding of when someone may need further help
- starting a conversation and developing communication skills in a non-judgemental and supportive manner
- the ALGEE action plan, which guides the mental health first aid through the following steps:
  - **Assess** the situation and the person's safety
  - **Listen** non-judgementally and with empathy
  - **Give** reassurance and offer support

- **Encourage** professional help and guide them towards resources or professionals
- **Enact** a safety plan if needed, to ensure their wellbeing until help arrives
• specific first-aid skills – depending on the training programme, there may be the opportunity to learn specific techniques to manage situations like suicidal thoughts, panic attacks or psychotic episodes.

Mental health first-aid training empowers those trained by giving them the confidence and knowledge to intervene and potentially make a difference to the life of a person in crisis. It can also reduce stigma by enabling a greater understanding of mental health difficulties, and may encourage adults and children to seek help from their recognised mental health first-aider. In addition, it furthers mental health literacy with a knowledge- and evidence-informed approach.

Who should undertake the training? The adult-focused course should certainly be undertaken by at least two senior members of staff, to be available in a supportive role for the staff, especially if they experience an issue with pupils, parents or colleagues that requires immediate attention. There should also be a balance through both teaching and support staff to be there for each other at times of crisis. Consider also those staff who face parents each day, such as the office staff and family support, who may be called upon to use this training to support a parent or carer who may come to the school experiencing an episode of mental ill health and is asking for help. For the youth-level training, again look for a balance across the school, but also ensure that at least one midday supervisor receives the training, as lunchbreaks are often the time at which the most vulnerable children feel more exposed and may be at greater risk.

Ensure too that colleagues who undertake training want to take on the role. Never make it an obligation or part of the performance management process, and recognise that colleagues can step away from the role if they wish. It is also essential to communicate to adults and pupils who the mental health first-aiders are and how they can support; don't just leave it to a poster or a link on the website, but consider use of assemblies and curriculum time, to ensure that there is knowledge and understanding of the role.

Emotional literacy support assistant

The emotional literacy support assistant (ELSA) is a member of support staff who has received specific training over several days from a recognised provider.

Once trained, the ELSA works with identified young people to support them with issues such as bereavement, friendship issues, bullying, anxieties, social skills, emotional regulation and the management of feelings. Referrals to the ELSA can originate from the class teacher or SENDCo, a parent or the pupil themselves. The scope of this role should only cover what the practitioner has been trained to do; concerns arising outside their training experience should be referred to their supervisor, a qualified educational psychologist or an outside agency. ELSA-trained staff require regular supervision to support them in their role and this is key to good practice, enabling them to share and discuss problems and issues that have arisen in their role.

Staff put forward for ELSA training should show warmth and kindness and be aware of the barriers that children face in achieving their social, emotional and academic potential. The success of the intervention depends upon the strength of the relationship between the ELSA and the child. They understand the barriers to learning that some children and young people might have and can help them by supporting emotional development and coping strategies. ELSAs will also help children and young people to find solutions to problems that they might have. An ELSA is not there to fix problems but to help children to find their own solutions and offer that important support to a child or young person. ELSA interventions are short periods of support, usually over a term or half term, working on specific targets such as the child being able to recognise coping strategies, triggers for angry outbursts or feelings of anxiety. An important caveat for the ELSA role – and indeed for all specific training mentioned here – is to help the child reach their own solution to an issue rather than direct the child to a solution.

Drawing and talking therapy

Drawing and talking therapy is a child-centred one-to-one intervention focusing on supporting the social and emotional wellbeing of children and young people. The process recognises that children are not able to verbally express their feelings and responses to specific events, struggles or ongoing trauma, and the technique allows the young person to play, to draw and to process any emotions that they are feeling internally, at their own pace and in a non-confrontational way. Sessions typically last for 30 minutes over a half or full term, and children are asked to draw what they choose, to talk about their feelings and to use storytelling language to make sense of their internal world. Practitioners do not interpret the pictures or ask any questions about what has been drawn, and it is essential that they are trained and qualified. Like

ELSA interventions, this is something that might be put into place before more specialist intervention such as CAMHS is engaged. Again like the ELSA role, this is a position that a willing member of support staff can be trained to deliver.

Play therapy

Play therapy is a form of therapy that uses the power of play to help children to express themselves, explore their emotions and work through challenges. The approach recognises that play is a natural way for children to communicate and learn. It enables children to communicate at their level, especially if they may not yet have the language skills to fully express their thoughts and feelings. Play therapy provides a safe space for them to use toys, games and creative expression to communicate their inner world. Play therapy can help children to cope with various issues, like anxiety, depression, trauma, grief, family conflict or social difficulties. It is also a means of processing experiences that they may not be able to articulate verbally. Play therapy can also develop coping skills and build self-esteem.

Play therapy can be used to support children who are experiencing bereavement and grief, those witnessing or experiencing conflict in the family, or those who have social, emotional or behavioural difficulties. Its benefits include enhanced communication skills and emotional regulation, reduced anxiety and improved social skills.

A play therapy session typically takes place in a space equipped with a variety of toys, games and creative materials. The therapist follows a child-centred approach, meaning that the child leads the play and chooses the activities they engage in. The therapist will create a safe and supportive space using techniques such as mirroring (to reflect the child's feelings and emotions), open-ended questioning (to encourage elaboration and further expression) or storytelling (using stories and metaphors to create connections and explore their experiences in a safe way). Some schools may buy into local play therapy provision, but it may be more cost-effective and personalised to the school to train an appropriate colleague, often in a pastoral or family support role, to support the young people and to offer the service to other schools if time permits.

LEGO® Therapy

LEGO® Therapy is a form of collaborative play therapy that uses LEGO® bricks to help children to develop social, emotional and communication skills. It is most commonly used with children on the autism spectrum, but it can also be beneficial for children with other developmental delays or social difficulties. The range of benefits are broadly aligned with those of play therapy, the principal difference here being working in a group situation.

During a LEGO® Therapy session, a therapist will typically provide the children with a set of LEGO® bricks and instructions for building a specific model. However, the therapist's main focus is not on whether the group completes the model correctly but rather on the process of building it. The therapist will observe the child's behaviour and communication, and provide them with prompts and support as needed. Children can work in a range of roles, giving instruction, supplying bricks, construction and as a facilitator of positive interactions. Roles are often swapped during a session.

Nurture provision

Many schools now have nurture provision, based on the training provided by Nurture UK (www.nurtureuk.org), an evidence-based approach that has been used for over 50 years. The nurturing approach helps children to develop social skills, confidence and self-esteem, and highlights the importance of social environments that have an influence on their wellbeing and behaviour. Schools that engage in the nurture approach use it with children who may have missed early childhood nurturing experiences, and require trained practitioners to be aware of attachment theory and the impact of early trauma.

Nurture training and provision is driven by the six principles of nurture:

- **Safety**: This is provided by the safe space that the nurture classroom offers.
- **Wellbeing:** Nurture is important for the development of wellbeing, for the self and for others.
- **Language:** Language is the most important channel of communication.
- **Behaviour:** Nurture acknowledges that all behaviour is communication.
- **Learning:** Learning is a developmental process, of which social and emotional learning is a part.
- **Transitions:** Nurture recognises the importance of and impact of transitions on children's lives.

Nurture may sit in the school as an intervention or support, but should be viewed very much as part of the whole-school approach to mental health and wellbeing, and not sit in isolation from what is happening in the classrooms. The graduated approach to nurture, detailed on the Nurture UK website, emphasises that every child should have access to the support that they need when it is needed. If the school chooses the nurture approach, all colleagues should be informed of the role of practitioners and the benefits for all the pupils in the school.

Counselling for children

Some schools are in the fortunate position of having a counsellor to support the children, perhaps for a few hours a week or maybe shared between other schools nearby or by other settings within the same trust. Schools with the healthiest budgets may have a full-time counsellor engaged on the staff or through a service-level agreement. There are also schools that are encouraging staff to train as counsellors, with counselling skills training typically at level 2. This is training at an introductory level, covering developing core counselling skills and theory, building relationships and understanding attachment theory, improving practitioners' communication and self-awareness with children, and developing creative strategies to support children. These skills offer a foundation in counselling, maybe as a stepping stone to further qualification.

Final thoughts

All the aforementioned interventions offer the opportunity for staff – principally support staff – to develop their skills and to provide intervention and support for the whole-school approach to mental health. These will also strengthen the whole-school ethos, especially when the roles are discussed with the staff body and where their impacts and benefits are shared. All are evidence-informed and important to consider in terms of cost-effectiveness, and also whether there is any challenge to the decision to engage in this training.

THINK about staff professional development and training

Time

- Never imagine for a minute that one day will suffice for your training. Even if you are in a school with well-established practice, mental health needs to be a regular feature of the CPD agenda to maintain focus and identify areas for development.
- Be clear that this is not an overnight process – placing mental health and wellbeing at the heart of everything that happens in a school

is going to take time, and be dependent upon context and upon culture. Neither are fixed, but context is determined by community, of which the school is just part, while culture can change sooner, determined by a shift in mindset and ethos. At the heart of this is the communication of the sense of 'why'.

Holistic

- Any whole-school training needs to emphasise that the whole school means every colleague and every child, and that this means the development of the whole child.
- Intervention or support should be recognised as just part of the mental health offer, alongside the broader curriculum offer.

Inclusive

- Staff training should emphasise the universal offer and the fact that what is available to every child is more than the taught curriculum. Every child has the right to be heard, to be respected and to have access to every aspect of support if it is needed.
- Inclusivity extends to staff too, allowing them to develop their professional expertise if they wish to embark on any aspect of more specialised training.

Non-judgemental

- Always challenge stigma, but not in a confrontational manner. Regard it as an opportunity to develop staff.
- Children seeking help shouldn't be regarded as lacking resilience, but as having agency and understanding of emotional literacy.
- Children who do not yet possess a level of emotional literacy may express themselves through their actions and responses. Behaviour is a form of communication.

Knowledgeable

- Make yourself familiar with the evidence behind different programmes of support, of the benefits that they bring in general and how they can specifically work in your setting.
- Take every opportunity to grow your whole-staff vocabulary around mental health. Make it a regular feature of CPD meetings to keep it centred in the practice of the staff team.

Case study: The power of language and kindness, Hillborough Junior School

Hillborough Junior School in Luton was judged as 'outstanding' by Ofsted for the second time in November 2023, having previously been judged at the same grade in January 2010. The first paragraph of the report references that 'it is the language of kindness that is spoken most loudly' and that the kindness the children bring has a way of 'boomeranging back' to them, making the school, and the world, positive places to be. The compassion shown in the words of the pupils and the care demonstrated in their actions obviously struck a chord with the inspection team.

I spoke with David Bradshaw, the headteacher, Liam O'Donnell, who is deputy headteacher, SENDCo and assistant headteacher Penny Whelan and assistant headteachers Morag Howes, Suzanne Bradshaw and Jack Stevens about how Hillborough Junior School has developed such a positive and community-focused school.

What makes Hillborough a kind school?

Kindness is very much part of the school culture. Teachers and support staff are kind to each other, especially when colleagues are away from school unwell, and the sense of family permeates down to children, who see this too. Kindness is one of the most basic and simple things of life, but it has such an impact. Four of the colleagues I spoke to had been at the school at the previous inspection in 2010, the headteacher had been there for 25 years and one colleague for even longer. The length of service speaks much of the school and the sense of community and family that all the staff felt. The headteacher was told that he ran 'a tight ship with kind hands' by the lead inspector. Succession planning by the previous incumbent of the role has ensured that the culture of kindness is deeply embedded in every aspect of the school. 'Culture eats strategy for breakfast' is an oft-used phrase that David added to the conversation; the school works as it does because of the culture that is lived by everyone. There have been very few changes of staff in recent years, but when a new colleague arrives, they are inducted into the culture rather than policies and procedures. Within six weeks, they have a definite sense of what the culture looks and feels like.

Children are supported so well that new staff would be hard pressed to think that there was a level of challenge in their behaviour or attitude. The school prides itself on its frank, open and positive relationships with children and parents. The feedback that the staff receive from parents is honest and touching. When staff do move on, it is for reasons of professional progress or relocation and is a wrench for both sides. The school buys into the Richard Branson philosophy of training staff so well that they can leave, but treating them so well that they don't want to. The school has also taken the decision not to jump on and undertake every educational initiative, but to evaluate them and consider whether it is right for the school and has a valid place in the education of the children.

The power of positive language

The language used on the school website stands out because of the very child-friendly and child-focused vocabulary. This is particularly noticeable in the 'Bullying and other worries' drop-down on the 'Children' section of the website. The school took the very deliberate decision to make the language suitable for all but accessible for children, including other places to come to for support, links to follow, and encouraging children to know their trusted adults. Bullying is discussed in its terminology and defines the difference between nasty comments and bullying over a sustained period. The page includes the words of one pupil, who says that when meeting someone new, you don't know whether they might be a good friend, and 'you have to be a bit careful at first' – wise words from a young mind. The careful choice of language extends to PSHE, which is known in the school as 'Growing Up' and regarded as an essential part of the learning, fitting in health education, relationships and sex education, although a deliberate decision was made not to use the terminology 'sex education' out of sensitivity to the community.

Respect for the community: Listening to voices

The school serves a diverse community, of which the largest group is of Pakistani heritage, followed by White 'others', of European heritage, and then White UK children, with a small but growing number of children from Nigerian families. Eighteen nationalities and 31 languages are represented across some 360 pupils in a three-form-entry school. The diversity of the school is regarded as an opportunity to celebrate the full range of festivals; children are experts in their faith and culture and can articulate their beliefs. Respect features very highly across the website, Ofsted reports and the lived culture of the school.

Student voice is well established, with a strong school council and play leaders. When the Eco Warriors were restarted after Covid, a three-page-long list of volunteers materialised. Children have plentiful opportunities to speak up, including at the Vision for Luton 2040, talking about their thoughts about the town in the future, particularly around clean streets and knife crime. All children, especially the children with SEND, speak eloquently about concerns for the future.

Strategic moves after lockdown

In discussing a shift in mental health after the return from lockdown, everything seemed to be in a good place in the early days. It took some weeks before the realisation set in that socialisation and the way in which children played were very different, and that anxiety was much more apparent. In 2022, the school employed a psychotherapist for one day a week because of identified children who wouldn't meet a CAMHS threshold. This has also impacted the quality of training for staff, who are trauma-informed and understand behaviour as communication and not as an outcome.

The psychotherapist also supports staff in terms of clinical supervision. Two family workers support family learning and also in completion of forms. Teachers also provide close support to parents. To address anxiety in children and parents, there has been an investment in play and art therapy and in ELSA-trained staff. Hillborough has a strong understanding of children and where they are, supporting those children where and when it is needed most. Hillborough embodies empathy, compassion and kindness in everything that it does.

7 Enabling the student voice

Chapter overview

In this chapter, we will consider:

- the power of the voice
- what is impacting the emotional wellbeing of our pupils
- issues specific to the needs of boys
- how students can contribute to the whole-school ethos
- other ways to empower children through communication.

The power of the voice

We need children to have powerful voices: not loud, but reasoned and rational, honest and heartfelt, empathetic and emotive. They need this powerful voice for their own futures and for that of society. In school, we can develop this voice, which can be spoken or written, with language development, through the ability to develop an argument and to be persuasive, to be an active listener, to respond to a statement with a question and to recognise that sometimes things are said that might be wrong and how to correct this. These are curricular skills and life skills: academic and pastoral sitting alongside each other.

Young people will express their voices in a range of ways. Some will be eloquent and confident to share their thoughts, others more reluctant, reticent or shy in a larger group but expressive with trusted peers. There will, of course, also be children who, when asked or expected to talk, may be unable to do so because this triggers anxiety or panic and who may learn to anticipate and avoid situations leading to the freeze response.

Children may express their 'voice' through means other than the spoken word: by their body language and facial expression, through the written word, through drawing or by the way in which they play and interact with others. Our culture of noticing can appreciate and amplify this voice, respect and respond to it, while also giving it value and validation. In this chapter, we will discuss giving power to the voice of young people, but first will consider the barriers and challenges to their mental health.

What is impacting the emotional wellbeing of our pupils?

As part of a mature, informative and meaningful conversation with our young people, a regular part of discussion with individuals, classes and year groups needs to focus upon what is concerning them. The answer isn't an easy one, being influenced by a web of complex and interlinked factors, with no one single cause being identifiable because of this complexity. Societal and cultural changes will no doubt be an impactor, as will economic and financial concerns, issues around identity and image, and stresses originating from school, peers, family and external influence. Ask your children, collectively and individually, what is of concern to them, and their answers may fall into one of the ten general categories below, although there may, of course, be others reflecting your local context.

Academic stress

With the pressure of schools to 'perform' academically and achieve high grades and progress, the pressure is being transferred to our students. In English schools, Key Stage 2 SATs are a high-stakes formal examination with the impersonal terminology of 'working at the expected standard' and also, for some children, 'working towards the expected standard', which is not the language to encourage positive emotional wellbeing. Although it doesn't say so, the implication is 'good enough' or 'not good enough', which, for the children who spend the whole of primary education working towards the expected standard, seems like a discouraging label. SATs should be a measure at a point in time, but some schools are testing the children on previous papers from January in their final primary school year or, in some cases, from September, and the year becomes focused on turning out a performance in English and mathematics, perhaps at the cost of the wider and more character-forming curriculum.

The pandemic period saw a time of teacher-assessed grades followed by a full return to examinations, meaning that in 2022 we had students sitting A level papers (Highers in Scotland) in what would have been their first experience of a formal examination – one that might make or break their university aspirations.

A degree of examination stress will be felt by any pupil, as any kind of test brings a level of pressure around recall of learned material, but this period emphasised just how much expectations were adding to the cognitive burden of the students. Teachers, school leaders and parents all wish for children to do their best academically, but how much are we adding to the emotional burden of pupils with the pressure of expectations, by additional classes that are compulsory in all but name?

Long-term impact of the pandemic period

A once-in-100-years public health emergency wasn't a blip, but a period of substantial social, economic and emotional impact, not least on our children. A first lockdown, with a sense of the unknown and separation from friends and peer relationships, a return to school in 'bubbles', with strict hygiene rules and class closures as the virus spread again, and the absence of so much of the normal and routine aspects of school life, removed much of what was familiar and reassuring. A class of Year 5/P6 children at the start of lockdown in 2020 would not have had an uninterrupted year until Year 8/S2, missing out on the rite of passage of moving on from primary and moving to new schools in a manner restricting their social interaction with their newer peers. Children who were of pre-school age missed out, with nursery and playgroup provision being closed down and the opportunity to socialise taken out for what would have been a substantial percentage of their life at the time. The ongoing result of this has been poorer social and communication skills, with additional emotional support having to be offered and planned for through EYFS and beyond. School attendance, as already discussed, has also been lower since the pandemic, but the other substantial impact has been the increased reliance of young people on their digital connections, driven in part by having to spend so much time online during lockdown.

Social media, phone use and digital wellbeing

To an outsider, it would look like secondary school children in particular are obsessed with their phones. Just a cursory glance at pupils leaving at the end of the day would appear to show a phone in the possession of everyone – on a call, scrolling or taking photos or video. Increasingly, primary-aged children have access to a smartphone, with all the risks that such a device brings with it. One of the greater risks is peer pressure and fear of missing out (FOMO), which may be a driving factor behind children accessing social media platforms and other material, including pornography, with children as young as eight years old having seen pornographic material on a phone (Wain, 2023).

With sharing links at the touch of a screen, material on apps such as TikTok can spread around a group nearly instantly. The types of material alarming parents and teachers on this platform include videos leading children to self-diagnose mental health conditions, such as borderline personality disorder, depression and anxiety, and others that seem to glorify acts of disruption and disorder in the classroom and corridors. The latter example would have been filmed in schools, which a ban on phones in school might see reduced or eliminated. The former, however, the content of which isn't produced in schools, is the type of material that, once having been exposed to it through a group, children might be accessing more secretly. The work of the Molly Rose Foundation, set up in memory of Molly Rose Russell, campaigns for suicide prevention, particularly drawing attention to the influence of social media on the lives of young people. It draws attention to the failings of social media companies in controlling suicide and self-harm content and the working of algorithms that show similar content to that which has been searched for.

Bullying and cyberbullying

Bullying happens when and where there are opportunities for it to occur. Ask your children where bullying happens and the answers will largely be what they consider the unsafe spaces: the toilets, changing rooms, unsupervised areas of the playground or maybe the classroom when the adult's attention is with other pupils. Rarely will bullying occur in plain sight, as the last thing that a bully wants is to be caught in the act.

Schools put substantial resources into making their spaces as safe as possible, but the one space that they cannot protect is the online space – the one occupied by so many children after school hours. Cyberbullying can occur through WhatsApp, social media applications and gaming sites, even though most of our children fall below the recommended age for use. Life online does not have the same filter as real life, responses are instant and often not thought through and language choices can be shocking, from the full gamut of swearing to offensive emojis. Children who might not be bold enough to speak out of turn in class could act completely differently through a digital platform. Cyberbullying can include threats from individuals or groups and can also take the form of orchestrated pile-ons from others in a group. The subjects that weren't discussed by children in previous generations, such as self-harm or suicide, can be brought into interactions by cyberbullies, presenting a heightened level of risk for young people and a need for school to introduce a greater awareness of children vulnerable to such influences.

Family conflict and instability

Schools may not always be informed of family breakdown or domestic violence, the first indication often coming from a child appearing more withdrawn or more readily upset, as their fears at what is happening at home spill into their emotional cup at school. An unstable family relationship can affect a child in many ways, from struggling to comprehend what is happening to blaming themselves for the breakdown. The communication of emotion is as likely to come through behaviour and non-verbal signals as from the child trying to articulate their feelings. Children may seek the reassurance that someone at school is prepared to listen and, crucially, be a stable presence for them among familial uncertainty.

Neglect or abuse

A level of neglect may have been in a child's life from birth, but could also be something that has developed through economic hardship, familial changes, relocation or substance misuse. Abuse, physical, emotional or sexual, can occur within the family setting, but increasingly there is concern about the extent of peer-on-peer abuse. This is something that may be linked to what the children see online, such as misogynistic content on social media or images portrayed in pornography. The student voice here again may come from non-verbal communication, but also via a trusted adult or peer.

Financial insecurity

The cost of living crisis, high inflation, substandard accommodation and increasing use of food banks will have impacted much of your community. You may know this in particular if you are in a school that offers food-bank-style support to your families, and your families may be comfortable in discussing their financial issues with you. Where parent–school relationships are poor, where families are reluctant to discuss such matters or if there is a feeling that social divisions among pupils may result in bullying or social isolation, we may be in an under informed position about the hardships that our pupils face. This gives further justification to why our children must have a respected and heard voice, however they need to express it.

Inequality and discrimination

Where children are well informed about discrimination, they can identify when and where it may happen. If they are less informed, they may believe something not to be discriminatory or that their words and actions are neither offensive nor inappropriate. Do we dismiss this, deal with it only under school sanctions or take it as a learning opportunity? Many secondary settings have set up an LGBTQIA+ support group in response to student voice, and such groups are essential to give representation but also to further promote respect, tolerance and a knowledgeable base for what inequality and discrimination look like from a pupil perspective.

Identity

Increasingly, there are students who are questioning their gender identity and their choices of pronouns, and although some may find it easy to blame social media and increased internet activity around the subject during the pandemic, we again need to be respectful of emotions and feelings and ensure that we as a school act from a knowledgeable position. Social media scaremongering – about schools supposedly promoting certain agendas, or about schools with whole groups of children choosing to identify differently and blaming this on peer pressure – needs to be put aside to consider what is happening in your context, and what your young people have to say, and to ask about gender identity alongside the current guidance at local and national level.

Uncertainty about the future

Possibly influenced by what they see in the media, by listening to their peers and parents and by misinformation from social media, there is much that our younger generation have to think about for their adult futures. Given the financial uncertainty in the first years of the 2020s, they are going to be concerned about the jobs that they may have and whether they will be able to afford to live away from their family home. Older pupils will have concerns about the costs of university education and paying this off once in the workplace. Children worry about the environment and how they might afford an electric vehicle or whether there will be enough capacity to charge it. We need to allow them to express these fears and not to keep them to themselves.

Additional factors that can impact young people's mental health include:

- **Mental health stigma:** Feeling ashamed or afraid to seek help for mental health problems can prevent young people from getting the support that

they need. Although there has been progress towards addressing stigma, within certain communities this remains.
- **Lack of access to mental health services:** Many young people do not have access to affordable or quality mental health services.
- **Substance abuse:** Drug and alcohol use can be a coping mechanism for mental health problems, but it can also exacerbate them.
- **Influence of local gang culture:** Pressure can come from older children and young adults, especially around petty crime and drugs.

Issues specific to the needs of boys

In being inclusive, we need to consider that there will be issues specific to the needs of boys and girls in school, but need also to be aware about perceptions and stereotyping that lie equally in our communities, as well as among our student cohorts and our school staff. NHS statistics for England from 2023 (Marcheselli et al., 2023) show that between the ages of eight and 16, rates of a probable mental health disorder are approximately equal for boys and girls, but for the 17–25 age bracket, the rate for young women is twice as high as that for young men. Eating disorders are often stereotyped as a female issue, and while the majority of support is for young women, one-fifth of reported cases for 11- to 16-year-olds are boys. Issues around body image, self-harm, bullying and online abuse affect girls and boys, but at the root of addressing this is knowing the school and community context, what influences there are upon the young people in your setting and how these influences manifest themselves in the behaviours and language expressed by boys in school.

A recurrent theme in secondary schools in particular is boys demonstrating sexist and misogynistic behaviour. Concerns often relate to boys being influenced by the social media activity of Andrew Tate. Although his detention in Romania significantly reduced his online activity, schools have been aware of how Tate and others who share his views have impacted the behaviour of some young men, which in turn has had an effect upon the mental health of female pupils and staff. Disrespectful attitudes to women teachers, along the lines of thinking it acceptable to challenge the authority of a teacher just because they are female, are one aspect of the Tate influence; being physically or sexually threatening is another more sinister side that social media has contributed to. A seemingly more innocuous but nonetheless concerning aspect is boys making the hand symbol that Tate often makes on his videos and in interviews.

It represents not an innocent positioning of the fingers but a communication of control, of perceived power and influence. I know of at least one school that had to cancel orders of year group photographs because of boys making this sign to the camera.

The issue here is not necessarily one of the influence of people like Andrew Tate but of the traits of toxic masculinity and how some of our young men feel they have to act in this manner. Bringing up Tate's name in lessons may draw further attention to him, and many schools don't mention him but address specific and contextual behaviours. A focus on respectful behaviours is one aspect that schools pursue, which draws upon how we affect others positively or negatively by our thoughts, words and actions. Respectful language is a starting point, but schools can also consider lessons on the respect of personal space, on staring and unwanted eye contact, on how body language and gestures can also make others feel uncomfortable. By extension, these themes can be extended into lessons about online etiquette, particularly the way young people communicate with each other on their mobile phones, through smartphone apps and through gaming devices. Lessons on digital safety may refer to online pornography. There are concerns that children as young as eight have seen pornography on a mobile device (Wain, 2023). There are two issues here, one being the access to something that is clearly for an audience over the age of 18, but more important is the influence that it could have on attitudes to women and particularly on themes of consent. This is discussed in further detail in Chapter 10.

Another aspect of toxic masculinity is the language in expressions that may be heard in the home or the community, such as 'man up', 'grow a pair' or 'big boys don't cry'. Actually, boys do cry and so do adult men; it is a natural and emotional response to joy and relief as much as to sadness and grief. Tears are an expression of emotion, a sign perhaps that some support may be required, but also an indication of a level of emotional literacy. In two contrasting contexts, both former US president Barack Obama and Keith Brymer-Jones, known for *The Great Pottery Throw Down*, have shed tears in public. Male staff reading this: have you demonstrated this in school – showed that you are an emotional being? Or do you maintain the persona of the hard-faced disciplinarian? Which presents the better emotional role model?

Boys also do not want to be stereotyped as the boorish thugs responsible for disruption in the class, nor as potential future sex pests. While there are a minority of our male students who do not behave well in school and who are disrespectful to female students and staff, it is a minority; know your class, analyse the behaviour and you will see that this is the case. Boys will also point out that girls are equally responsible for poor behaviour and can behave in an inappropriate and disrespectful manner too.

Roman Kemp: *The Fight for Young Lives*

In November 2023, the media personality Roman Kemp presented a documentary for the BBC called *The Fight for Young Lives*, in which he detailed how young people were contacting him about struggles with depression and suicidal feelings after a previous programme that he had made about the death by suicide of one of his best friends. He wanted to know what was going on in the lives of young people and what he could do to help, because they felt that, despite speaking up about their struggles, they did not receive the help and support that they needed.

A heartbreaking and upsetting programme, empathetically presented by Kemp, it explores youth suicide and the support that is offered through CAMHS and how, despite support, some young people continue to attempt and complete suicide, in some cases after support has ended. In some cases, CAMHS was so stretched that it could only be of help at the point of extreme crisis. A CAMHS professional felt that young people regarded the service in a negative light because of the struggle to find support, although there was a suggestion that the reduction of stigma and the willingness of young people to talk more about their mental health has been a contributory factor to the increase in demand for CAMHS services, an increase of 75 per cent from 2019 to 2023, adding substantially to waiting lists.

One of the concerns expressed in the programme was of suicidal ideation affecting children at younger ages, as young as 11. Social media was raised as a contributory factor, a place where young people went if they didn't have a trusting relationship with adults, including parents and mentors. A further issue raised was the closure and disappearance of youth clubs, meaning that a level of support has been eroded and lost.

Visiting the mental health charity YoungMinds, which at the time was organising a lobby of members of Parliament, Kemp listened to young people, who articulated their anxieties and panic attacks but explained how they were told by CAMHS that they did not reach the threshold for support. One young man described his experience, aged just nine, of depression and suicidal thoughts being dismissed and brushed aside by his GP as 'attention-seeking behaviour', with him not feeling heard and not being seen. He eloquently expressed his desire to see youth clubs reopened and a counsellor in every school, both to give his peers the level of support that they needed so that they were not left isolated. Kemp left this meeting with two core ideas in mind: specialist support hubs in the community and better access to mental health care in schools.

Kemp then visited Grace Academy in Coventry, a school that takes responsibility for the mental health of the children, with specialist members of staff. The school provides a safe space where young people can be heard. The safe space also has a 'nurture dog', and the staff described the students talking about releasing happy hormones as a result of interacting with the dog. One pupil explained that the safe space allowed them to escape the sensory overload of people and of noise elsewhere in school. Another felt that it gave the opportunity to have people to speak to – or not to speak to if they so chose – detailing how it helped her to deal with the grief of losing her mother. The principal of the academy recognised that many of her pupils were concerned about 'what ifs' in expressing their concerns, and that many had low levels of self-esteem and heightened anxiety, especially when they recognised that they only had their teachers and support staff to speak to about their worries. Pupils felt safe and in a position where they could trust the adults in the school.

The programme moved then to Sandwell and to St Michael's Church of England High School. This school supports young people through Student Voice, the platform of some 100 pupils from across the school that allows them to share ideas, articulate their thoughts and create change across the school and the wider community. I have had the privilege of hearing the Student Voice body present what they do and how it benefits them as individuals and the student body as a whole, and it is a model for engagement and consultation. The school also has 'Unmuted Radio', which broadcasts monthly on Black Country Xtra Radio, with content created by 11- to 16-year-olds to raise awareness of mental health and wellbeing.

Before leaving for the lobby session at Westminster, Kemp expressed concern about what happens in the schools that don't have such support, and that he could not believe that many schools were having to rely on their work with charities to support the growing mental health needs of students.

At the lobby session, the young people had an hour to discuss their concerns with the Parliamentarians in attendance. Maria Caulfield – at the time of writing the government minister whose portfolio of responsibility included mental health – declined to be interviewed on camera but, in addressing the meeting, committed to introduce waiting times for mental health support so that young people could hold local services to account. Olly Parker, head of external affairs at YoungMinds, felt that mental health was not high on the government agenda. The target, as of September 2023, was for 35 per cent of children to have access to mental health support teams in schools.

Kemp closed the documentary with an open letter sent to the UK government and to members of Parliament, calling for all children to have access to mental health support teams in their schools, arguing that they were cost-effective, saving £1.90 for every £1 spent on mental health services for young people. Maria Caulfield replied by letter, committing the government to coverage of 50 per cent of pupils by March 2025.

How students can contribute to the whole-school ethos

The voices of our young people can be amplified and validated through a range of strategies, including leadership and representative opportunities, as well as the means that children have to speak to their trusted members of staff. In the same way as we value our staff, we should be doing the same with our children in our policies, procedures and practices. Do these respect the opinions of young people, and recognise that practices have an impact upon emotional health and that sometimes this impact can be positive but at other times detrimental? Empowering and enabling give the children the tools to speak up and challenge what they don't believe is helping them; this is not a case of challenging authority, but one of enabling the taking of responsibility, growing resilience and having a sense of autonomy.

Owning the statement of intent

Developing a permanent display to demonstrate the significance mental health plays in the school is a means of communicating the positive message and positive language. Are our displays staff-driven or child-centred? You could try placing the children in charge of the mental health and wellbeing display, determining the content, the language and the status of mental health from their perspective. If we give our students their voice, the wider definition of voice will allow them to express their opinion through display, through written work and through other means of communication.

Take your intent statement, which will originally have been written for an adult audience – for staff and for parents – and shared on newsletters and on the school website. The statement of intent is for the benefit of the children, but have you ever shown them and talked to them about it? Do they recognise the sentiments in the intent statement from their experience in the school? Does it do what it says on the tin? This is an acid test of the commitment to mental health in the school. There is, after all, no harsher critic than a child.

Depending upon the ages and experiences of the children, some degree of adult explanation as to what the statement means might be required. This opens the opportunity for the statement to be rewritten in child-friendly language, in shorter sentences or with bullet points. Headings along the lines of 'The school promises to…' or 'The adults will…' give clarity as to what the intent statement means to do for the children. The students themselves may agree to what is expected of them, as emotional health and wellbeing is 'done with' rather than 'done to' our young people. If we take this perspective, it is paramount that we ask our children what they want and what is concerning them. For the children, the statement of intent can become more like a charter – a series of promises and obligations to which adults and pupils alike have signed up. The charter could then become a central feature of the mental health display.

The school council or pupil parliament

Article 12 of the United Nations Convention of the Rights of the Child (UNICEF, 1990) says that children and young people should have a say in decisions that affect their lives. The school council is thus a meaningful way of voicing opinion and having their views taken into account. A school council that is not only supported but also well trained in its role and tasks can be an effective conduit between the pupil body and the staff and leadership. Elections to the school council are not a popularity contest, as American college-set movies may lead us to believe, although inevitably there are going to be occasions when the perceived 'popular child' is elected to a leading role.

A school council that is nurtured and supported in its responsibilities might have an important role in promoting positive mental health and wellbeing. Depending upon the age and understanding of the children, it can be written into its constitution and take a regular place on the agenda. The council could address specific student wellbeing issues, such as bullying or online safety, but with support may also look at issues around behaviour and the wellbeing programmes that the school has on offer. The school council could also be the driving force behind expressing the statement of intent in child-friendly language, discussed earlier in the chapter.

The council might be styled as a 'pupil parliament', in which case it might encompass other groups such as wellbeing ambassadors, environmental leaders and sports captains. Such a model may be better in a larger secondary school, where each group can work with a degree of autonomy within its own area of concern but contribute to an agreed format on occasions where they all meet.

If each class or tutor group has one or more school councillors, they can feed back to a class council in the days after a school council session, which can then involve each child in discussion at an age-appropriate level. The class representatives can then, in turn, take the class response back to the whole council. Schools that do this well are embedding their ethos into the practices and responses of their children. This model can be incorporated into part of the PSHE curriculum and within the support for oracy skills in developing the children's emotional vocabulary and literacy.

Wellbeing ambassadors and mental health champions

'Wellbeing ambassador' is a broad term and is used in workplaces as well as in schools. For adults, it involves the promotion and support of staff wellbeing, directing staff to resources and acting as an advocate for wellbeing in the workplace; for the adults in school, there may be someone who has volunteered to take on this role, most likely without training.

For children and young people, the role of a wellbeing ambassador involves training that then enables them to support peer wellbeing through activities at break and lunchtimes, through providing information and by providing a safe space for children to talk. In some ways, the wellbeing ambassador role in primary school is an extension of the position of play leader or peer mediator – the transferable skills of active listening, validation of opinion and appropriate and considered responses to what they have been told.

The role of mental health champions is different in the specific mention of mental health. If the school is going to have children in both roles, there needs to be a specific definition of each, as we have seen in earlier chapters. Schools may choose to have either or both roles, depending upon the size of the school and the experiences of the school population. Mental health champions are advocates for mental health, and their roles could include the following:

- Raising awareness through workshops, presentations, assemblies and displays that draw attention to the support available in the school and which direct peers to resources. They could also present to adult audiences, including governors and parents.
- Challenging stigma if there is discrimination or stereotyping; the voices of young people can be effective in challenging this because they can share their lived experience of this in their terms, often more impactful than being lectured by an adult. Facilitating safe spaces and encouraging others to seek adult support challenges the fear of being judged. Challenging stigma might also take the form of calling out name-calling and the use of such terms in bullying behaviour.
- Promoting positive mental health by being an advocate for the resources and support offered by the school and speaking for the benefits that such initiatives offer.
- Offering support and encouragement to peers suffering challenges, and supporting a sense of community and belonging.
- Promoting positive language around mental health, as modelling such language normalises it and gives it a place within the emotional vocabulary of the student population.

Proper and qualified training is paramount, as is the need to ensure feedback to adults of what they have done and who has come to them for support.

The benefits of having either wellbeing ambassadors or mental health champions – or both – are substantial. They can increase awareness and understanding of mental health and wellbeing at a pupil level. They can challenge and reduce stigma and empower individuals to seek help for their needs. Having such roles is also beneficial for the inclusivity of the school community, by providing another means of promoting the whole-school profile of mental health.

Other ways to empower children through communication

The value of journalling

For adults, journalling can have a profound impact on their mental health. The simple act of putting pen to paper or typing onto a phone or keyboard to express thoughts and feelings creates a safe psychological space in which to unload emotional burdens, untangle complex thoughts and gain a fresh perspective on challenging or frustrating experiences. Increasingly, there is a movement towards encouraging young people to journal, for a record of their own feelings and for their emotional autonomy. There are several core benefits to keeping a journal.

- **Reduction of stress and anxiety:** Writing down worries can help to release them from the mind. Journalling can act as a calming and therapeutic tool, enabling emotions to be processed and understood in a healthy way.
- **Improvement of mood:** Journalling can help to identify negative thought patterns and challenge them. By focusing on the positive aspects of life and expressing gratitude for people, acts of kindness and appreciation of the natural world, mood can be boosted and feelings of sadness faced and overcome.
- **Self-awareness and reflection:** The act of journalling provides a space in which to reflect on and learn from experiences. The regular writing down of thoughts and feelings can enable a deeper understanding of self and of motivation.
- **Boosts creativity and problem-solving:** Writing down thoughts is a means of generating new ideas and brainstorming solutions to problems. Writing freely without the constraints of a rigid thinking pattern or structured writing framework enables creative freedom and expression.
- **Promotion of emotional regulation:** Journalling can help to identify and manage emotions in a healthy way, and this may be particularly useful for children who are having difficulty in this regard. By writing about feelings, they can be expressed in a constructive way and avoid unhealthy coping mechanisms.

- **Strengthening of memory and cognitive function:** Writing and reflecting can help to improve memory and cognitive function, as well as keeping organised and focused.
- **Provides a sense of accomplishment:** Progress over time can be a great motivator and provide a sense of accomplishment. This can boost your self-esteem and confidence.
- **Builds resilience and coping skills:** By reflecting on experiences, this can be used to learn lessons and to show levels of resilience.

If the school is going to take the decision to promote journalling as a means of pupils taking ownership of their emotionally healthy voice, there are some points to consider. Firstly, it is a commitment, and so very much needs to tie in with the ethos and culture of the school. If just one member of staff doesn't give it the same priority, then the long-term impact could be lost. Journalling needs to be part of a routine. It is not aimed at perfection – there is no right or wrong – but it is about self-expression and not feeling judged. Writing could take other forms, through doodles and pictures, photographs or mementos. Journalling should also be modelled, with the adults in the school also taking part in the process. While a blank exercise book might be a cost-saving option, commercially produced and age-appropriate journals provide model guidance for the children, ideas to stimulate thinking and space for different forms of writing.

Sociograms for children

Sociograms were covered in Chapters 3 and 4 in relation to staff mental health and to planning for intervention, but there is a place for the pupils to use these too, particularly in considering their relationships with their peers and their standing in the class. At an EYFS level, the children could draw lines or link string or wool from themselves to others they have played or interacted with, and this can be a motivator to play with others. As the children mature through primary school and become more self-aware, they may understand that their interactions are limited to closer friends and that they may not interact with some children. This may be of particular use if there are issues around gender or bullying within a class. Similarly, if a child is feeling isolated and expressing this to adults, the teacher should refer to their own sociogram record; if there is a genuine knowledge of the class, the document will have noted the paucity of interactions for this particular pupil. At secondary level, the sociogram can be used by pastoral leaders to support young people with uncertainties about their relationships with others and to demonstrate that they interact and associate with more of their peers than they might think.

Final thoughts

There are a plethora of means for children to express their voice, and each child needs to feel equally valued, from the seemingly confident to the most reticent. Whether as a group or as individuals, each pupil brings their personality and character to their voice, whether it is heard in a representative forum or expressed for private reflection in a journal. In our culture of positive mental health, their voices need to be accepted, authenticated and amplified.

THINK about enabling the student voice

Time

- The passage of time allows for the voice of our young people to mature and become more reflective, which can enable the adults to reflect on the effectiveness of the support that they offer.
- The profile of the student body will change each year, with arrivals each September and departures in July, coupled with in-year transfers too. Changes over time bring challenges but can also refresh the student voice.

Holistic

- The student voice for the whole pupil community needs to speak on a range of issues affecting the breadth of mental health and wellbeing. Allow for wide-reaching discussion, be it on behaviour, bullying, curriculum and assessment, pastoral support or the experience of breaktimes.
- Any aspect of school life that individual pupils feel is affecting their happiness may be subject to reasoned discussion. This implies that the school should be modelling and teaching the art of reasoned discussion.

Inclusive

- Do you hear the voice of all your children?
- Children with a diagnosis of autism or ASD are more vulnerable to risk factors around mental health and may have some difficulties in expressing their concerns. Children who are non-verbal or elective mute should have their voices enabled in ways that they can access and understand.
- Some children are quiet, shy or introverted, less confident or wary of speaking up. Answering an annual survey does not necessarily represent giving them a voice; planning for opportunities to share what they have to say, verbally or in writing or drawing, shows that their thoughts are valued.

Non-judgemental

- If we dismiss the phrase 'All behaviour is communication' as a mere cliché and as the ignoring of poor behaviour, we miss the point that behaviour refers to good conduct too.
- Reference to the 'compliance' of children can also be judgemental. Is a child compliant because they understand the norms and expectations of the school, or are they compliant because of the fear of the consequences of not doing so, from teachers or from family?
- A more informed view of behaviour comes not from how children behave when you are watching but from how they behave when you are not.

Knowledgeable

- The sociogram is an effective tool for understanding the pattern of relationships in a class or group. Used well, it can identify the children on the margins, or those more vulnerable or isolated from their peers. It is these children's voices that must not be lost.
- Knowing our pupils is at the heart of our relationship with them; not knowing them reduces them to mere statistics.

Case study: Hearing the voices of students, Altrincham Grammar School for Girls

Altrincham Grammar School for Girls is part of the Bright Futures Educational Trust. Rhianne Bond, vice principal with responsibility for pupil and student development, guided me through life at the school and how wellbeing and mental health are supported for the young women who make up the student body.

Knowing the context: Specific challenges

The challenges around mental health are largely reflective of the national picture, and in terms of mental health, there is little noticeable difference between the core issues seen at a national level and those within the school. It has been noted, though, that from the outset the girls are quite competitive. Being a grammar school with an entrance examination to be sat in Year 6, it has been noticed that children in Year 7 compare their scores from the entrance tests, as do the parents. There is an element of unspoken competition – a pressure to perform at a certain level and a fear of failure. Having explored this issue further, the school has recognised that this is pressure not from teachers but from the children and families themselves. In comparison to other contexts, there are different kinds of pressures experienced by the young people, many of whom travel from outside Altrincham, from across Greater Manchester and beyond. These children come to the school with high expectations; there are indications that even at primary school age, conversations are being held about careers and the role of education in their futures. This has seen a high level of interest in the STEM (science, technology, engineering and maths) subjects, which is positive given concerns about the numbers of young women taking scientific, technical and engineering subjects beyond GCSE, with aspirations from parents that their daughters go onto medicine, dentistry or other science-based careers. What has happened at the school, though, is a leaning away from the arts subjects and the students talking about how they might be perceived by their peers over their choice of subjects at examination level.

The school has noticed that its Muslim students are often more reluctant to discuss their mental health or that they report that mental health is not discussed or taken seriously at home. Sometimes this reluctance has extended to asking the school not to mention to parents if they have sought support from the school counsellor or if reference has been made to working with the educational psychologist. This echoes one of the key themes that I have explored in this book: awareness of the school context, respect for the beliefs and practices of the community and a sensitive but informed approach to wellbeing and mental health.

We discussed whether the girls at the school had encountered any problems – particularly through social media – with misogynistic attitudes shown by boys. Rhianne felt that this was not a particular issue, with only a minor number of incidents occurring and being discussed with staff at the school. Rhianne believes that the girls have a sense of agency and strong viewpoints around this issue and possess confidence in dealing with boys who might act with a lack of appropriate respect.

Student agency and wellbeing

The 'Wellbeing' tab of the school website further encourages student agency and self-referral and encourages them to be aware of their own wellbeing and mental health. Under the heading 'The Guide to a Healthy Mind', there are a series of questions with four tiers of response: A, B, C and D. Questions focus on mood over recent days, being sociable with friends, being confident to talk with family, and patterns of sleep and energy. Children whose answers are mostly D are urged to speak to someone about how they are feeling, acknowledging that this may feel difficult and make them fearful but that mental health professionals can provide the tools to recover and to manage anxiety. Included in this tier are both self-help exercises and a list of services in school, including in-school and external counselling services and support from a senior tutor. Tier C children may be feeling low mood and heightened anxiety; they are told that this is not an unnatural or abnormal feeling and are offered similar levels of support. Tier B acknowledges those children experiencing ups and downs, but encourages them to seek support if they feel that things are not improving or getting worse. Tier A describes mental health as good but, again, recognises that self-help and making use of the services in the school is the entitlement of those students too.

As part of the universal offer, Altrincham Grammar School for Girls has teams of student leaders, including wellbeing ambassadors and anti-bullying ambassadors. There is a SharePoint site for all staff to access, which allows them to signpost materials to children and parents. Mental health and wellbeing are also covered through, and influenced by, tutor support and assemblies.

There is a termly mental health and wellbeing survey completed by all students, featuring a general wellbeing section asking about friendships, relationships, sleep and diet, while the second half is more mental health focused, based on

NHS questions around anxiety and depression. The pastoral team analyses the data produced and identifies children needing form tutor support and a regular check-in, those needing reference to a senior tutor and possibly the school counsellor, and finally those in need of more intensive support, possibly from external agencies. The school has very clear referral pathways, with safeguarding software used to record every concern, even the smallest ones, recognising that each of these pieces of information builds into a bigger picture for each child.

Zones of regulation are employed in the school. Some girls have sets of cards to communicate if they are having some issues in self-regulation, which allow them to have some time out at the pastoral office; this has become part of the school routine. A sensory room and wellbeing room are also available for those struggling to self-regulate. Staff are aware of whether the girls need to be escorted to the room or can take themselves independently. Students are seen quickly and know that staff take their mental health seriously.

Mental health in the curriculum

Teaching about mental health is covered within citizenship lessons as part of the core curriculum, and not within tutor time, which is the case in some secondary schools. Wellbeing Wednesdays, mindfulness sessions and mental-health-specific assemblies take place in addition to the content covered in lessons. In regard to the holistic approach within other subjects, because of the high profile around mental health across school, all staff are aware of and are good at dealing with concerns that arise in class. To return to the fear of failure, addressing this has been part of the school development plan, looking at creating confident learners and taking the approach that mistakes are a learning opportunity – very much a growth mindset approach.

The school was judged by Ofsted as 'outstanding' in 2022. The report mentions personal development in particular. Inspectors observed that students felt they belonged and had a voice, a sense of agency and extensive extra curricular opportunity to engage in music, sport, dance and drama, much of which was student-led. The school is focused on the development of the whole person, which can be regarded as a protective factor.

Staff wellbeing

Staff wellbeing is considered within leadership strategy and decisions made in consultation with staff, whose feedback is listened to and acted upon. Staff receive supervision from an educational psychologist each half term, and a genuine open-door policy means that staff are unafraid to approach Rhianne and Stephanie Gill, the principal, with any worries. Like the other schools covered in the case studies elsewhere in the book, staff are long-serving, with promotion and change of personal circumstances being behind any decision to move on.

Reaching out

The school supports other schools in the trust in a number of ways, including transition from primary school. Key departments visit primaries and run transition projects. The pastoral team visits each new pupil in their primary school, and further support comes with days in school and parental support evenings. New Year 7s have a residential trip in the early days of September. Of the year groups impacted most by the pandemic lockdowns, Year 10 in 2023–24 were most vulnerable in terms of emotional-based school avoidance. Year 9 had shown some issues with immaturity in the previous year, but the intervention of the pastoral team in restorative work around friendships, lunchtime clubs and engaging student leadership sums up the approach that Rhianne and the staff at Altrincham Grammar School for Girls take: be proactive in noticing, responsive in anticipating and holistic in delivering.

8 Enabling parent voice and working with parents and carers

Chapter overview

In this chapter, we will consider:

- promoting a positive culture with parents
- the importance of effective family engagement
- promoting a culture of wellbeing outside of school hours
- barriers that prevent engagement
- parent WhatsApp groups – a modern challenge
- useful strategies to engage parents.

Promoting a positive culture with parents

Although many schools may feel that they are just beginning their journey in supporting parents around their own and their children's mental health, truth be told every school has a baseline from which to start the process. Even a school that is only recently established will be offering a programme based upon the knowledge of the context in which the young people and their parents and carers live and the expectations they may have of their new school.

In Chapter 1, we discussed how a culture supporting mental health in the school could be created, with a focus on 'why' and also on knowing your context. A school is a community of staff, children and parents, and the strength of this triangle relies upon the joints between all three. Knowing your context and your parents is crucial, because this can contribute to your 'why' but also your 'how' when it comes to communication and engagement. You may be reading this chapter in a school in a leafy suburb, with low levels of socio-economic deprivation and high levels of parental expectation around academic progress. Equally, you may be in an area where the cost of living crisis has hit hardest, where many families are accommodated in below-standard social housing and attitudes to schooling and attainment are very different. More likely, your cohort will be in some combination of both. Is the 'why' the same for each? It may be, but the 'how' will certainly differ. Talk from a headteacher or adviser that they have a guaranteed and proven method of improvement, development and communication can be taken with a cynical pinch of salt; one size certainly does not fit all.

Parents need to be in a position where they feel psychologically safe in discussing their children's and their own mental health. The safe space that we discussed for staff in Chapter 2 applies with parents equally. They need to feel that they are not being judged, that the information that they may share will not be used against them or their children, and that they are being taken seriously. Parents need to be assured that they are respected and their opinions are valid and not feel patronised or overwhelmed; as teachers with a degree-level qualification, we must remember that we may be speaking to parents with different levels of literacy and communication, and we need to be able to pitch our language appropriately.

If the school has a fractured relationship with parents, the process of rebuilding trust and respect takes time. Readers familiar with *The Wellbeing Toolkit* (Cowley, 2019) will recall a case study on Lessness Heath Primary School, where Kelly Hannaghan was responsible for family liaison and staff wellbeing. Relationships with parents had been broken under previous leadership, and the reconstruction of the link with parents depended on one family engaging with Kelly's Family Matters programme and for these parents to spread the word that the school was supportive and could be trusted. There is an explanation of Family Matters from Kelly on page 150.

As already discussed, attendance has been impacted by mental health, especially since the return to school after the Covid lockdowns, although other factors can affect the children, such as diagnoses of ASD or ADHD. 'The missing link' report in early 2024 from the Centre for Social Justice shows that nearly three in ten parents surveyed agree that Covid and lockdowns have shown that it is not essential for children to attend school every day. Fewer than three in four parents are confident their child's needs are being met at school, with confidence dropping to 61 per cent among those with a child in secondary school. Children from disadvantaged backgrounds, with parents with lower levels of parental engagement, are likely to have the lowest attendance. The pandemic period has seen an erosion of the trust between school and parents, a situation not helped by disruption caused by industrial action; although teachers felt that this was justified, for parents it was an inconvenience, with financial implications if they had to miss shifts.

The importance of effective family engagement

Families can be empowered through successful engagement with the school, which will enable their voices to be heard. This has obvious advantages all around if we are just considering the academic picture, but we are considering the whole child. Parent voice is of paramount importance in regard to mental health, for the simple reason that we need all stakeholders involved to inform us, and we need to keep them aware of any aspects of a child's life at school and at home that contribute to their difficulties. Parents and carers need to be valued, to feel respected and to be able to contribute as equals to any meetings and shared conversations.

Do you ever dread meetings with certain parents? Have staff been told that they can be 'difficult' or 'intimidating', with a reputation for inappropriate language and gesture? If this is the case, your body language or tone of voice might betray your discomfort.

Now think again. Are the parents 'difficult' or are they seeking the best for their child? Are they 'intimidating' or do they find expressing their coherent thoughts a challenge, leading to frustration? Maybe they are dreading meeting with you?

There are going to be parents who do offer a level of challenge in their behaviour and language, enough perhaps to warrant a ban from the school premises. They are, however, a small number, and our positive language needs to emphasise to our colleagues that they are a minority – that most parents appreciate the support of the school, but they might not have the skills and tools to express this appreciation. We should also be aware in our staffroom conversations that many of our support staff may live in the community and know families out of school, and may not want to hear them spoken about in a negative manner.

Family Matters: Parent empowerment programme

Kelly Hannaghan, the founder of Mind Work Matters, describes the way she has empowered parents and families through her Family Matters programme, first initiated at Lessness Heath Primary School in Bexley.

Empowering partnerships

The landscape of education has long been shaped not only by leaders and teachers but also significantly by parents and families. The partnership between schools and families is crucial, not merely as good practice but also as a cornerstone of educational effectiveness. Research consistently shows that when parents and carers are actively involved in their children's education, the children are more likely to achieve academic success. This piece explores the vital role of parental engagement in schools, underlining its impact on student outcomes and delineating a framework for establishing an effective parent empowerment programme within your schools. It is out of this need that my journey of embarking on developing the 'Family Matters Programme' began.

The significance of parental partnerships in education

Parental involvement in education is multifaceted, encompassing activities such as helping with home learning, attending school events and participating in the learning journey. The influence of these activities is profound. Research by the Education Endowment Foundation (cited in Wood, 2023) shows that effective parental engagement results in an additional two months' progress a year for children, with approaches where a parent works one to one with their child having an additional five months' progress a year for children. There is a positive and convincing relationship between family involvement and student success.

When parents are involved in their children's education, children do better on a wide range of measures, including behaviour symptoms, greater confidence and self-esteem, higher attendance rates and higher attainment. When schools and parents listen to each other and work together, they have a positive impact on attainment and student wellbeing. This is why it is so important that schools work in partnership with their parents.

Factors to consider in setting up a parent empowerment programme

Recognising the diverse background of families is vital; the programme should be culturally sensitive and inclusive, providing materials and resources in multiple languages if necessary and respecting different cultural perspectives on education and parent–teacher roles.

In establishing effective and accessible communication channels between the school and families, it is helpful to consider various methods, like emails, newsletters, social media and communication apps and platforms, to ensure that all families are informed and can participate.

When considering flexibility and accessibility, try to schedule events and meetings at various times to accommodate different work schedules. You may even want to consider an online offer for the family empowerment programme.

Questions to explore:

- Who will facilitate the programme?
- When and where will the sessions be held?
- How can we recruit parents and carers into the programme?
- What topical issues should we cover within the content of each session?
- How can we set up a working group agreement?
- How can we manage endings?
- What mechanisms can we use to measure the impact of the programme?

Components of a successful parent empowerment programme

Before embarking on your design journey, it's important to outline your goals and desired outcomes of providing the sessions, while ensuring that you have appropriate feedback mechanisms to encourage a collaborative approach and measure the impact of the programme. Parent voice is vital for shaping the structure and content of the sessions, ensuring that you are providing a menu of learning that is aligned to the desired topical issues that parents and carers may be facing. Regular surveys, suggestion boxes and parent councils can provide parents with a voice in the growth of the programme. Projects where parents and teachers collaborate can help to build trust and mutual understanding.

Case study

Within the Family Matters programme, I encountered a case study that profoundly illustrates the programme's impact. A mother joined our sessions, grappling with challenges in her relationship with her eight-year-old daughter. Her struggles were deeply rooted in her own turbulent childhood, which had unknowingly shaped her approach to parenting and left her unequipped to address her daughter's emotional needs effectively.

Through her journey in the programme, she gained invaluable insights into recognising indicators of her child's wellbeing and gained various emotional regulation techniques. More importantly, the programme provided a supportive and non-judgemental environment. This safe space was instrumental in allowing her to confront and process her own emotional difficulties, a step that was crucial for her personal growth and healing.

The knowledge and skills that she acquired were transformative. They not only equipped her to better understand and respond to her daughter's emotional distress but they also empowered her to start mending and strengthening their relationship.

The progress that they have made since is a testament to the power of informed and compassionate parenting. Today, both mother and daughter are enjoying a much healthier and happier relationship, thriving in their individual lives and as a family unit.

Conclusion

The adage that it takes a village to raise a child holds particularly true in education. Empowering parents to take an active role in their children's

> education is not just beneficial but essential for fostering an environment where students can thrive academically, socially and emotionally. By establishing effective parent empowerment programmes, schools can harness the potential of this collaborative force, ultimately leading to a more holistic and enriched education experience for students.
>
> 'Parental partnerships in education are like roots to a tree; they nourish and stabilise, allowing children, parents and educators to grow strong together.' (Kelly Hannaghan)

Promoting a culture of wellbeing outside of school hours

School may finish at 3.30 pm or so, but our pupils' interactions with their peers continue long after this, on the journey home and online, gaming or through social media or WhatsApp. We know that children shouldn't be using such applications, many with an age limitation of 13, 16 or 18, but we know that children do access this aspect of digital life, sometimes without the knowledge of their parents. We cannot police what children do online at home, but we can offer support to families that demonstrates that our culture for positive mental health extends beyond school. This can include discussing protective factors, such as tracking phones, checking online behaviour or even turning off the Wi-Fi, a service now offered by some broadband providers.

We know too that children will also engage in risky online behaviours, from chatting with unknown and anonymous people in gaming or on social media to sharing images of themselves, and that these scenarios leave them at risk of predatory abuse. Whether the school is first made aware of this by a concerned parent, or the child makes a disclosure in school, your response to the parent should be the same: support but don't confront. Parents are not always aware of what their children do online until they are faced by an unexpected credit card bill for online and in-app gaming purchases, or when they are shown screenshots by another parent of language and emojis deemed offensive. Both situations are best addressed through conversation with parent and child together, going through the risks and protections that could be put in place. What would be inappropriate would be a knee-jerk reaction, such as an assembly or whole-class intervention on the matter, which might draw attention either to the behaviour – leading others to do the same – or to the child concerned, possibly leaving them isolated and exposed. Your response, of course, might be different if this was a pattern of behaviours involving several pupils, with cyberbullying or multiple children sharing or accessing concerning content online being the most likely triggers.

Barriers that prevent engagement

Language and communication is an area where school–home relationships can founder. Families who do not have English as their first language may find it difficult to participate in school activities or to communicate with the school without the support of translation services or dual language communication. Schools may also use complex language, educational jargon and acronyms in their newsletters and emails. Be wary too of language that might seem patronising, like 'as a parent myself', which sounds like you are telling them how to parent. The school may also be guilty of one-way conversations, giving out information but not readily listening to concerns or suggestions.

There may also be cultural and socio-economic barriers to parental engagement. Past negative experiences with schooling themselves may make parents hesitant to engage with their child's school. They may have had learning needs that were unmet, felt they were let down academically or had issues with bullying and bad behaviour, either as a victim or as a perpetrator. These aren't issues that parents would readily share, but a positive school culture might anticipate them. There may also be a lack of trust in the school system or a belief that they have little say in their child's education, especially in a school where pastoral care appears to have been marginalised at the expense of attainment. For some families, it is also the case that cultural differences and personal values may not align with the school's culture, which can make parents feel uncomfortable or unwelcome.

Barriers based around the school itself include an unwelcoming climate for parents. This could be due to a lack of outreach in areas of deprivation. Parents may also feel that there is a culture of blame directed at them around behaviour in school, anti-social conduct outside of school or low levels of interest or engagement in the children's learning. Lack of resources to support parents, such as translation services or wraparound childcare, can also add to parental disengagement, especially when they are aware that other schools in the vicinity may offer these facilities. Poor relationships that some staff have with pupils may well extend to parents. Young and inexperienced staff or those who are not yet parents themselves cannot be labelled as the culprits here; more often than not, it is staff who are perhaps set in their ways that create the barrier, which can discourage parents from getting involved.

Communication around mental health in particular may not be the best with parents. Over half of the parents I surveyed advised that they were unaware of whether the school offered any support for their child's mental health, and a similar number were not aware that it was taught in any way. Others became aware of the support that was available after they sought help over issues such as a lack of confidence or fear of bullying, and these parents were, in the main, satisfied with the school's response to them. However, there were several who expressed alarm at the language used to describe mental health concerns from staff – for example, 'His self-esteem is worryingly low', which is the sort of comment that will worry parents but also lead them to ask how long this has been the case, what has been done and why they weren't made aware.

Parent WhatsApp groups – a modern challenge

A phenomenon of recent years, the parent WhatsApp group emerged initially as a communication tool for sharing key information – reminders for parents who have lost track of letters and need reminders about homework. In many ways, these have been a positive and additional layer of communication for the school, albeit out of the school's hands.

Many headteachers I have spoken to raise their eyebrows at the mention of such groups, and have found them problematic when the content of discussions is reported back to the school, either in person or through emails with attached screenshots. Sometimes these are reported straight to the teacher – the 'Look what they are saying about you' conversation, which can make many teachers anxious and concerned, whether this reporting is done with good intentions or otherwise.

WhatsApp groups can be harmful. The broadcasters and inclusion campaigners Carrie and David Grant (2019) tell of a parent group set up by the other parents in their adopted son's class to discuss him and his behaviour. Eventually, this led to a petition calling for him to be excluded. In primary schools in particular, WhatsApp is used by a vocal minority to vent about the teacher, from their use of discipline and their style of teaching to criticism of their clothes, hair and make-up or speculation about their private lives. Social media groups such as those on Facebook discuss such concerns, but they represent the views of a minority, and any reasonable headteacher or governor wouldn't take any complaint of this nature seriously. They may bat it aside, but will record it and won't ignore it, as it does give a valuable insight into the mental health of the parent and the way they interact with a larger group.

Principle issues with WhatsApp groups (and this could include your staff group and your street or community group too) include:

- When the group reaches a certain size, at least into double figures, there will be certain figures who tend to dominate posts and discussions.
- Without agreed rules and moderation, the group could become burdensome or intrusive into the digital lives of its members.
- The posting of misinformation can be an innocent mistake or a deliberate provocation.
- Some people will believe anything that is posted.
- Although some members will leave a group if the content becomes questionable, others will feel pressured to remain and also to go along with the actions of the dominant voices.
- Some opinions are expressed in the group because there is a feeling that they aren't listened to or are talked down to by teachers or school leaders.
- The phone numbers of individual group members are available for all members to see, sometimes leading to unpleasant and intrusive personal messaging.

A strategy that the school may wish to consider is how to get the louder voices onside. Don't use language like 'ringleaders' or 'troublemakers' and avoid letters and emails as a point of contact. Sometimes, having them in the office for a meeting, kept formal without a desk separating you, and speaking to them with a sense of respect and from a position of equality can go a long way to winning over even the most reluctant parent.

Useful strategies to engage parents

- Take the opinions and thoughts of your parents and carers with regular surveys but, more importantly, share what the surveys indicate, positive and negative, warts and all!

- For areas raised as a concern through the survey and through formal or informal complaints, make clear the choice of action taken and publicise it; a 'You said, we did' board or newsletter feature is a simple form to communicate this change.
- A good family liaison officer (FLO) colleague is worth their weight in gold. Seen as separate from the teaching team by parents, they can be a source of confidence and advice and are often the first point of contact with the school if there is a concern around their child's or their family's mental health. A good FLO is non-judgemental while remaining professional, and regarded by some parents as their most trusted contact, because they are the most consistent contact over a period of years.
- The mental health lead, together with the FLO and SENDCo, can draw up a list of support networks locally to signpost parents to if they need additional resources. These could include NHS resources such as CAMHS, local groups offering specialist provision or sources of individual therapy, while other parents may benefit from support groups, workshops or online resources.
- Ensure that there are clear channels of communication for parents, especially if they feel that they have to make a complaint. Ideally, the first point of contact should be the school, as all schools make clear in their complaints policy. However, some parents report directly to Ofsted, more so since Gavin Williamson announced that they should do so over the quality of online learning in 2021 (Roberts, 2021). Others bypass the school and may take a complaint to the local authority, while some make contact with local or national press to air their concerns. Rather than have the parents search the school website for the complaints procedure, an open door culture and being available to listen and act can often head off a more challenging scenario.

Final thoughts

Parents and carers complete the third side of the triangle of community, adjacent to children and staff. A strong triangle is stable and supportive, and our parent body should be engaged with and welcomed, enabled and valued, so that they feel that they are very much in a partnership with the school in terms of their children's and their own mental health and wellbeing.

THINK about enabling parent voice and working with parents and carers

Time

- Relationships with parents take time as a new leader, if the school is newly opened or if there has been a historic fractured relationship with the school in the past.
- Any parent will be appreciative of time given to them, be it by school leaders, class teachers or support staff. The willingness to give them time amplifies and validates their voices.

Holistic

- Consider your communication with parents as a means of opening conversation around all aspects of schooling, whether academic, social or cultural, to ensure that mental health doesn't stand alone in their eyes when concerns are raised. Positive relationships make any subsequent challenging conversations easier to handle.

Inclusive

- Remember the needs of your parents as much as those of your children. Choose your language and communication to reflect the fact that you may have parents with poor literacy skills, with little or no spoken English or with special needs identified in their own days at school.
- Some parents will be wary at the mention of the words 'mental health', perhaps making them defensive or withdrawn. Parents need the same positive language around mental health and wellbeing as the children; a shared language is for all sides of the community to use – parents, children and staff.

Non-judgemental

- Avoid terms like 'difficult' about parents and remember that your most challenging parents are a minority. The vast majority, even if largely silent, are supportive of what you do.
- A parent who might appear challenging probably has challenges of their own around their social and economic circumstances, their

own mental and physical health and/or in their understanding of what the school has told them. The majority of parents who might raise a voice, send a hastily worded email or an impromptu text message will apologise the next day, having reflected upon their actions with another family member.

Knowledgeable

- Know your community. What works in one school might not function in another; there is not a 'one size fits all' model with mental health.
- Consider that parts of the community will be more reluctant or reticent to discuss the term 'mental health', perhaps for cultural or faith-based reasons. Your shared language may use the term 'wellbeing' instead.
- Know your families by building relationships; know their histories and acknowledge that some families have an influence in the community through their leadership of local groups, such as in places of worship, sports clubs or Beavers and Scouts groups. Such influences can help to promote the school message of positive mental health.

Interview with Ellie Costello of Square Pegs: Developing the relationship between schools and parents

Ellie Costello is director of Square Peg, a parent support organisation particularly concerned about pressures that schools are facing around attendance. Her interests lie in developing ACE-aware best practice, service-planning and provision for all those working with children and families, in order to build cohesive, holistic, attachment-aware, trauma-informed frameworks and services. Passionate about mental health and neurodevelopment, Ellie envisions a world where happy, emotionally resilient, curious and creative children thrive equally; where improved health, education and life outcomes are delivered and sustained. We spent an afternoon discussing parental views of the picture of mental health in schools.

Do you believe that schools talk enough to children about mental health in general and to parents about their child's mental health in particular?

The conversation around mental health is improving. Mental health and wellbeing wasn't on the landscape when we entered education as a family with a child in Reception in 2010. Covid very much legitimised this conversation around needs and levels of need around poor mental health, but there isn't enough of a conversation around what wellness and wellbeing is, as opposed to spotting mental health and mental ill health as emerging themes in children; these are two separate subjects. I have been concerned about the amount of self-diagnosis on social media, TikTok in particular. Children are very aware and alert to their emotional state, and that of their peers and adults around them, as we are wired to survive based on the happiness of the clan. There is a pushback that mental health awareness campaigns are causing poor mental health in children and that having these conversations is a bad thing, which speaks to the deficit and fear and lack of capacity in the tools of the adults, who don't know how to respond to and support a child in distress, or how to contain a child's distress. Learning how to do this is needed to help our children navigate the world safely.

I'm very aware that educators are the only frontline service professionals who do not have clinical supervision, but believe that any professional working up close and personal with families and young people needs this level of supervision, for reflective practice and to offload. Good supervision for staff can help in working on toxic staffroom cultures, and the gossipy element can be dissipated. It is no wonder we have so-called 'culture wars' within schools with so much going on, and layers of 'us and them' in the staffroom and negative comments about parents, children and colleagues. Done well, and possibly delivered at a group level, supervision can enable staff to share their deepest, darkest thoughts and their despair, without any reporting back. It differs from coaching, which is solutions-focused and tools-based, but clinical supervision is a very specific place, which can support some key individuals in the school.

Supervision is woven into the standards for social workers, emergency medicine, doctors and CAMHS professionals. It can be an effective route, written into standards for school staff too. The case for supervision is firstly that you aren't doing anything wrong and secondly that it is evidence-based. It works with other sectors and probably has a place in education.

[A note from the author: I think that putting supervision into place needs to be there, although it will be a huge professional and financial commitment. We need

to be looking at major radical solutions here, because of the numbers of teachers and leaders that we are losing from the profession. The long-term future of the profession depends on such radical solutions.]

Is the priority given to academic attainment and progress overshadowing the importance of our children's mental health?

Without a doubt. We are chasing the wrong KPIs [key performance indicators]. Grades are clearly important but they come at a cost. It narrows our focus and is a false narrative. Thirty years ago, we were all told to qualify with a fistful of GCSEs and A levels and you will have a secure and well-paid job and career satisfaction for life, but we know there is no such thing as a job for life and that a bag full of grades doesn't equate to job security – nor does it equate to mental fitness. I heard Sir Anthony Seldon speak at the Rethinking Education conference in 2023, saying how the high drop-out rate from university was alarming, with complex and considerable reasons, but one reason being that we aren't schooling or equipping our children to be independent critical thinkers or to be prepared for independent living. Children are alert to the fact that school doesn't prepare them for life, so what and why are we doing this, with pushing the high-grade agenda? My work with local services, where we try to evaluate the effectiveness and satisfaction with the service – I suggest that we ask children if they are happy, often met with 'How do we measure that?', to which I respond that we can trust what they say and we hope that it is consistent, which we can tell by asking them at one point in the year, and then again later. If they are happy, everything else improves: attendance improves, their grades go up, they are more optimistic for the future, they have a sense of trust in their autonomy, and agency over their own life outcomes. Everything goes up when children are happy, so why on earth don't we value children's happiness and wellbeing, and why don't we want the same for our school staff too, which will also see grades rise and improve? There are huge opportunities that we are missing with obsessive observation and assessment, which can be adjusted with more outdoor learning, inquiry-based or play-based opportunities, working together and not directly instructing. What we are seeing is wellbeing in decline and mental ill health on the rise, and we need to do things differently and urgently.

[A note from the author: There was a major opportunity lost in 2010, with the quashing of the Rose and Alexander reports, which would have led to a more flexible and less prescribed, richer and more spacious curriculum.]

Are the pathways for children and families seeking support clear enough for them and for teachers to follow?

No, unfortunately, although we have a diverse offer in all of the options for a child, professionals and parents to seek support. The diversity is interesting but not standardised, because of the different ethos and culture, the socio-economic profile of the school or postcode. The offer is a mess, but we also cannot discount the stigma around seeking support. It's not OK to not be OK, even though we say that it is. As soon as a child, parent or colleague finds themselves struggling and in need of support, there is so much stigma, and not least institutional structural barriers. Human beings by nature don't automatically enjoy falling into seeking help; we are independent autonomous beings and children, particularly in the Early Years, are fiercely independent. Most people from this starting position will choose independence over support, but are also naturally drawn to the collective and community. How do we give permission to allow for autonomous and independent thinking when some people don't want or accept support, even when it is freely offered? I spoke to a headteacher recently who offered pupil premium support to a proud working-class family who were of the opinion that they were only chosen because of where they lived and didn't feel there was a need for the offered interventions. On reflection, despite the entitlement to the offer, the headteacher thought that the family were absolutely fine.

[A note from the author: Stigma comes up as one of the biggest barriers, within both the school and the community. Sometimes stigma is cultural, sometimes it is prejudiced and discriminatory and sometimes it boils down to lack of knowledge. A reaction to lack of understanding is sometimes just to close up. Positive conversations are one way of addressing this, particularly with staff who are demonstrating a degree of stigma; the best solution here is not the path of capability or disciplinary, but the path of training.]

This approach ensures that the conversation is inclusive and solutions-focused. Keeping policy-led and professional means you can quite quickly get onto the pathway of admonishment rather than taking it as a learning or reflection opportunity.

I am concerned from what I hear that members of mental health support teams are suffering a degree of burnout and not completing their qualifications, but also that they are being rolled out over a wider area, where there aren't enough hours to share out, and that they are taking on involvement and giving advice for children with very complex and high-end needs, at Tier 3 or 4. There is a concern that the teams aren't keeping their staff because they feel very exposed, the situation is unsustainable and/or they couldn't get access to their supervisor.

Some headteachers describe a 'sense of entitlement' from some parents, whom they describe as 'difficult' or 'challenging'. Do parents have this sense or are they just seeking the best for their child?

Parents are seeking the best for their child. Schools sometimes have a dim view at times of children and aren't very family-friendly, and the narrative around parents is poor and leads to a sense of separation and segregation between schools and families. Parents may think why should they do their best with schools if educators fall into the trap, in the way they present to parents, that they think they are uneducated, ignorant, illiterate, lazy, feckless and lacking in aspiration, or if they think they are a pointy-elbowed middle-class type who wants the moon on a stick. Teachers wouldn't speak to each other in these ways, and this goes back to staffroom gossip, which can be unsavoury, unprofessional and not very grown-up. Parents who believe this to be teachers' attitudes will respond in kind, often defensive, angry and frustrated at the way they feel spoken to.

In the same way that the teaching profession wants to feel respected, parents want exactly the same thing. There is a parallel in the case of Ruth Perry, in how teachers and leaders spoke of their experience of Ofsted, with what parents have said of their experience of schools: so sick with worry that they couldn't sleep, not feeling included, feeling alone and lonely, not feeling listened to. There is so much common experience. We need to stop lecturing, sermonising and finger-pointing in education; the tone of letters and communication from schools is outrageous at times. Do we think enough of those parents with English as a second language or those parents who were wounded by their own experience of education and of life? We need to scaffold and support communication to enable us to speak to parents regardless of socio-economic background, but also be grounded in humility; education isn't there to homogenise families, but to work with the families they have and deliver a service for the whole community. There is also a feeling of entitlement in the profession too, but entitlement is born from a sense of not feeling represented, not being understood, feeling blamed and isolated. This is a habit we just need to get out of. There are always opportunities to repair relationships, particularly working with key and influential connections.

What is the most positive experience about supporting a child's mental health that you have heard of?

The best example is this. I was involved from bid level in a key worker service, part of a pilot project out of the NHS long-term plan, the purpose of which was to prevent or reduce Tier 4 admissions for young people aged 14 to 25 with a diagnosis of autism or learning disability. We have reduced admissions, which was our key target, prevented family breakdown, prevented completion of suicide, returned children to education, training and employment, avoided youth justice sentences, and got young children off the streets and into secure accommodation. This has all been built by experts with lived experience. Evaluation and constant review by the same professions ensures professional challenge but also ensures that principles and values are embraced. We had the most incredible team, a team still in place.

9 Developing external provision

Chapter overview

In this chapter, we will consider:

- CAMHS – child and adolescent mental health services
- mental health support teams
- working with other external services, including charities and the third sector
- communication and relationships with external agencies
- reaching out and sharing good practice.

In Chapter 5, we discussed the three levels of mental health support: the universal, representing the offer available to every pupil, regardless of need; the selective, being the support or intervention arising from assessment and observation, which the school can provide through its own resources and appropriate expertise; and the intensive, being the external and more expert provision that the school is able to access for the pupils with the most pressing level of concern. It is this upper tier where the greatest inequalities lie, depending upon local provision and access to programmes of support and levels of funding. External support will be the upper level of support and as such, this will be reflected both in any intervention map that a school may produce, and in the referral pathway that will articulate the services the school can refer to and the staff with responsibility for making any referral to this level of support.

CAMHS – child and adolescent mental health services

School mental health initiatives are a vital part of a child's pastoral and academic journey. These initiatives aim to promote and support the emotional wellbeing of students and help them to develop the skills needed to manage challenges and difficulties. However, implementing successful mental health initiatives in schools requires collaboration between educators, parents and mental health professionals. CAMHS is the name of the NHS services that assess and treat young people with emotional, behavioural or mental health difficulties. Another acronym, CYPMHS, stands for children and young people's mental health services. This is a new term and it includes all the services that might be available to help young people in addition to CAMHS. CAMHS teams comprise multidisciplinary professionals, including psychiatrists, psychologists, social workers and nurses, who work together to provide a comprehensive range of services.

CAMHS is able to support young people with the following:

- anxiety
- depression
- eating disorders
- obsessive-compulsive disorder (OCD)
- post-traumatic stress disorder (PTSD)
- attention deficit hyperactivity disorder (ADHD)
- autism spectrum disorder (ASD)
- conduct disorders
- self-harm
- bullying
- family problems
- bereavement.

CAMHS offers a range of services, including:

- assessments and diagnoses
- individual therapy

- group therapy
- family therapy
- medication
- support groups
- early intervention services.

If there is concern about the mental health of a child or young person, they can be referred to CAMHS by speaking to their GP, school nurse or social worker. Concerns can also be raised by contacting CAMHS directly. Schools need to be very clear in their referral pathways; in theory, any adult in the school could make a referral to CAMHS, bypassing the mental health lead, senior leadership and the parent or carer. While such a scenario is unlikely, it emphasises the importance of training and everyone taking responsibility, but also respecting guidelines and protocols.

CAMHS services are divided into four tiers, with thresholds defining access to each.

- Tier 1 covers universal services, addresses initial concerns and includes the work of GPs and health visitors, as well as the universal provision from schools in supporting and promoting wellbeing. CAMHS has no direct involvement in Tier 1 but can add capacity to this tier by the offer to schools of training for staff.
- Tier 2 is targeted services and early intervention, which includes mild to moderate concerns that might have been raised by school staff, educational psychologists or counsellors.
- Tier 3 covers *specialist* services for moderate and severe concerns and includes specialist multidisciplinary teams working in a community mental health setting. This tier includes psychiatry outpatient service and support for eating disorders.
- Tier 4 is the place of *specialised* services for severe concerns. This includes day and inpatient services and crisis treatment services.

Successful partnering with CAMHS experts has several benefits in implementing school mental health initiatives. CAMHS brings specialised knowledge and evidence-based expertise in mental health and child development. Working alongside CAMHS experts provides opportunities for staff to enhance their skills and knowledge in mental health and emotional wellbeing. Also, CAMHS practitioners can help to develop and implement strategies to support students with mental health challenges, creating a more inclusive and supportive school environment.

However, the reality of the experience of many schools is determined and overwhelmed by the sheer volume of cases that CAMHS has, the capacity of both the school and the CAMHS practitioners to give their time or resources, and the thresholds for support not being met because of cases not being deemed sufficiently severe for Tier 3 or 4 intervention. As Roman Kemp discovered (see Chapter 7), the attitude of some professionals also impacts the effectiveness of and access to intervention at this highest level. Building a relationship is one thing, but for all the efforts that the school is making in determining the ethos around mental health, external forces can operate against this, adding to the challenge and to waiting lists. In researching this theme, I have heard of waiting lists varying from 17 weeks, which is still long enough in the life of a young person, to three years, meaning that if this is the case for a child in Year 3 in primary school, they are almost at secondary transition when help may be available. This means that schools need to be looking creatively and widely at other opportunities to provide expert-level support for the children who need it.

Mental health support teams

Mental health support teams (MHSTs) began to be rolled out in England, with similar provision in the rest of the UK, from 2018. MHSTs are initiatives dedicated to providing accessible and early-intervention mental health support for children and young people. In England between 2018 and 2022, some 14 pilot sites were rolled out (NHS England, n.d.) and, as we know from Chapter 7, there was a target of 36 per cent of children having access to the work of an MHST, rising to a target of 50 per cent by March 2025.

There are three core functions of MHSTs. The first is to deliver evidence-based interventions for mild-to-moderate mental health issues – in other words, Tier 2 of the CAMHS thresholds. Secondly, the teams support the senior mental health lead in each school or college to introduce or develop the whole-school or college approach, which requires the school to have a designated lead for mental health who has undertaken appropriate training. The third function is to give timely advice to school and college staff, and liaise with external specialist services to help young people to receive the right support.

Where schools have access to an MHST, they may have the support of professionals such as clinical lead practitioners and education mental health practitioners, likely at a trainee level. The team can offer evidence-based interventions for issues like anxiety, low mood or exam stress. They can also support the school in developing whole-school approaches to mental wellbeing. Benefits of using the services provided by the MHST include providing accessible and early-intervention support for mild-to-moderate mental health concerns. Access to the MHST can also reduce stigma around mental health by normalising the seeking of help. When the team works effectively in school, it can add to the toolkit of resources and skills of the staff in supporting and promoting positive mental health strategies and language. Teams can provide one-to-one sessions of support, based on principles of cognitive behaviour therapy, as well as group sessions and workshops that promote emotional wellbeing and provide strategies for coping with emerging difficulties.

The intention is that MHSTs can bridge the gap between community resources and specialised mental health services. However, even with a 50 per cent target, one barrier to effective use is the location of the school – a 'postcode lottery' as it were. An internet search for mental health support teams in your part of the country will show whether the service is locally available. Even in areas where teams operate, they may be limited in the numbers of schools they have capacity to support. A further barrier is the numbers of staff available and the quality of training and support that they receive. Given our awareness of staff mental health and wellbeing, we don't want to see our MHST trainees overwhelmed by the number of schools by which they are engaged and the potential caseload within each setting.

Working with other external services, including charities and the third sector

As a result of challenges around timescales and capacity with NHS mental health provision, many schools seek support from what is known as the third sector, which can include charities, but also local and national groups supported by public or private funding. They can be used as a way of supporting both young people in school and also their families, by signposting them to suitable agencies and support networks. There are also a number of other agencies and organisations, both local and national, that can offer support around specific issues. The third sector is not a substitute for Tiers 3 and 4 of CAMHS, but does offer a valuable level of expertise to which our resources and budgets in schools may not allow access otherwise.

Charities

A good starting point is mental health charities. Mind, for example, has over 100 Local Mind initiatives across England and Wales, each different in what they are able to provide but covering such topics as talking therapies, crisis helplines, advocacy, counselling and befriending services. Local Minds groups can be signposted to families, as they can provide specific support for new mothers and fathers, non-judgemental peer support and support for issues around employment. They also offer confidential signposting for young people and adults facing an element of fear or stigma. Some local groups – Mind Lancashire, for example – provide a package of support under their Thriving Schools programme, to support both the primary and secondary sector. YoungMinds, as the name implies, is specifically aimed at the mental health of young people; it also provides programmes of support for schools and can also be used for signposting to parents and carers and their children.

Football clubs in the community

Local football clubs also offer community programmes, of which schools are a major beneficiary. Providers aren't only the most successful clubs in the Premier League; clubs throughout the English Football League, National League and Cymru Premier have community projects, as do clubs across the Scottish league system. In Northern Ireland, the Irish FA Foundation Football Community Hubs has 12 centres, with the aim of promoting health and education alongside football. What the clubs provide is much more than sports coaching, upon which Sports Premium funding may have been spent, but a wider level of community engagement and support. One of the most remote senior clubs in the UK, Inverness Caledonian Thistle, explicitly states on its ICT Trust website page: 'The ICT Trust's primary objective is to promote and improve the physical and mental health of both young and old through activity and provide an opportunity for everyone in Inverness and surrounding areas to participate in football!' That their primary objective concerns physical and mental health aligns with the holistic model of mental health, fitting into the broadest definition of curriculum in our schools. Such initiatives are not limited to the world of football; rugby clubs of both codes and the county cricket clubs also run community programmes, which can be found through links on their websites.

Charlton Athletic Community Trust was founded in 1992, and on three occasions in the intervening years, the club has been awarded Community

Club of the Year by the English Football League. In addition to coaching sports in PE lessons and after-school clubs, coaches can work with boys who are not engaging in reading and writing through Premier League Stars, which encourages reading but which can also develop self-esteem and provide a positive younger-adult role model. The trust also works through the Charlton Athletic Race and Equality Partnership, established after the murder of Stephen Lawrence, in promoting anti-racist initiatives. In partnership with Oxleas NHS Foundation Trust, the club works in the community and with schools in a variety of programmes promoting mental health and wellbeing. The club works prominently in the reduction of street violence, and has promoted community cohesion and positive relationships, particularly after the murder of Lee Rigby. The club actively promotes the LGBTQIA+ community, having the first LGBTQIA+ team with the name and badge of a professional team in CACT Invicta FC. Representatives of the community trust speak regularly to meetings of senior leaders across South-East London and Kent about their work and what they offer to schools. Schools that haven't yet accessed what their local professional clubs can offer need only consider the impact that a club with community at its heart, like Charlton Athletic, can have.

Healthy relationships

There will be few schools that do not have children impacted by domestic violence and relationship breakdown. In supporting these young people, schools can consider reaching out to local branches of organisations such as Women's Aid. Women's Aid are able to offer free sessions offering support around healthy relationships through workshops and games. Although the school will be aware of the purpose and intention of the workshops, with the children there is no mention of abuse or violence. The organisation is also able to run support sessions for children who have disclosed domestic abuse in their homes. Project workers talk through with the children what they have experienced, and discuss how to control anger, understand their feelings and how to keep safe and disclose secrets safely to their trusted adults. Women's Aid programmes are focused upon preventive education.

Another organisation worth considering around healthy relationships is Tender, a nationwide charity that uses drama and the arts to educate young people and adults about what healthy relationships look like, aiming to equip them with the skills and knowledge to identify unhealthy relationships. Content covered includes elements of the relationships, sex and health education (RSHE) programme, with appropriate age-level input at both primary and secondary level. There is also the opportunity to explore the impact of the digital world and how phones and social media can be negotiated safely. Tender also very much promotes the concept of a healthy and positive community, emphasising the role that individuals play within society. The organisation provides specialist support for alternative provision settings, special schools and sixth-form colleges, in addition to the primary and secondary school offer.

Keeping our children safe

Two organisations worth looking at, both born from tragic circumstances, are the Molly Rose Foundation and the Mizen Foundation. The former, established by Ian Russell after the death of his daughter, is aimed at suicide prevention in the under-25 age group, helping them to reach out for support and practical advice. Although providing resources around various aspects of mental health awareness, at the core of the foundation's work is online safety, because of the material that Molly had been accessing in the months prior to her death. The Mizen Foundation, established in memory of Jimmy, who was killed in 2008, reaches out to schools, pupil referral units, youth groups and the broader community. Margaret and Barry Mizen speak openly about what happened to Jimmy and the history of bullying and anti-social behaviour of the young man that took the life of their son. Their message, though, is one of dealing with anger, understanding the consequences of our own actions, taking personal responsibility and, most powerfully, the ability to forgive.

Other local groups

The school could consider other groups, knowing the context and the local offer, such as the following:

- young carers support
- young violence reduction services
- local substance misuse services
- school nursing service
- attendance services, some of which are private and others, through education welfare officers, run through the local authority
- advice around eating disorders

- police and paramedic services, particularly around the impact of youth violence
- local safeguarding board.

The availability of local networks is variable, with more rural locations less likely to have access to services because of distance from larger population centres and fewer organisations available in the immediate area. Due to much lower population density, there are inevitably going to be fewer people to work for and with such groups. Although there are fewer children in more rural areas, they have as much entitlement to support around mental health as their peers in our larger towns and cities. School leaders with a sound knowledge of their community and who have built relationships will reiterate the golden thread that there is no 'one size fits all' model. For this reason, the importance of building channels of communication and of reaching out will be paramount.

Communication and relationships with external agencies

Establishing strong communication channels with external services is crucial for ensuring mutually positive relationships and successful collaboration. Schools that do this best within their own setting are probably able to build these relationships, because a positive culture around wellbeing in a school ought naturally to flow into the manner in which staff relate to external providers. This can enable efficient sharing of information and productive collaboration.

A starting point is to consider the needs around communication, both the school's own and those of the service provider. A larger organisation may have an administration ensuring the efficiency of the business, but if working with a sole trader, such as a self-employed therapist, it is important not to overwhelm them with burdensome communication. Consider the communication methods and protocols that the provider may prefer, alongside how the school communicates. If a provider receives multiple emails from several schools, the sheer volume of them may cause a backlog. The relationship between the school and the practitioner may begin through email, but maintaining a professional relationship relies in part, in the same way as it does with staff and parents, on not creating such a volume of communication to cause vital points to be missed.

How the relationship between the school and the professional subsequently develops can impact the communication process. Schools want a productive and collaborative environment in which to work with external providers, but the practitioner needs to feel welcome in the workplace. If a therapist or counsellor is engaged by the school, it is essential to communicate with staff who they are, what they do and why they are there, even if they are not working with children in that staff member's class. Successful schools may make their outside professionals feel like part of the team, inviting them to the staffroom and even to social events. The school could be equally successful with a purely business and professional relationship, but should consider visiting staff as part of the wider school community; a frosty relationship could be a sign of underlying toxicity or of an issue with the commitment to the ethos of the school. Part of the communication with external providers therefore needs to involve sharing and communicating the ethos of the school, regardless of the length of their contract and hours on site.

Reaching out and sharing good practice

While the focus of this book concerns schools establishing the culture and ethos that promotes positive mental health and wellbeing in their community and addressing the needs of their stakeholders, there will be schools where the work of the team could and should be shared more widely as an exemplar and as a model for others to learn from, be that within a local authority, in a MAT or at a national level.

Schools that provide the best examples of good practice usually go about their business quietly, and rather than promote what they do, it is the words and reactions of those that notice the impact of actions that tend to draw positive attention to what is taking place. This could, of course, come from an Ofsted inspection, where inspectors may report on the positive and supportive relationships and culture in a school and how wellbeing and mental health is given a prominent place in the personal development of the pupils. Inspectors may be influenced by the voice of parents, through the questionnaire and by face-to-face interaction – and the voices of parents, if amplified positively through social media channels, can also promote the school, especially in a catchment where a number of schools are competing for pupil numbers. Parents want to see their child achieve well academically, but they also want them to be safe and to thrive, and for themselves as parents to be respected. Visiting professionals, be they educational psychologists, counsellors, therapists or members of the mental health support team, will recognise good practice and, in visiting other schools, may share what is working well in other settings. School improvement partners and advisers, at both local authority and MAT level, providing that they buy into the wider holistic picture of positive mental health supporting good learning health, rather than a 'results are everything' ethos, can also act as a conduit in which the word about the excellent practice can reach a wider audience.

Once other professionals become aware of the nature of the work taking place in school, a number of other opportunities may present themselves. This could involve speaking to local headteachers and other school leaders at termly or annual conferences, or it could be at a national event run by one of the education unions, other professional organisations or educational publishers. The school may also find itself invited to contribute a blog post, to write for the educational press or to contribute a chapter to a compendium piece. Such an opportunity – sharing with schools that may not have the same culture and ethos and may possibly have a cynical point of view – offers the chance to answer these questions:

- Why do we do what we offer?
- What do we do?
- How do we do it, how do we resource it and how do we finance it?
- Who does what and when does it happen?
- When and how is the programme evaluated?

Be wary of ill-advised, poorly timed and provocative social media posts about the qualities that the school has to offer. High-profile and somewhat controversial leaders and teachers can promote posts that attract a level of critique and contentious debate. Let others publicise and promote the impact of good practice in a school, rather than the school promote itself.

A school that is able to share its good practice, positive language, ethos and culture in effect becomes an external provider itself. If the school has staff able to speak to and to train colleagues in other settings, not only does it offer another layer of support, but it also generates an income stream for the original school and broadens the scope of the community supporting positive mental health and wellbeing.

Final thoughts

There is going to be variation in the local offer, with urban settings possibly having more ready access to resourcing than more rural areas with a widespread population and differing budgets. Cooperation, collaboration and carefully curated professional relationships can facilitate a culture where good practice can be shared and promoted.

THINK about developing external provision

Time

- The referral process in the school needs to be set out and understood, and not rushed and bypassed. There is a difference between a timely intervention and a hurried intervention. Has every appropriate step been addressed first?
- Any school involvement with CAMHS needs patience and resilience. Waiting lists vary between different localities and from months to years, due to under resourcing and overwhelming demand.

Holistic

- Remember that any intervention isn't an end in itself, but part of the support for a young person to engage them as positive and emotionally healthy learners. Having an intervention doesn't impact learning; it enables it and allows access to learning with the support that the allocated programme allows.

Inclusive

- Any child may need an external intervention, regardless of their background and their previous learning.
- Keep to the suggested referral pathways that the school has. Some parents may seek independent assessments, but a school with clarity on the referral process can act effectively in informing parents of what is regarded as best practice in a school setting.

Non-judgemental

- School staff should not judge or criticise CAMHS and MHST staff, who are also working to tight budgets, time-limited interventions and a volume of referrals beyond their capacity.
- A school that builds channels of communication, considers the wellbeing and mental health of its external providers, and balances a professional and business-minded approach with the reality of working with people with emotions and feelings, will be a school that truly embraces a positive culture of mental health for all.

Knowledgeable

- Know your local context. What services are offered outside of NHS provision? How else can the broader community support the school, and what can the school offer back to the community?
- The third sector offers support at a variety of levels of expertise, experience and emotional intelligence. Embrace every opportunity, build and maintain relationships and share what works well.

10 Developing the curriculum and learning experience

> **Chapter overview**
>
> In this chapter, we will consider:
>
> - mental health in the statutory curriculum: PSHE and RSE across the four nations
> - mental health in the Early Years
> - the place and value of PSHE
> - mental health across the curriculum
> - the power of a good assembly
> - the power of language.

When we consider curriculum, we need to think beyond the narrow confines of what the children learn in class and the content of each subject. Of course, teacher subject knowledge is important, but if we don't reach beyond when we teach about gravity, the point in the year when decimals are introduced or when we cover oxbow lakes, we risk our curriculum being 'cold' and isolated. Let's think of curriculum as every learning opportunity, each minute of the day, from the moment the children are greeted at the gate to the moment they leave, and arguably beyond this point, with digital learning and positive online interactions in their own time.

Every point in the day should be considered a learning opportunity. Speaking to a member of staff on the gate or the class teacher on entry to the classroom is both a social opportunity and a social skill. We would never consider greeting a five-year-old with a nod or a grunt; we would at the very least welcome them with a smile and warmth, to enable them to feel settled at the beginning of the school day. In time, this age of children will repeat these behaviours so that they become a habit, a positive habit that will be embedded and reflect the values of the school. Walking to the hall for assembly, leaving class for the next lesson or for breaktime, how the children wait in line for their lunch and conduct themselves at their lunch tables: regard these not merely as part of the school day but as part of the learning experience – of life skills, of embedding manners and courtesy. If we can have schools teach children about opening a door for others or making an apology for inappropriate behaviours, we can have them learning about the positive impacts that such actions have on the emotional health of others.

In the pages of this closing chapter, we will consider ways in which mental health and wellbeing can fit into the curriculum by drawing on the threads covered through the book. It is not an exhaustive list, but one to encourage lateral rather than linear thinking about the holistic nature of learning. A starting point for this discussion is what statutory requirements are in place for PSHE and RSE.

Mental health in the statutory curriculum: PSHE and RSE across the four nations

The nature of PSHE

In England, PSHE is a non-statutory subject. It is compulsory to cover relationships education in primary school, relationships and sex education in secondary school, and health education in both sectors. In primary education, children are taught about characteristics of healthy family life, about respectful and caring relationships and also about online relationships and keeping safe.

The requirements for secondary schools include sex education. There is nothing in the first section of the guidance to link relationships and mental health, but as we have discussed through the earlier chapters, all aspects of family life and relationships contribute – positively or negatively – to the mental health of our pupils.

In the second half of the DfE guidance (2024), mental health is specifically mentioned, interlinked with physical health, encouraging schools to promote mental wellbeing as a normal part of everyday life and health. Further on, the document mentions making good decisions, urging schools to help pupils in recognising what is normal and in promoting self-control and self-regulation, alongside perseverance. This is supported by encouraging schools to adopt a whole-school approach and to consider the positive impact on behaviour and attainment, to reduce stigma and to encourage openness.

Emotions, feelings and the broader view of good health

In the guidance for primary school, mention is made of the normal range of emotions, including happiness and sadness, fear and anger, surprise and nervousness, and that there is a scale of emotions that are felt in different situations. Mention is made also of a wide and varied vocabulary to discuss feelings, which leads to making choices about behaviours being appropriate and proportionate. There is recognition too of what can impact mental wellbeing: isolation and loneliness, bullying and cyberbullying. The documentation also recognises the benefits of exercise, time outdoors, voluntary and community-based activity and self-care.

Both primary and secondary schools should encourage their pupils to discuss feelings with adults and to seek help and support. The secondary guidance, while modelling the same recommendations as primary but at a more age-appropriate level, extends into recognising the early signs of mental health concerns. There is also the recommendation to teach young people to be critically evaluative of something that they do or are involved in having a positive or negative effect on their own or others' mental health. This is probably the most powerful statement in the documentation, and it mirrors my most frequently used sentences in presentations that I make:

> *'Everything you think, say or do has the capacity to impact the wellbeing of others, negatively, neutrally or positively. You may not consider your thoughts impacting anyone, but thoughts determine attitudes and attitudes can determine words, deeds and actions.'*

PSHE in Scotland, Northern Ireland and Cymru

Education in the UK is devolved, with the DfE guidance only covering schools in England. It is worth readers considering recommendations in the rest of the four nations, which, while also promoting a curriculum around, and sound leadership of, mental health in schools, take slightly different approaches. The Scottish guidance about health in schools breaks health and wellbeing into six sections, of which mental, emotional, social and physical wellbeing is the first category, and although all have equal weight, being listed first implies that it has some priority.

The Northern Ireland curriculum, organised similarly to the discarded English curriculum of 2010, mentioned in my interview with Ellie Costello, is quite specific in what should be covered: children should be taught to understand their own and others' feelings and emotions; to develop the ability to talk about how they feel; to develop their motivation to learn and their individual creative potential; to listen to and interact positively with others; and to explore and understand how others may respond differently to themselves.

In Cymru, the Welsh curriculum makes early and specific reference to the need to take a holistic approach. It identifies that all staff have a role to play in supporting the mental health of young people, and that the ethos and organisation of the school has a pivotal position in providing this support. The Welsh document is the only one to make reference to emotional intelligence and its potential to have an impact on children and young people's personal and social effectiveness, both in the present and for the future.

Mental health in the Early Years

Sophie Smith-Tong is a teacher, EYFS specialist and founder of Mindfulness for Learning – the wellbeing centre for educators and families. She has 15 years' experience of inner-London classroom teaching, and leading on mental health and wellbeing. She now runs Mindfulness for Learning alongside teaching her Reception class in London. Sophie kindly agreed to share her expertise.

Mental health and wellbeing in the Early Years Foundation Stage by Sophie Smith-Tong

So how are we currently doing in terms of Early Years mental health and wellbeing?

- 'In our YouGov poll of parents, 2 in 5 parents (42%) in England with children 0–4 years said they have been worried about the social or emotional wellbeing or behaviour of their child.' (UNICEF, 2022, p. 16)
- 'Nearly three in ten children are not reaching all areas of cognitive, social and emotional development by the end of Reception.' (UNICEF, 2022, p. 17)
- The formal learning model is trickling down into our Early Years spaces.
- Professor and play researcher Peter Gray is one of many experts who believes that there is a correlation between the demise of

play in children's lives and the sharp uptick in 'anxiety, depression, suicide [and] feelings of helplessness' among children (Gray, 2011, pp. 443–63).

I had a child in my class. I was 'warned' about his energy. He loved to move, full of life, enthusiasm. His eyes shone with excitement and an eagerness to play and learn. Reception carpet times are becoming longer, more focused and even scripted. This child wasn't ready for that. Most aren't. The only outcome of carpet times for this particular child was erosion of self-esteem – if every time he came to the carpet I was asking something of him that he was not developmentally ready to do, he would feel like a failure, every day and for extended periods of time. Imagine how that might feel: at work, you are given the lead in a topic you are not equipped or ready to lead on – it may be quite anxiety-inducing. That anxiety may grow and develop into an anxiety disorder or depression. Let me clarify: I am not saying that all children will become anxious or depressed as a result of forced carpet times, but it can't be good for mental health and wellbeing, can it? I didn't pressure this child to join in at carpet times, but for many children this is a daily reality. As the rules and rigour of Key Stage 2 are gradually moving down (they are already in our Year 1 and 2 classrooms), they are now invading our Early Years settings. We are seeing more challenging behaviours and, of course, Covid will have undoubtedly had an impact, but we need to open our eyes to the unachievable expectations we are placing on our youngest children.

With an increase in high-stakes accountability pressures, the focus is often moved away from the three very important prime areas of learning to questioning 'are children academically ready for Year 1?' With this pressure for product, we are seeing:

- more carpet time
- more scripted and prescriptive schemes
- baseline assessments/regular phonics assessments
- restrictive themes and progression maps
- little time to facilitate children's play and really connect with them.

For happier and mentally healthy Early Years classrooms, we need to address the above challenges, and here is how we begin:

Reduce carpet times

More exploratory 'up on our feet' learning is needed. Physical activity improves brain functioning. Sitting still isn't a sign of children absorbing what we are saying. We need to question why we are asking children to sit still for such long periods of time, and reflect upon new and more experiential ways we can offer this kind of learning.

Minimise scheme use

Many schemes are scripted and dictate the way we teach. Connection and being vulnerable are vital for wellbeing. Vanessa King states that 'active listening is one of the most effective relationship and communication skills we can develop' (2016, p. 59). Following a script means we are unable to pause, engage and organically interact with children.

Avoid worksheets

Some children come to Reception having never been to a previous setting or having held a pencil. Worksheets lack imagination and exclude many who are not developmentally ready to succeed in completing one.

Sidestep prescriptive planning and a limiting curriculum

Learning is not linear, and nobody will have the same learning journey. 'Child development cannot be accelerated' (Pica, 2022, p. 17) through inflexible planning and progression maps. The education system went on without me because I did not fit its expectations – listen to the children in your class, trusting that they will learn if it comes from them.

Allow time to connect

Pressure to progress disrupts the road to real progress. Do not pack your days out with adult-directed tasks – give the children space and time in which to explore their own interests and experience their school life, with adults to facilitate the learning in each moment.

Weave wellbeing into your day

A parent of one previous reception child wrote:

'The ritual of being met at the door every morning by the teacher, with genuine curiosity and care, was very supportive and helped her feel secure. She benefited hugely from the "calm corner" as a cosy base for quiet activities. The Magic Hat ritual taught her language and skills around giving compliments, which I think boosted both her empathy and self-esteem.'

These observations show us that there is no one discrete lesson to teach mental health and wellbeing to young children. Learning is modelled through individualised responses and genuine care, patience and love for each child. It doesn't come with a mark, a grade or a product in mind; it's process- and life-experience-driven – from the heart.

Discrete mental health and wellbeing sessions

Deliver discrete moments that introduce children to ways they can manage their mental health and wellbeing. I regularly deliver circle times where we look at Dan Siegel's hand model of the brain, discuss the amygdala and what happens when we are feeling frustrated or cross, and explore ways they can manage these feelings. Children often feel a lot of shame for feeling emotions such as anger or jealousy. A level of understanding as to why they are feeling these emotions can allow them to accept them as part of being human.

Daily mindfulness

Offer daily mindfulness sessions. We have mindfulness with our class puppet, Mindful Mo, who teaches us a new breathing or movement technique every day. Children use the techniques throughout the day when needing space to calm or refocus.

The place and value of PSHE

PSHE is a subject that, in many ways isn't a subject, not being examined or tested, and in some places not timetabled but left to dedicated days and weeks. In tandem with SMSC (spiritual, moral, social and cultural development), it has the potential to be taught discretely, on its own and in its own right, but has the equal potential to sit both alongside and within other areas of the curriculum if we think holistically. The PSHE Association is a starting point for many schools, as are a number of commercial providers who provide planning for the long and medium term, as well as individual lesson plans and even scripted lessons within their schemes of work.

Scripted lessons or context-specific learning?

Scripted and off-the-shelf lessons may have a place in some subjects with a knowledge-focused approach: earthquakes are the same, whether taught in Exeter or Edinburgh; fronted adverbials look the same in Frome and in Folkestone; subtraction in Stirling or Southampton will still give the same answer. However, the place of an off-the-shelf lesson on this aspect of personal development must be in question. Mental health doesn't look or feel the same in Manchester, Melrose or Market Rasen; resilience will differ for children in Redruth and Rhyl. Contexts differ, communities differ and the mental health needs of all these communities differ, as much as they will differ between schools in these communities.

For this reason, while staying with the given schemes of work for PSHE for some of the programme, for the parts referencing mental health, schools should be looking at local need and be responsive to changes that can be impacted by local factors, such as gang culture, crime or racism; national factors, such as the cost of living crisis; or international influences, such as the wars in Ukraine and Gaza, for children who are from the affected nations and also those worried by the crises in these regions. The broad overall headings, such as health and wellbeing, healthy relationships, being a good citizen and life skills, can still be included but need to be specific to local needs. Economic wellbeing lessons may look very different in areas where many families are relying on food banks or where there are higher levels of unemployment. Lessons should also be planned to reflect the racial diversity, gender balance and LGBTQIA+ community in the school. Off-the-shelf lessons give a start, but may need adaptation to reflect the needs of the community.

Delivery of PSHE content

How the lessons are delivered needs consideration. In primary schools, the PSHE lessons, much like other stand-alone subjects such as religious education or music, may often be left for a cover teacher while the class teacher takes regular release time. Isn't it the class teacher who knows the class best? In the subject where knowing your class is most pertinent, where children may share their thoughts or where they are encouraged to consider the emotional impact on themselves and others of what is happening around them, the adult with the greater knowledge of them should be teaching this most important of lessons. For secondary colleagues, there are two points of potential delivery. The first is a regular place on the timetable, although with the pressures on the timetable of examined subjects, even with a two-week timetable, and a shortage of staff in the subject, this could be squeezed or pushed aside. A more workable model employs the use of tutor time, using this time as less of an equipment check and more of a daily check-in and a means of covering the PSHE requirements. With many tutors having a pastoral background or a pastoral responsibility in addition to their subject role, not only does PSHE have a place and is given value and respect as a subject, but the children also have the opportunity to discuss issues arising from the lessons with their most trusted adult. A good tutor can ensure that the time is also used to check in with identified vulnerable pupils, and on a rota basis with every pupil over a two- to three-week period, ensuring that the universal offer around mental health is being delivered as promised.

At the outset of this section, the matter of coverage of PSHE on specialist awareness days or weeks was raised. If the school is choosing to deliver PSHE only on dedicated pre-planned dates – such occasions as Children's Mental Health Week and Safer Internet Day in the same week in February, Anti-Bullying Week in November and Mental Health Awareness Week in May – or acknowledging kindness either on Random Acts of Kindness Day in February or World Kindness Day each November, the key question is going to be: 'Is this enough?' If this chosen delivery isn't enough, the diet of support for the pupils' mental health may be insufficient and, rather than representing thorough coverage, it could appear as little more than ticking a box. Internet safety and digital literacy need to be constantly on the agenda in lessons and assemblies. In the same way, even if the school is delivering a full programme of PSHE support, the question that we might ask about the awareness days and weeks is 'What happens next?', because children don't use the internet for one day in February, bullies don't reserve their conduct for weeks other than Anti-Bullying Week and children's mental health is not only an issue in Children's Mental Health Week. Placing these on the calendar without any planned evaluation is not sufficient, and impacts over time need to be considered, as does keeping mental health on the agenda of staff and children throughout the year.

Mental health across the curriculum

Aside from PSHE, there are a number of subjects where mental health can be taught as a discrete part of learning or built into the broader cross-curricular approach. This should not be shoe-horned into the curriculum. Mapping out the opportunities to consider how and when mental health can be covered within the curriculum will take time, possibly a complete year to pick out the pinch points where staff and pupils will have busy times, especially around assessments, but also where there might be an increased need for support, which again could fall at periods of transition, starts and ends of term and during the examination cycle. Schools may well need a further year to evaluate this programme in more detail, to ensure that coverage is thorough and relevant. There are no instant solutions; one staff meeting or a training day will not be sufficient time.

Physical education

PE teachers are often in a prime position to identify concerns around safeguarding, especially if the school has a clearly established culture of noticing. With young people in PE kit, their teachers are likely to be the first to notice any marks, scratches or bruises (possible signs of self-harm or physical violence), weight loss or gain (possible signs of eating disorder or neglect) or lack of cleanliness (also a possible sign of neglect). Each of these possible signs could also be an indicator of an emergent issue around the young person's mental health.

Being physically active, alongside being outside, is known to be beneficial to mental health and wellbeing. Physical education has three core aims: to play sport to a competitive level, which, although theoretically open to all, in reality will only include some children; to teach skills, which is universal in its reach; and to lead a physically active lifestyle, again universal but arguably the most crucial, as it is those young people who never get the chance to represent their school, and who might enjoy PE the least, who need to appreciate the long-term benefits of physical activity. PE teachers can be actively involved in promoting the proven impacts of physical activity on mental health, particularly in the discussion of endorphins, the hormones released during exercise that can relieve stress, reduce pain and add to an overall sense of wellbeing.

Science

Although the specific and examined science curriculum does not cover mental health, there is every reason why, in any off-curriculum times such as awareness days and weeks, this should be covered. Science teachers can contribute hugely to the language around mental health by raising awareness of the correct terms to use and developing the understanding of what they mean and how the brain and hormones function.

The working of the human organs forms part of the curriculum, and understanding of the brain and its functions will at the very least cover the roles of the four lobes.

- The frontal lobe is associated with reasoning, motor skills, higher-level cognition and expressive language.
- The parietal lobe is located in the middle section of the brain and is associated with pressure, touch and pain.
- The temporal lobe is located on the bottom section of the brain and is the location of the primary auditory cortex, enabling us to process sounds and language. The temporal lobe also contains the hippocampus.
- The occipital lobe is located at the back portion of the brain and is associated with interpreting visual stimuli and information.

The parts of the brain that are linked to mental health are part of the limbic system:

- The amygdala is involved in the brain's response to threats, and as such plays a role in anxiety. Its functions are linked to memory, emotion and the body's response to 'fight or flight'.
- The hippocampus receives information from the amygdala, which might prompt a response to outside threats. The hippocampus is the part of the brain associated with memory and with fear-learning – the prediction of adverse events.
- The hypothalamus controls the release of hormones.

The hormones that impact mental health include:

- Cortisol is the primary stress hormone, released by the adrenal glands into the bloodstream. The right cortisol level is essential for overall health; too little or too much can lead to a variety of health problems.
- Endorphins can relieve stress and reduce pain.
- Dopamine acts on areas of the brain to give feelings of pleasure, satisfaction and motivation. Dopamine also has a role to play in controlling memory, mood, sleep, learning, concentration, movement and other body functions. It is associated with reward and motivation.
- Serotonin also regulates mood and sleep, in addition to appetite, digestion, learning ability and memory. It is associated with focus and calmness.
- Oxytocin is essential for strong parent-to-child bonding and can promote trust and empathy, help children to develop social skills and reduce repetitive behaviour.

The arts

Art, music, drama, dance and creative writing are all driven by emotions, feelings and a sense of purpose – or feeling a lack of purpose in the case of some artists. In studying key characters from history and across the arts, pupils can gain an understanding of how mental ill health has impacted people, how they have dealt with it and how it has not been a barrier to achievement and reputation. This can also lead to some important and sensitive discussion about issues such as the choice of coping strategies and of suicide.

- Vincent van Gogh suffered from anxiety and depression throughout his short life, and he once wrote, 'I put my heart and my soul into my work, and lost my mind in the process.' His works show his talent with a limited palette, and can lead to discussion about how they show his inner torment. Van Gogh, of course, took his own life.
- Mark Rothko also took his own life, having suffered from depression most of his life. His coping mechanism was to turn to alcohol, but he also smoked heavily, failed to exercise and ate unhealthily, ignoring medical instruction after a diagnosis of a heart condition.
- Georgia O'Keefe suffered from depression, linked to her husband's infidelity and also after a planned artwork had to be abandoned because the plaster

to which the paint was to be applied hadn't dried. This led to her becoming socially withdrawn, not eating and extremely tearful for long periods.
- Edvard Munch's *The Scream* is possibly the most famous work illustrating mental health. It was painted after a walk through Oslo at sunset, where the sky suddenly turned blood red, leaving him trembling with anxiety, from which he suffered his entire life. The painting is often interpreted as representing human anxiety in the modern world.

History and geography

History and geography can lend themselves to discussion about the impact of human actions and being critically evaluative of behaviours and decisions. The examples listed below could be starting points for discussion in both primary and secondary settings.

History

- The First World War can lead to discussions about shell shock, now known as post-traumatic stress disorder or PTSD, alongside how soldiers felt at the loss of their friends and the sheer fear of life in the trenches. This allows links to the English curriculum, in studying the war poets such as Wilfred Owen or Rupert Brooke. The final episode, especially the closing scene, of *Blackadder Goes Forth* is a powerful resource. The impact of facial injury and the pioneering work of Harold Gillies in reconstructive surgery may also be addressed here.
- In relation to the Second World War, evacuation and its direct impact on families can show children how quickly events can impact their mental health, as does a study of aerial bombing and its impact on Britain and on Germany. For older pupils, the lifelong impact of the Holocaust on survivors can stimulate some important debate. Both wars can allow children to relate to events in Ukraine and Gaza and other areas of international crisis. Texts such as *Goodnight Mr Tom* by Michelle Magorian and *Carrie's War* by Nina Bawden delve into the emotional impact on children.
- Study of poverty in the Tudor or Victorian periods, or in the twentieth century, with events such as the hunger march known as the Jarrow Crusade, can generate an understanding of the cost of living crisis of 2022 onwards and a consideration of the impact that poverty has on physical and mental health. *Street Child* by Berlie Doherty or age-appropriate

versions of the works of Charles Dickens can also be used to illustrate the impact of poverty.
- Significant individuals and the impact on them of human actions can also form the basis of debate. Alan Turing, the computer genius whose work was essential in the Second World War, was prosecuted for homosexual acts and accepted hormone treatment, colloquially known as chemical castration, as an alternative to prison. He was stripped of his previous security clearance. Two years later, he ingested cyanide, ruled as suicide, a verdict that his mother did not accept. It was not until 2009 that an official government apology for his appalling treatment at the hands of authority was given.

Geography

- What is the wider impact of a particular building project? This can be linked to a local issue, such as a new tunnel, bypass, housing estate or factory. Impact can be positive as well as negative, and also allows for discussion of the impact on the environment, on the local economy and on schools and families, as well as how mental health could be impacted.
- The impact of climate change and of catastrophic weather events can be discussed. This can be local or global, such as the impact of river flooding, which has impacted towns across the UK, or how rising sea levels affect the east coast of England and low-lying islands in the Indian and Pacific Oceans. Mental health can be discussed in terms of the uncertainty and feelings of lack of support that such events can generate.

Mathematics

Mathematics is perhaps the subject where it would seem most difficult to consider the place of mental health within the curriculum content, aside from making calculations based on some of the mental health statistics available, which may be counterproductive. Returning to our broader definition of curriculum, and also how good mental health supports good academic health, then the place of the mental health of the pupils becomes more apparent.

Take, for example, a Year 4 lesson on comparing and ordering fractions. Fractions, decimals and percentages take up a larger part of the number and calculation part of schemes of work as the children advance through their school years, and both primary and secondary colleagues will recognise that it is an area that causes worry and concern for some pupils. The teacher will have delivered the initial input and set the children off on their tasks. There will be a group that understands straight away, who are able to work quickly and can identify their own errors and misconceptions, through their own capacity or through shared talk. Another group of children may be supported by a teaching assistant, working on a differentiated activity with appropriate resources. Then there might be the group who are usually comfortable with other aspects of maths, but this time either get started but don't understand the concept or meet you with a stare that says that they are struggling. The good teacher in you will return to the first part of the lesson, but will set out the whiteboards and the manipulatives, go through the misconceptions the children have, perhaps make an error yourself for the children to identify and correct, and provide the one-to-one or small-group support that some children might require. This is nothing new; every teacher does this every day. It is a learning intervention but it is also a mental health intervention. It is a mental health intervention because it is giving those children a sense of success and a level of understanding; even if they might have less on the page than some of the others in class, that makes them feel better about the lesson than they might have done 30 minutes earlier. It eases their passage through the rest of the day.

English

Think of any work of fiction and the narrative is driven by the characters and their interactions with each other – the levels of empathy demonstrated and how levels of resilience change. Just consider how, in Kenneth Grahame's *The Wind in the Willows*, Mole transforms from a nervous and reclusive figure to one full of confidence, or in *The London Eye Mystery* by Siobhan Dowd, Ted, a boy with Asperger syndrome (now considered part of the autism spectrum), grows in confidence throughout the book to solve the mystery. There are some inspiring texts to use in discussing the emotional health and wellbeing of the characters, perhaps in a way to relate to the context of the pupils in school. These also offer ways into writing – fiction, non-fiction and poetry – where the young people can develop and demonstrate their empathy and their confidence to write about their own emotions.

Holes by Louis Sachar

Holes is an excellent text to use across upper Key Stage 2 and Key Stage 3 and, if the text is returned to, offers a higher level of analysis.

- In which ways does the opening chapter create a sense of fear about Camp Green Lake?
- What might Stanley's emotions be like as he travels alone to Camp Green Lake?
- Imagine Stanley's internal monologue as he first meets Mr Sir. What do you imagine his overwhelming emotions to be?
- Is Mr Pendanski a genuinely empathetic character?
- Zero (Hector Zeroni) is bullied for his inability to read or write. Do you believe that he is aware of this bullying?
- Is Mr Sir a bully or a victim of bullying?
- Are there issues around race and racism in the story?
- What are the impacts on a person and their family of being wrongly accused and sanctioned?

Romeo and Juliet by William Shakespeare

Shakespeare has a place in later primary as well as into secondary. *Macbeth* or *A Midsummer Night's Dream* both offer opportunities to discuss the mental health of the characters, but the tale of the star-crossed lovers has a few themes that may relate to the local context.

- The play opens with a gang fight. How and why did this fight begin? Why did each participant act the way they did?
- Is the Prince's proposed sanction of execution excessive or appropriate? This could form part of a discussion about the reasons for sanctions and what they are intended to achieve.
- The Capulets hold a party but deliberately do not invite the Montagues. What is it like and how might someone respond to being deliberately socially excluded?
- How might people feel if the relationship that they are in is disapproved of by family or friends?
- The play could also form a powerful discussion around suicide, principally about prevention and support networks to reach out to. Any discussion of suicide should be within the policies and values of the school.

Other texts that could be used

An exhaustive list would cover an entire chapter, but by keeping context and community in mind and responding to changes in both, a school can ensure that its choices of literature reflect the real lives and experiences of its pupils. Books that discuss issues around the impact of racism include the works of Malorie Blackman, especially *Pig Heart Boy* and *Noughts and Crosses*, and of Kiran Millwood Hargrave, whose text *The Girl of Ink and Stars* has some of the same themes as *Noughts and Crosses*. The works of the late Benjamin Zephaniah or of the poet Lemn Sissay are also accessible across a range of ages. Specific texts around mental health include *Sad Book* by Michael Rosen and *The Goldfish Boy* by Lisa Thompson, in which the lead character rarely leaves his room because of crippling OCD. There are high-quality texts supporting LGBTQIA+ themes: *And Tango Makes Three* by Justin Richardson and Peter Parnell and *Nen and the Lonely Fisherman* by Ian Eagleton are just two suggestions. A number of commercial schemes produce lists of texts to support work around the English subject curriculum or as part of a creative, project-themed approach. Schools may wish to choose books based on these principles, but please never forget the value of reading a book aloud because it is such an enjoyable and engaging piece of work. The case study of Meadowbank Primary School references their use of 'Our Favourite Five', and it is well worth a look at their website for further suggestions.

The power of a good assembly

Assemblies can be very much part of the curriculum, especially if they are linked to what is happening in the school and the community. Assemblies should not be viewed simply as a means of ticking the box of a daily reflection or act of worship, but as part of the broad programme of support for young people in every aspect of school life, of which mental health is one part. Schools should be planning their sequence of assemblies over a whole year and on a termly basis, using the latter to tweak the content to address current concerns. Of course, every assembly cannot be about mental health, but the school should have the capacity for one assembly a week on this theme, leaving the others for celebration and reward, class presentations, visitors and the headteacher's weekly assembly. A model that the school could have – and this would work at a primary level, as well as in secondary school with year group assemblies – is one of three weeks out of four having a pre-planned programme of content, which might include respect, kindness, resilience, digital safety and other aspects of pastoral support, including how to speak to adults in the school about support. Every fourth week can be used to address issues that have arisen in the school or community, or it could be used for young people to present to the school as part of their leadership roles. While many schools use some of their assemblies to allow some additional assessment and preparation time for their staff, any mental health-themed assemblies should have everyone in attendance, as this reinforces the message that there is a whole-school approach.

The power of language

Throughout *The School Mental Health Toolkit*, the emphasis has been on positive language and upon challenging negative terminology, phrasing and attitudes. As was discussed earlier, schools should not be producing a list of banned words, because banning a word can have the reverse effect of making it more prominent. What we need to consider is the power of positive language – the language that promotes good mental health and wellbeing, which recognises that there will be mental ill health among our community, and which challenges stigma and prejudice and normalises discussion around a subject that in the past has not been discussed.

A starting point could be with the positive language of the 'five ways to wellbeing', promoted by the NHS and mental health charities (see Mind, n.d.). The language used can be incorporated into classroom and corridor display, to provide a visual focus and reminder of the whole-school approach to mental health that is being undertaken.

- **Connect:** Relationships give a sense of belonging and of self-worth. They allow people to share positive experiences and to offer and seek support. It is important to build strong relationships, take time with friends and family, turn off digital devices and talk. Connection also recognises that some people prefer one-to-one interaction rather than small groups.
- **Be active:** Physical activity raises self-esteem and releases endorphins. It increases strength and flexibility. It doesn't mean being talented at sports or running a marathon, but undertaking something that can help sleep, ease anxiety and reduce stress.

- **Notice:** Noticing, being in the moment, being mindful – each concerns taking a positive approach to making changes and facing challenges. Noticing helps in the recognition of what may trigger stress and anxiety, and how coping and distraction techniques can help.
- **Learn:** Learning goes beyond schooling. It could include developing new skills, learning a new sport or pastime, learning to cook or finding a new challenge. The sense of feeling that something is being learned adds to a sense of self-esteem.
- **Give:** Giving isn't simply the giving of gifts and money, but could include giving of time to others and volunteering services to those in need. An act of kindness is an act of giving. Giving can also include giving thanks, showing good manners, recognising others for their actions and contribution to the wellbeing of others.

The language used should be shared, should be positive and should become part of habit, embedding it in the vocabulary of the school. The language chosen will reflect the correct terminology, used correctly for accuracy and for the avoidance of stigma. Stress, anxiety and depression are words that should be understood, the signs of each identified and recognised, and support highlighted. The school that does this well will see children, parents and staff aware of what help the school can offer and how to reach out for it. The true power of language is that it enables the broadest definition of curriculum around mental health to be embedded in the school and its practice.

Final thoughts

Curriculum is much more than the documents containing the statutory requirements for content. It is a living and breathing experience for the children, from EYFS to A level and indeed beyond. A mentally healthy curriculum will be part of that lived experience, covering every aspect of the child's time at school. Any curriculum review should consider this.

THINK about developing the curriculum and learning experience

Time

- Allow plenty of time to develop the mental health curriculum. Anything rushed or seen as an instant solution will appear to shoe-horn mental health into the curriculum and risks not having the buy-in from staff, especially those who are reluctant to engage.
- Time also means taking time to evaluate. What works well? Does the school need to do more or less of something? How does this become better?

Holistic

- Consider curriculum in its very broadest sense: the entire time during which the children are on site and engaged with the school and their peers, which could include homework and online/interactive lessons.
- Support colleagues who are finding it a challenge to structure their curriculum for opportunities to cover mental health.
- Always think, 'What happens next?'

Inclusive

- Language needs to be inclusive. Neurodivergent children – and adults – may interpret language differently to others.
- Differentiated approaches, as in any other lesson, should be considered to facilitate access for all children.

Non-judgemental

- Some pupils will come from backgrounds where mental health is not discussed or where parent and family attitudes may not support or understand what the school is teaching. Neither brush this aside nor be confrontational, but take time to explain the positive intent and the role that understanding mental health plays in being a responsible and responsive member of society.

Knowledgeable

- Knowledge of curriculum and language will become a habit that will embed itself in interaction, in behaviour and in the attitudes of all stakeholders.
- Knowing the children means knowing who needs more support and time than others. It also means knowing that even those appearing the most resilient need the time for an emotional check-in. This will show a truly whole-school universal approach to mental health.

Conclusion

Where do we go from here?

When, many moons ago, I passed my driving test at the second attempt, my instructor congratulated me, shook my hand and told me, 'Now, you need to learn how to drive.' My lessons on the quiet roads of Southport may have taught me how to reverse around a corner and to remember stopping distances in the wet, but they had given me no experience of winding country lanes behind a tractor, negotiating a city centre ring road or how to drive on a motorway. It took time for these to become second nature. The same advice could equally apply to how the role of mental health leader develops in our schools; we have had our training and read the theory, but now need to put all this into practice. Much of what we do in our roles is common, but our contexts, cultures and communities aren't; and neither is the degree of compassion, as any teacher who has moved schools will attest to.

What this book has done, I hope, is to enable you to consider your context and consider how the principles of positive mental health apply within your school community and how you intend to drive the culture in a compassionate way that will shape mental health and wellbeing for all your stakeholders. There are challenges – not least financial – limiting what we can offer within school, there are services stretched to the point where waiting lists are months and years long and there is still a lingering stigma around mental health in some communities, families and for individuals. What we can offer, and which comes with no financial cost, is a principled and values-led approach, one that is proactive and responsive, which anticipates and identifies trigger points and which has in place strategies to handle concerns and crises when they emerge, rather than working in a way that seems like we are constantly battling fires.

A mental health journey

Whatever stage of developing the mental health provision in your school that you are at, you are on a journey. A journey of a thousand miles may begin with a single step, but that single first step needs to be in the right direction, because even just a few steps the wrong way can lead you awry and to not meeting the needs of those with the greatest concern. A broken compass makes reading a map near impossible; a faulty moral compass could equally send you on a more difficult path. There are no off-the-shelf solutions, no tick-box exercises that will meet the needs that our school community presents. There is no guaranteed and proven method of improvement, but there are common principles, problems and practices, which may have been recognised from reading the earlier chapters.

But what of the journey itself? Are you the kind of person who plugs into their laptop on the train, missing the beauty of the natural landscapes that pass by, or are you the one who spends three hours on work calls, which everyone in the carriage overhears? Or do you set out in your car and never stop to appreciate the view? Your journey is part of your travel experience; your mental health journey is part of the emotional health and wellbeing experience. Stopping, appreciating, evaluating, observing, reflecting – all form part of the overarching enjoyment of achieving something and recognising the way to the final destination. The journey isn't simply about the destination, but about the way there; the highlights and the pitfalls are part of the experience. The roadworks, potholes, weight of traffic, delays and accidents all happen, but we don't give up because of these; we seek solutions and support to overcome them.

Context, culture, compassion and community

Context

In Chapter 1, we asked the big question, 'What does positive mental health look like in our school and in our context?' – and although there will be a commonality of practice between schools in supporting the mental health and wellbeing of our children, contexts aren't homogenous. Even in two schools a few hundred metres apart, the catchment and cohorts will differ, as will the reputation of the schools among parents and children. Those two schools will also be contrasting in their cultures.

Culture

Culture doesn't change overnight. It develops and grows, through nurture and a sense of belonging, through shared purpose and a communal understanding of 'why' and being able to answer the question. Why? The answer shouldn't be 'Why not?' and certainly must not be 'Because I said so!' Neither of these communicate a sense of purpose, and the latter implies a dictated or imposed culture, one of fear and not one where relationships can flourish. Relationships thrive where there is a sense of compassion.

Compassion

A compassionate school will promote a profound feeling of empathy, of understanding, of support for all stakeholders. Compassion may be regarded as a soft skill, but in reality it is hard and realistic, and promotes reflective practice and a shared sense of purpose. The compassionate school is one that not only supports those times of loss, grief and challenge, but also demonstrates this sense of kindness and warmth at all times and to all members of its community.

Community

Community is a word that we heard much of during lockdown. Schools were at the heart of this, and for every school that was featured on local television news delivering food parcels, there were dozens more doing the exact same and more – touching base with families with phone calls and on Zoom, keeping the flow of communication going, sharing positive and supportive messages. Community wasn't forged by the pandemic, but may have been changed by it; only history will tell. What the Covid period did do was to help society consider the meaning of community, especially as this time made all of us very much more aware of ourselves and of others. To paraphrase the words of President John F. Kennedy at his inauguration, 'Ask not what my community can do for me, but what I can do for my community.' (JFK Library, 1961)

Communities are about people. What can each of these groups of people bring to our commitment to mental health and wellbeing?

Commitment

You may be reading this as a school leader. Have you reflected upon your practice, your leadership and your management of the school? Leaders need to know their school but also need to know their team and the ways in which they function. You work with people – human beings and not human doings. The staff are the engine room of the school, but do you lead from behind or lead from the front? Lead them or work with them? Are you able to take constructive criticism of your actions, policies and practices, to review them and yet still remain authentic to your values? Do you practise what you preach, model empathy and keep that literal and metaphorical open door as open as it should be?

You may be a class or form teacher or head of department. Perhaps you were one of the staff expressing reservations about the impact of a programme of mental health upon your curriculum subject or were challenged over your perceived stigma around mental health. Have you now embraced the holistic view of emotional health, bought into the way in which good learning health is supported by the children being as mentally healthy as possible? Can you see where positive mental health fits into your curriculum, but also supports and enables it?

You may be reading this as a member of support staff. In many ways, you will be on the frontline of mental health in school, often the first person to whom a young person with concerns or in the first stages of a crisis may turn, as you may be their trusted adult, with a slightly different relationship with you than with their teachers. Very often, you will be running the interventions with individuals and groups, as an ELSA or a practitioner trained in one of the commercially available support schemes the school has invested in. If you live in the school community, you may also be a trusted point of contact for parents, quite possibly parents you knew as children in the school. Do you realise the powerful impact that you can have on pupils by promoting positive language around mental health, as well as by offering the appropriate support?

You may be reading this as a governor. How does mental health fit into the strategy of the school development plan and the accountability of the headteacher? Do you have the professional curiosity – whether you have an educational background or come from public service or the commercial sector – to question what you observe or have been told as a 'critical friend', offering support but asking questions to further your understanding of how mental health supports the academic health of the school community?

You may be reading this as a parent. How is your relationship with the school? Are your questions taken seriously and are you given a straight answer? Does the school provide you with a simple and transparent means of communication? On the other hand, do you understand that the school is meeting the needs of a diverse range of hundreds of other pupils, a tricky balancing act? Have you considered how you interact with the school?

You may be reading this as a student in initial teacher training or as an ECT. I hope that this has given you a taste of how mental health fits into the curriculum and of what we mean when we talk about the whole child and how holistic thinking allows you to consider all the barriers and protective factors that the school can offer to its young people.

Final thoughts

Each chapter of this book has encouraged the reader to THINK about how mental health and wellbeing can be promoted and supported through the school, among the community of children, parents and carers, and the whole staff. Take time and patience; take a holistic approach; be inclusive of the needs of every member of the community; be non-judgemental of the attitudes and words of others, but act to develop these in a positive way; and ensure that the school works from a secure knowledge base, knowing children, parents and staff.

In his *Nicomachean Ethics* (2004), Aristotle wrote of *eudaimonia* as 'doing and living well' and also that 'happiness depends upon ourselves'. As educators, we do more than teach our subjects; we teach about life, of which happiness is part, and some parts of our community need our support in attaining this happiness. We may not THINK like Aristotle, but we can THINK like a leader for mental health, and pursue the path of excellence in our own settings.

Appendix 1

Practitioners

Sophie Smith-Tong

Sophie is a teacher, EYFS specialist and founder of Mindfulness for Learning – the wellbeing centre for educators and families. Following over a decade of inner-London classroom teaching, leading on mental health and wellbeing and training in mindfulness and yoga, Sophie decided to quit teaching for a while. She was becoming fed up with being part of the problem.

Sophie launched Mindfulness for Learning during a break from the classroom, in order to have a proactive response to the problematic systems and policies in place. Sophie now runs Mindfulness for Learning alongside being back in the classroom, putting into practice all that she preaches.

Kelly Hannaghan

Kelly is a mental health and wellbeing consultant and the director and founder of Mind Work Matters Ltd. She puts wellbeing and people at the heart of education. She is an award-winning motivational speaker, school improvement advisor, published author and founder of the Family Matters empowerment and engagement programme.

Kelly has worked systemically throughout her career as a director of wellbeing, working with local authorities, MATs, senior leaders, pastoral teams and governors to help to create healthy work cultures and environments. She is an expert trainer and coach for senior mental health leads and supports some of the most challenging communities with preventive and early help measures in education.

Kelly develops the strategies to help people in education to thrive from adversities. Her work with schools and organisations raises aspirations, engagement, attendance and outcomes. She has recently led on the DfE Wellbeing for Education Return project and leads on education development processes, creating outstanding outcomes and awards for many organisations. She is recognised by the DfE, NCB, Anna Freud Centre and Education Support as a lead influencer of mental health and wellbeing in education.

If you would like to explore more information and training opportunities for the Family Matters Programme, please do connect with Kelly at kelly@mindworkmatters.com or visit her website, www.mindworkmatters.com

Kimberley Evans

Improving your staff's wellbeing can have a huge impact on the outcomes of a school, but tackling this important task yourself can lead to increased workload and stress for you. Kimberley offers practical assistance by providing targeted surveys to get you the information you need and guiding you to make effective changes, with recommendations grounded in her extensive experience. She also provides support and training to help your staff to be the best that they can be, through professional development courses and training.

www.nourishtheworkplace.com

Frederika Roberts

Frederika is a trainer, speaker, author, lecturer and researcher, who brings the science of wellbeing to life in a variety of schools and other educational settings in the UK, continental Europe and beyond.

As a PGCE-qualified teacher with an MSc in applied positive psychology, she is currently undertaking practical doctoral research (towards her EdD) into 'appreciative inquiry' as a process for improving whole-school wellbeing. She has written *Recipe for Happiness* (2013) and *For Flourishing's Sake* (2020), co-written *Character Toolkit for Teachers* (2018) and *Character Toolkit Strength Cards* (2020), and co-edited *The Big Book of Whole School Wellbeing* (2022).

Where to find/contact Fredericka:

- www.happiness-speaker.com
- fred@happiness-speaker.com
- www.linkedin.com/in/frederikaroberts
- www.x.com/Frederika_R

Steve Waters and Suneta Bagri

Teach Well Toolkit (www.teachwelltoolkit.com) was founded by Steve Waters and Suneta Bagri. They support schools to develop a whole-school culture of staff mental health. Their belief is that if schools focus first on staff mental wellbeing, they will be able to teach effectively and look after the children and young people in their care. They are a DfE-approved provider of senior mental health lead training.

Their offer to schools includes:

- Senior mental health lead training: https://teachwellall.samcart.com/products/senior-mental-health-lead-training
- Mental health lead toolkit (enables schools to build a whole-school culture of staff and mental health): https://teachwellall.samcart.com/products/mental-health-lead-toolkit-building-a-school-culture-of-staff-wellbeing-and-mental-health
- Student wellbeing ambassador training (video-recorded course for Years 5 to 10): https://teachwellall.samcart.com/products/student-wellbeing-and-mental-health-ambassador-training
- Level 2 first aid for mental health: (age 14 to adult): https://teachwellall.samcart.com/products/first-aid-for-mental-health-schools-level-2
- Level 2 first aid for youth mental health (age 14 to adult): https://teachwellall.samcart.com/products/level-2-award-in-first-aid-for-youth-mental-health-online

Steve is also the editor and inspiration behind *Cultures of Staff Wellbeing and Mental Health in Schools*, published in 2021 by Open University Press.

Thérèse Hoyle

Thérèse Hoyle is founder of Thérèse Hoyle Consultancies Ltd. Thérèse supports primary schools to dramatically improve the quality of day-to-day playtimes and lunchtimes, with a consequent beneficial impact on lunchtime behaviour, engagement, learning and social, emotional, mental and physical health and wellbeing. She is recognised as the UK's leading training provider of playtime and lunchtime programmes, with her 'How to be a lunchtime supervisor superhero' workshop, Positive Playtime Essentials and award programmes and Positive Playtime Online Academy.

Thérèse has over 25 years' experience in education and is author of *101 Playground Games*, *101 Wet Playtime Games*, *How to be a Peaceful School* (contributing author) and *The Big Book of Whole School Wellbeing* (co-editor and contributing author).

To find out more, go to www.theresehoyle.com or contact her at support@theresehoyle.com.

Sarah Johnson

Sarah is a keynote speaker, president of PRUsAP and founder and director of Phoenix Education Consultancy (www.phoenixeducationconsultancy.com). Sarah has been invited to share her expertise and experiences, or represent alternative provisions and vulnerable children, at a number of events at a national and local level. Sarah is able to provide engaging keynotes, commentary and workshops on topics including, but not limited to, behaviour, mental health, supporting medical needs, neurodiversity and inclusion. Author of two books in the 'All About SEMH' series and of *Behaving Together in the Classroom*, Sarah is also a 'go-to' voice on the topic of emotional-based school avoidance.

Appendix 2

Useful websites

Anna Freud Centre (mental health support for schools and colleges):
www.annafreud.org/
Charlton Athletic Community Trust (community engagement):
www.charltonafc.com/charlton-athletic-community-trust
Mind (mental health support for adults): www.mind.org.uk
Minds Ahead (mental health support in schools and colleges):
www.mindsahead.org.uk
Mizen Foundation (young people as changemakers):
http://mizenfoundation.org/
Molly Rose Foundation (youth suicide prevention and online safety):
https://mollyrosefoundation.org/
NHS (mental health charities for children and young people):
www.nhs.uk/mental-health/children-and-young-adults/mental-health-support/mental-health-charities
Place2Be (for mental health services for staff and children):
www.place2be.org.uk
Tender (healthy relationships): https://tender.org.uk/
The Happy Confident Company (for journalling resources):
www.happyconfident.com
Women's Aid (healthy relationships and domestic abuse):
www.womensaid.org.uk/what-we-do/training/
YoungMinds (mental health charity for young people):
www.youngminds.org.uk

Appendix 3

Further reading

Of the publications on mental health on the education market, these are a handful to which I have turned for regular advice:

Erasmus, C. (2019) *The Mental Health and Wellbeing Handbook for Schools: Transforming Mental Health Support on a Budget*. London: Jessica Kingsley.

Erasmus, C. (2021) *The Designated Mental Health Lead Planner: A Guide and Checklist for the School Year*. London: Jessica Kingsley.

Foulkes, L. (2022) *What Mental Illness Really Is… (and what it isn't)*. London: Vintage.

Garai, A (2022) *Being With Our Feelings – A Mindful Approach to Wellbeing for Children: A Teaching Toolkit*. London: Routledge.

Knightsmith, P. (2000) *The Mentally Healthy Schools Workbook*. London: Jessica Kingsley.

Lathan, S (2024) *Creating a Trauma-informed Classroom*. St. Albans: Critical Publishing.

Morgan, F. and Costello, E. (2023) *Square Pegs: Inclusivity, Compassion and Fitting In: A Guide for Schools*. Carmarthen: Independent Thinking Press.

Naish, S. et al. (2023) *The A–Z of Trauma-Informed Teaching: Strategies and Solutions to Help with Behaviour and Support for Children Aged 3–11*. London: Jessica Kingsley.

References

Aristotle (2004), *The Nicomachean Ethics*. London: Penguin.

BBC (2023), *Roman Kemp: The Fight for Young Lives*. BBC iPlayer. [online] Available at: www.bbc.co.uk/iplayer/episode/m001s1mm/roman-kemp-the-fight-for-young-lives [Accessed 30 July 2024].

Brown, B. (2013), Brené Brown on Empathy. [online] *YouTube*. Available at: https://www.youtube.com/watch?v=1Evwgu369Jw&t=30s [Accessed 11 September 2024].

Carrie & David Grant (2019), *The boy who found his tears*. [online] Available at: www.carrieanddavidgrant.co.uk/latest-news [Accessed 30 July 2024].

Children and Young People's Commissioner Scotland (CYPCS) (2024), *Annual report 2023–24*. [online] Available at: www.cypcs.org.uk/resources/annual-report-2023-24 [Accessed 30 July 2024].

Close, G. (2010), Mental illness: The stigma of silence. *HuffPost*. [online] Available at: www.huffpost.com/entry/mental-illness-the-stigma_b_328591 [Accessed 30 July 2024].

Cowley, A. (2019), *The Wellbeing Toolkit*. London: Bloomsbury.

Cowley, A. (2021), *The Wellbeing Curriculum*. London: Bloomsbury.

de Souza, R. (2023), *Everyone must obsess over full attendance from day one*. [online] Schools Week. Available at: https://schoolsweek.co.uk/everyone-must-obsess-over-full-attendance-from-day-one/ [Accessed 11 September 2024].

Department for Education (DfE) (2023a), *School workforce in England: Reporting year 2023*. [online] Available at: https://explore-education-statistics.service.gov.uk/find-statistics/school-workforce-in-england [Accessed 30 July 2024].

Department for Education (DfE) (2023b), *Keeping children safe in education 2023: Statutory guidance for schools and colleges*. [online] Available at: https://assets.publishing.service.gov.uk/media/64f0a68ea78c5f000dc6f3b2/Keeping_children_safe_in_education_2023.pdf [Accessed 12 August 2024].

Department for Education (DfE) (2024), *Draft relationships education, relationships and sex education (RSE) and health education: Statutory guidance for governing bodies, proprietors, head teachers, principals, senior leadership teams, teachers*. [online] Available at: https://consult.education.gov.uk/rshe-team/review-of-the-rshe-statutory-guidance/supporting_documents/Draft%20RSE%20and%20Health%20Education%20statutory%20guidance.pdf [Accessed 11 September 2024].

Department of Health (DoH) and Department for Education (DfE) (2017), *Transforming children and young people's mental health provision: A Green Paper*.

[online] Available at: https://assets.publishing.service.gov.uk/media/5a823518e5274a2e87dc1b56/Transforming_children_and_young_people_s_mental_health_provision.pdf [Accessed 30 July 2024].

Dweck, C. (2017), *Mindset: Changing the Way You Think to Fulfil Your Potential.* Updated ed. London: Robinson.

Education Support (2023), *Teacher Wellbeing Index.* [online] Available at: www.educationsupport.org.uk/resources/for-organisations/research/teacher-wellbeing-index/?gad_source=1&gclid=CjwKCAjwzIK1BhAuEiwAHQmU3 (rm29P6hdq5xswXFpIH9B2yiCq38zWe8LZDTFDJ1FXzsI_jtV77MeRoCuqMQAvD_BwE [Accessed 30 July 2024].

Equality Act 2010, c. 15. Available at: www.legislation.gov.uk/ukpga/2010/15/contents [Accessed 9 August 2024].

Gray, P. (2011), The decline of play and the rise of psychopathology in children and adolescents. *American Journal of Play*, 3, (4), pp. 443–63.

ICT Trust (n.d.), *About us.* [online] Available at: www.icttrust.org.uk [Accessed 30 July 2024].

JFK Library (1961), *Inaugural address.* [online] Available at: www.jfklibrary.org/learn/about-jfk/historic-speeches/inaugural-address [Accessed 30 July 2024].

Kerr, J. (2013), *Legacy.* London: Constable.

King, V. (2016), *10 Keys To Happier Living.* London: Headline.

Marcheselli, F., Mandalia, D., Ryder-Dalton, A. and McManus, S. (2023), *Children and young people's mental health in 2023.* [online] National Centre for Social Research. Available at: https://natcen.ac.uk/publications/children-and-young-peoples-mental-health-2023?gad_source=1&gclid=CjwKCAjw2Je1BhAgEiwAp3KY74Ep_pnsVZvUuRgvZ_VTxqAuHmz4KOPJE8PbQfK7DTDmj_uGsKpg9BoCAXsQAvD_BwE [Accessed 30 July 2024].

Martin, A.-C. (2023), Handwritten notes reveal headteacher's anguish over Ofsted probe before her suicide. [online] *The Independent.* Available at: www.independent.co.uk/news/uk/home-news/ruth-perry-inquest-ofsted-alan-derry-report-b2460018.html [Accessed 30 July 2024].

Mental Health Champion (2023), *Mental health in Northern Ireland: Fundamental Facts 2023 report launched.* [online] Available at: www.mentalhealthchampion-ni.org.uk/news/mental-health-northern-ireland-fundamental-facts-2023-report-launched [Accessed 30 July 2024].

Mind (n.d.), *5 ways to wellbeing.* [online] Available at: www.mind.org.uk/workplace/mental-health-at-work/five-ways-to-wellbeing [Accessed 14 August 2024].

NHS England (n.d.), *Mental health support in schools and colleges.* [online] Available at: www.england.nhs.uk/mental-health/cyp/trailblazers [Accessed 30 July 2024].

NHS England (2023), *Mental health of children and young people in England, 2023 – wave 4 follow up to the 2017 survey*. [online] Available at: https://digital.nhs.uk/data-and-information/publications/statistical/mental-health-of-children-and-young-people-in-england/2023-wave-4-follow-up [Accessed 30 July 2024].

NurtureUK (n.d.), *What is nurture?* [online] Available at: www.nurtureuk.org/what-is-nurture [Accessed 30 July 2024].

Pica, R. (2022), *Spark a Revolution in Early Education*. St Paul, MN: Redleaf Press.

Political TV (2023), Sunday with Laura Kuenssberg. [online] *YouTube*. Available at: www.youtube.com/watch?v=nh_3a8HgO_8 [Accessed 30 July 2024].

Public Health England (2021), *Promoting children and young people's mental health and wellbeing: A whole school or college approach*. [online] Available at: https://assets.publishing.service.gov.uk/media/614cc965d3bf7f718518029c/Promoting_children_and_young_people_s_mental_health_and_wellbeing.pdf [Accessed 30 July 2024].

Pye, J. (1988), *Invisible Children: Who are the Real Losers at School?* Oxford: Oxford University Press.

Roberts, J. (2021), Parents can report schools to Ofsted on remote learning. *TES Magazine*. [online] Available at: https://www.tes.com/magazine/archived/parents-can-report-schools-ofsted-remote-learning [Accessed 11 September 2024].

Scottish Government (2017), *Mental health strategy 2017–2027*. [online] Available at: www.gov.scot/publications/mental-health-strategy-2017-2027 [Accessed 30 July 2024].

Shafan-Azhar, Z. and Treloar, N. (2023), *The state of children and young people's mental health in 2023*. [online] Centre for Mental Health. Available at: www.centreformentalhealth.org.uk/the-state-of-children-and-young-peoples-mental-health-in-2023 [Accessed 30 July 2024].

Sinek, S. (2009), *Start With Why: How Great Leaders Inspire Everyone to Take Action*. London: Penguin.

The Centre for Social Justice (2024), *The missing link: Restoring the bond between schools and families*. [online] Available at: www.centreforsocialjustice.org.uk/library/the-missing-link [Accessed 30 July 2024].

UK Government (2003), *Every child matters*. [online] Available at: https://assets.publishing.service.gov.uk/media/5a7c95a4e5274a0bb7cb806d/5860.pdf [Accessed 30 July 2024].

UNICEF (1990), *The United Nations Convention on the Rights of the Child*. [online] Available at: www.unicef.org.uk/wp-content/uploads/2016/08/unicef-convention-rights-child-uncrc.pdf [Accessed 13 August 2024].

UNICEF (2022), *Early moments matter*. [online] Available at: www.unicef.org.uk/wp-content/uploads/2022/10/EarlyMomentsMatter_UNICEFUK_2022_PolicyReport.pdf [Accessed 30 July 2024].

Wain, P. (2023), Children's commissioner: Pornography affecting 8-year-olds' behaviour. *BBC News*. [online] Available at: www.bbc.co.uk/news/technology-65534354 [Accessed 30 July 2024].

Wood, E. (2023), *Strengthening parent engagement in UK secondary schools: Strategies for success*. [online] We Are In Beta. Available at: www.weareinbeta.community/posts/strengthening-parent-engagement-in-uk-secondary-schools-strategies-for-success [Accessed 30 July 2024].

World Health Organization (2021), *Mental health of adolescents*. [online] Available at: www.who.int/news-room/fact-sheets/detail/adolescent-mental-health [Accessed 30 July 2024].

World Health Organization (2022), *Mental health*. [online] Available at: www.who.int/news-room/fact-sheets/detail/mental-health-strengthening-our-response [Accessed 30 July 2024].

World Health Organization (2023a), *Anxiety disorders*. [online] Available at: www.who.int/news-room/fact-sheets/detail/anxiety-disorders [Accessed 30 July 2024].

World Health Organization (2023b), *Depressive disorder (depression)*. [online] Available at: www.who.int/news-room/fact-sheets/detail/depression [Accessed 30 July 2024].

YoungMinds (n.d.), *Understanding trauma and adversity*. [online] Available at: www.youngminds.org.uk/professional/resources/understanding-trauma-and-adversity [Accessed 30 July 2024].

Index

abuse 77, 129, 153
  domestic 171
  emotional 88
  online 88, 131
  peer-on-peer 74, 129
  sexual 74–5
  substance 22, 76, 131
accomplishment, sense of 140
adverse childhood experiences (ACEs) 5, 7, 41, 77–8, 88, 94, 159
ALGEE action plan 114–15
And Tango Makes Three (Richardson and Parnell) 195
Anna Freud Centre 3, 207
anti-bullying ambassadors 144
Anti-Bullying Week 187
anti-racist initiatives 171
anxiety 2, 52, 57, 64, 73, 81, 85, 102–3, 116, 125, 134, 139, 166, 190–1, 197
  addressing 123, 144–5, 196
  amygdala in 189
  and anxious, difference between 39
  and CAMHS 166
  and depression 2, 5, 37, 114, 117, 128, 190
  as disorder 39–40, 183
  learning anxieties 97–8, 169
assemblies 27, 42, 91, 115, 138, 144
  mental health specific assemblies 145
  power of good 195–6
  PSHE support programme in 187–8
attainment, and mental health 43, 72, 76–7, 80, 83, 111, 148, 150–1, 154, 161, 180
attendance 15, 75, 88–9, 97, 127
  during and after pandemic 22, 26, 53–4, 72, 127, 148–9, 161
  awards 73
  and mental health 21, 30, 31, 33, 72–3, 83
  mentoring 99
  services 172
attention deficit hyperactivity disorder (ADHD) 26, 75–6, 148, 166
autism spectrum disorder (ASD) 97, 117, 142, 148, 164, 166

behaviour 8, 9, 15, 23, 26, 31, 42, 64, 82, 94, 97, 100, 102, 112, 117, 180, 183, 190 *see also* bullying; cognitive behaviour therapy (CBT); oppositional defiant disorder (ODD)
  and adverse childhood experiences 7, 78
  aggressive behaviour 40
  anti-social behaviour 75, 154, 172
  attention-seeking behaviour 133–4
  boys' behaviour issues 131–3
  child's risky online behaviours 153–4
  classroom behaviour 56–7
  coercive behaviour 77
  and communication 21, 118, 120, 123, 129, 142
  disorders 5, 74–6
  dysregulated behaviour 40
  Golden Time, behaviour strategy 13
  intrusive behaviour 58, 156
  and language 80, 95, 149
  and mental health 20–2, 73–4, 111
  misogynistic behaviour 47–8, 104, 129, 131, 144
  policy 29–30, 56, 89
  positive behaviour 13, 16, 20–2
  rewards for good 90, 91
  staff behaviour 89
  support, selective intervention 98–9
  unpredictable 1, 3

belonging, sense of 9, 13–14, 16–17, 24, 91, 196, 202–3
bereavement 40, 78, 82, 100, 116–17, 166
bipolar disorder 2
Blackadder Goes Forth 191
body-shaming language 98
borderline personality disorder 128
Boxall Profiling, software 43
Brain Gym activities 113–14
breathing techniques 103, 185, 197
Brooke, Rupert 191
Brown, B. 112–13
Brymer-Jones, Keith 132
buddy bench provision 35
budgets 54–5, 82, 99, 105, 114, 119, 169, 176, 177
bullying 2–3, 10, 16, 36, 38, 48, 57, 74, 89, 97, 122, 128–9, 131, 140, 154–5, 181

carpet times 183–4
Carrie's War (Bawden) 191
celebration and reward 16, 195
Centre for Social Justice 148
challenging/difficult parents 148, 157–8, 163
charities and third sector organisations 68, 70, 135, 169–73, 196
chemical castration 192
child-centred approach 117
children and adolescent mental health services (CAMHS) 100, 116–17, 157, 176–7
 supervision 160
 support on youth suicide 133–4
 tier services 104, 166–8, 169
children and young people's mental health services (CYPMHS) 166
cognitive behaviour therapy (CBT) 113, 169
cognitive load 55, 64, 127, 140
communication 27, 57, 80, 88, 101–5, 119, 151, 203–4
 and behaviour 21, 118, 120, 123, 142
 communicating with 'why' 13–15, 120, 147
 conversation around mental health 160
 of emotion 129
 empowering children through 136, 139–41
 and language barrier 154–5
 with parents 155, 157–8, 163
 and relationships with external agencies 173–4, 177, 184
 skills 92, 114, 117, 123
 talking with pupils 95–6, 97
community support 170–1, 175, 177
compassionate school 78, 201, 203
conduct disorders (CD) 75, 166
confidentiality 35, 37, 104
context-specific learning 186
coping strategies 116, 131, 139, 169, 190, 197
 coping skills 117, 140
 coping with failure 93
 and resilience 77
cortisol 67–8, 190
counselling 37, 170 *see also* school counsellor; therapies
 services 144
 skills training for children 119
courage 16
Covid pandemic 5, 18, 42, 67, 92, 113, 122, 160, 183, 203
 and academic stress 77, 126–7
 and attendance 22, 72
 impacts on staff mental health 52–3
 lockdown impacts 26, 85, 102–3, 146, 148–9
 long-term impacts of 15, 127
 post-pandemic mental health crisis 10, 21
creativity, boosting 46, 139
culture of noticing 18–21, 44, 76, 79, 100, 125, 188
culture of positive mental health 9–10, 11–15
 beyond school hours 153–4
 context and challenges 17–18
 leading with values 15–16

Meadowbank Primary School (case study) 24–7
myths on mental health and wellbeing 11–13
Parable of the Sower, metaphor for building 10
with parents 147–8
positive behaviour 13, 16, 20–2
and relationships 10–11
safeguarding and attendance 22
school values, leading with 15–16
thinking about creating 23
culture wars, within schools 160
curriculum development 15–16, 30–1, 43, 105, 120, 179–80, 204
arts 190–1
curriculum mapping 24–5
Early Years 182–5
English subject 193–5
good assembly, power of 195–6
history and geography 191–2
mathematics 192–3
mental health in 46, 88, 103, 145, 188
'Our Favourite Five' initiative 25
physical education 188–9
PSHE 47–9, 85, 180–2
science 189–90
thinking about 198–9
cyberbullying 74, 128–9, 153–4, 181

decision-making 16, 78, 81
Department for Education (DfE) 51, 180–1
depression 40, 52, 114, 166, 197
and anxiety 2, 5, 37, 114, 117, 128, 145, 190
leading to suicidal feelings 5, 26, 74, 133, 183
de Souza, Rachel 73
detention 21–2
Dickens, Charles 191–2
digital wellbeing 26, 59, 69, 84
digital learning 179
digital literacy 187
digital safety 47, 48, 132, 137, 172, 182, 196
pandemic impacts on 15, 127–8
safety lessons on 132
social media and phone usage 127–8, 153–4, 172
discrimination 37, 74, 77, 88, 130, 138
domestic violence 76, 77, 97, 102, 129, 171
dopamine 190
drawing and talking therapy 116–17
Dweck, Carol 42, 93

early career teachers (ECTs) 2–3, 27, 54–5, 204
Early Years Foundation Stage (EYFS) 48, 79, 94, 127, 140, 197
mental health and wellbeing in 182–5
settings 84–5, 92, 162
eating disorders 5, 131, 166, 167, 172
educational psychologists 116, 143–4, 145–6, 167, 175
Education Endowment Foundation 150
Education Support 7, 51, 64
intensity of working and moral purpose 67
positive connections and interpersonal relationships 67–8
24-hour helpline 52, 68–70
education welfare officers (EWOs) 73, 172
emotional-based school avoidance (EBSA) 41, 73, 146
emotional literacy support assistants (ELSAs) 35, 99, 115–17, 123, 204
emotional wellbeing impacts, of pupils *see also* abuse
academic stress 126–7
concerns about 'what ifs' 134
cyberbullying 74, 128–9, 153–4, 181
family conflict and instability 117, 129, 166
financial insecurity 40, 78, 126, 129–30, 149
gender identity 130
inequality and discrimination 37, 77, 88, 130, 138
neglect 22, 77, 88, 129, 188

uncertainty about future and
   additional factors for 130–1
emotions 3, 10, 12, 25, 116, 185, 193–4
   and feelings 117, 130, 177, 181–2, 190
   managing and regulating 78, 85, 139
   misunderstanding 41
   positive and negative 42
empathy 1, 6, 8, 16, 20, 35–6, 55, 61,
      112–4, 123, 185, 193, 203–4
   lack of 75
   and trust, promoting 190
endorphins hormones 188–9, 190, 196
entitlement 49, 88, 144, 162–3, 173
Equality Act (2010) 48
Every Child Matters, document 3
evidence-based strategies 83, 113–14,
      118, 160, 167, 168–9
external provision, in mental health
      services 7, 82, 100, 165
   CAMHS 166–8
   communication and relationships
      173–4, 177, 184
   good practice sharing 35, 116,
      150, 174–6
   mental health support teams (MHSTs)
      135, 162, 168–9, 177
   thinking about 176–7
extracurricular activities 91, 145

family conflicts 117, 129, 166
family liaison officer (FLO) 32, 35, 81, 90,
      148, 157
Family Matters programme 148
   case study 152
   parental involvement in
      education 150–1
   parent empowerment
      programme 151–3
   schools and families partnerships
      150
favouritism accusations 56, 57
fear of missing out (FOMO) 127–8
Fight for Young Lives, The (Kemp) 133–5,
      168
fight or flight response 189

financial insecurity 40, 78, 126, 129–
      30, 149
food bank-style support 129, 186
football clubs, as community
      support 170–1
further education (FE) college 18, 66

gang culture 88, 131, 186
GCSE 46, 53, 77, 102, 143, 161
gender identity 130
Girl of Ink and Stars, The (Hargrave) 195
Goldfish Boy, The (Thompson) 195
Goodnight Mr Tom (Magorian) 191
good practice in school 35, 116,
      150, 174–6
Gray, Peter 182–3
Great Pottery Throw Down, The
      (TV show) 132

hand symbol 131
higher-level teaching assistants (HLTAs)
      46–47, 55
high morale 92
Holes (Sachar) 193–4
hormones impacting mental health
      134, 189–90

identification process, of needs and
      concerns
   awareness of staffs 79
   knowing your pupils 80
   knowledge through sociograms 79–80
   Obersee Bilingual School (case
      study) 84–5
   referral pathway and process 80–2
   review and evaluation of
      interventions 82
   thinking about 83–4
independent critical thinkers 161
insomnia 11, 66
intensive provision *see* external provision
intent statement 16, 21, 111, 136–7
intervention maps 81–2, 165
invisible children (Pye) 80
isolation 118

and loneliness 67–8, 112, 181
social isolation 129

Jarrow Crusade, hunger march 191
journalling 139–40

'Keeping children safe in education' document 83
Kemp, Roman 133–5, 168
key performance indicators (KPIs) 161
King, Vanessa 184
knowing and noticing staff 18–20
know your pupils 80, 84

language 54, 80, 107, 118, 151, 198–9
  body language 14, 19, 23, 80, 96, 125, 132, 149
  and challenging stigma 36–7, 65, 120, 138, 196–7
  choice of 95–6, 128
  and communication 154–5, 158–9
  confrontational language 96
  of kindness, Hillborough Junior School case study 121–3
  of mental health 108–9
  negative and inappropriate 26, 39–41, 47, 111–12, 131, 149, 156
  positive language around mental health 20, 41–3, 45, 47–8, 136–8, 169, 175, 189, 204
  positive language of 'five ways to wellbeing' 196–7
  power of 196–7
  skills 116, 117
leadership 10, 13–15, 17, 69, 107, 135–6, 146, 148 *see also* leading and managing positive mental health
  criticism on 60
  mental health lead and senior leadership 6, 13–15, 35, 39, 52, 56, 157, 159, 167–8
  roles and responsibilities of 61–2, 65, 92, 181, 196
  strategies 15, 145
  time 27, 49

  toxic leadership habits 57–8
leading and managing positive mental health
  Bramley Sunnyside Junior School (case study) 46–9
  building a team 31–3
  data collection and interpretation 43–4
  language, developing appropriate 38–43
  psychological safe space and provision 34–6, 108, 112, 134, 139, 148
  stigma, as a challenge 36–9, 65, 120, 138, 196–7
  strategic plan development 33–4
  team leading for change 30–1
  thinking about 45
  whole-school approach benefits 29–30
learning disability 164
learning opportunity 130, 145, 179
Legacy (Kerr) 14
LEGO® Therapy 99, 117–18
LGBTQIA+ community 25, 77, 130, 171, 186, 195
listening, value of 19, 32, 38, 84, 96, 110, 112, 122, 137, 154, 184
local safeguarding board 173
lockdowns, impact of 26, 53, 72, 85, 92, 97, 103–4, 146, 148
London Eye Mystery, The (Dowd) 193
loneliness 67–8, 112, 181

Macbeth (Shakespeare) 194
massage session 12
MAT 16, 81–2, 99, 107, 174, 175
meditation 11–12
meet and greet culture, at gate 19–20
mental disorder 4–5, 83
Mental Health Awareness Week 187
mental health champions 138
mental health first-aiders (MHFA) 38, 99, 103, 114–15
mental health services 69, 100, 131, 135, 169 *see also* external provision, in mental health services

mental health support teams (MHSTs) 135, 162, 168–9, 177
mentally healthy pupils 71
midday supervisor 17, 31–2, 51, 115
Midsummer Night's Dream, A (Shakespeare) 194
Mind (charity) 170
mindfulness 12, 103, 113, 145, 182, 185
Mindfulness for Learning 182
Mind Lancashire 170
mindset
    fixed 93
    growth 42, 76, 93, 145
    positive 32, 38, 42, 111
Mind Work Matters 150
mirroring techniques 25, 117
misogynistic attitudes 47–8, 104, 129, 131, 144
Mizen Foundation 172
mock inspections (Mocksteds) 54
Molly Rose Foundation 128, 172
mood improvement 139
myths on mental health and wellbeing 11–13

neglect 22, 77, 88, 129, 188
Nen and the Lonely Fisherman (Eagleton) 195
neurodivergent children 198
neurodiversity 36–7, 40, 65, 77, 80, 198
newly qualified teacher (NQT) *see* early career teachers (ECTs)
newsletters 136, 151, 154
NHS
    CAMHS, services of 166–7
    long-term plan 164
    mental health provision 169
    resources 157
    statistics 131
Nicomachean Ethics (Aristotle) 205
Noughts and Crosses (Blackman) 195
nurture training and provision 118–19
Nurture UK 118

Obama, Barack 132
obsessive-compulsive disorder (OCD) 166, 195
off-the-shelf lesson 8, 18, 186
Ofsted 24, 29, 69–70, 121, 122, 145, 163
    impacts on staff mental health 53–4
    inspections 174
online safety 172 *see also* safety
open-door policy 19, 145–6
open-ended questioning 117
oppositional defiant disorder (ODD) 75–6
Optimus Wellbeing Award 105
oracy skills 137
Our Favourite Five 25, 195
Owen, Wilfred 191
oxytocin 68, 190

paediatric first aid training 114
panic disorder 39, 115, 125, 133
parenting skills 26–7
parent–school relationships 129
parent voice 174–5
    barriers to engagement 154–5
    effective family engagement 149
    Family Matters programme 148, 150–3
    parent WhatsApp groups, challenges 155–6
    positive culture with parents 147–8
    strategies to engage parents 156–7
    thinking about 158–9
    wellbeing outside school, promoting 153–4
pastoral support 30–31, 95, 117, 141, 145–6, 154, 187, 195–6
pastoral support plan (PSP) 81
Peace Keepers 85
peer influences and friendships 91
peer pressure 16, 74, 88, 112, 127–8, 130, 132
perseverance 16, 180
personal, social and health education (PSHE) curriculum 2–3, 25, 30–2, 47–9, 85, 98, 122, 137
    Association 48, 186
    content delivery 187–8

context-specific learning 186
in England 180–1
in Northern Ireland curriculum 181–2
in Scotland 181
in Wales 182
personal values 15, 154
physical chastisement 2
physical first-aid training 114
physical health 2, 62–4, 71, 76, 158–9, 180
Pig Heart Boy (Blackman) 195
Place2Be 3, 102, 105
planning, preparation and assessment time (PPA) 27, 49, 55, 64, 79
play therapy 117–18
pornography 128–9, 132
positive attitude 93
positive classroom management 90–1
positive habit 179–80
post-traumatic stress disorder (PTSD) 166, 191
practitioners 42, 113, 116, 118–19, 173, 174, 204, 207–10
CAMHS 167–8
clinical lead practitioners 168–9
in cognitive behavioural therapy 99
education mental health practitioners 168–9
and school relationships 173–4
thrive practitioner 99
prejudicial attitudes 8, 20, 36, 37, 77, 112, 196
problem-solving 78, 139
protective factors in school environment 2, 47, 74, 78, 88, 90–3, 100, 145, 153
psychiatry outpatient service 167
psychological safe space 34–6, 108, 112, 134, 139, 148
psychological safety 74, 104, 108
psychosis 114
psychotherapist 123
pupil parliament *see* school council
pupil premium support 162
pupil progress meetings 43, 77
pupil-to-pupil interaction 41
Pye, James 80

quantitative and qualitative data, for academic progress 43–4, 99
quiet quitting 62

Random Acts of Kindness Day 187
referral 35, 116, 177
pathways and process 78, 80–2, 90, 98, 100, 145, 165, 167, 176
pupil referral units 172
self-referral 144
reflection 82, 108, 160, 162, 195
and evaluation, life skills 93, 202
in journal 139, 141
reflective ability 91, 93, 140, 203
regulation
emotional regulation 78, 116–7, 139, 152
self-regulation 78, 95, 145, 180
zones of regulation 40, 145
relationship breakdown 63–4, 88, 171
relationships, sex and health education (RSHE) 171–2
relationships and sex education (RSE) programme 30, 122, 180
resentment of staffs 56
resilience 16, 20, 36, 89, 91, 93, 98, 101, 135, 176, 193, 195–6
barriers to 112
and coping strategies 77, 140
lack of 36, 109, 120
during pandemic period 15, 42
parents 26
of pupil 8, 30, 74, 98, 186
of staff 61, 63
responsive practices 38
restorative practices 41
Rethinking Education conference (2023) 161
rewards 30, 90–1
risk factors in school environment 2, 74, 76, 88–9, 98, 101
Romeo and Juliet (Shakespeare) 194

Sad Book (Rosen) 195
safeguarding 8, 9, 19, 21–3, 29–30, 48, 82, 88–9, 94, 110, 188

safeguarding software 20, 44, 145
Safer Internet Day 187
safety 77, 88, 93–4, 98, 113–4, 118
   digital 47–8, 132, 137, 172, 182, 196
   plan or measure 104–5, 115
   psychological safety 74, 104, 108
SATs examination 24, 53, 126
schizophrenia 2
school council 92, 122, 136–7
school counsellor 68–9, 81–2, 85, 99, 119, 134, 143–4, 167, 174, 175
school development plans 15, 33, 82, 107, 145, 204
school–family relationship 97
school information management systems 72
school nursing service 172
school-parents relationship 150
   barriers to 154–5
   case study interview on 159–64
school refusal 41, 73 *see also* emotional-based school avoidance (EBSA)
Scream, The (Munch) 191
scripted conversations 20, 105, 183
scripted lessons 186
selective intervention in school 98–100, 165
self-awareness 103, 113, 119, 139
self-care 2, 12, 15, 181
self-harm 26, 80, 104–5, 128–9, 131, 166, 188 *see also* suicide
SENDCo 3, 32, 35, 81, 99, 107, 116, 121, 157
serotonin 190
service-level agreements (SLAs). 100, 119
Sissay, Lemn 195
SMART goals 33
social exclusion 36, 57, 80
social media 10, 58, 66, 88, 93, 171
   activities by Andrew Tate 131–2
   as communication channel 151, 156–7, 174
   cyberbullying 128–9
   issues/impacts 48, 105, 112, 127–9, 133, 144, 153–4, 160, 175

scaremongering 130
stigma in mental health 153–4
sociogram 58, 60–1, 97, 142
   for children 140–1
   knowledge through 79–80
special educational needs and disabilities (SEND) 24, 123
specific first-aid skills 115
spiritual, moral, social and cultural development (SMSC) 2–3, 186
Sports Premium funding 170
Square Peg 7, 159
staff mental health, negative impacts on 52–8
   budget restraints and additional responsibilities 54–5
   Covid-19 pandemic and its after-effects 52–3
   Ofsted inspections 53–4
   poor classroom behaviour 56–7
   staff absence and shortage 55–6
   toxic workplace culture 57–8
staff mental health and wellbeing 44, 137, 145–6, 169
   life events in lives of 63–4
   menopause awareness 62–3
   menstrual and reproductive health 63
   positive culture for 49
   prioritisation of individual 61–2
   raising concerns and complaints 89–90
   sociograms 60–1
   staff behaviour 89
   staff survey 58–60
   Teacher Wellbeing Index (TWIX) 7, 11, 51–2, 54, 57, 60, 66–70
   thinking about 64–5
staff professional development and training 20, 41, 100, 107–8
   counselling for children 119
   cultural shift to whole-school approach 111–14
   drawing and talking therapy 116–17
   emotional literacy support assistant (ELSA) training 115–16
   evidence-based strategies 113–14

know your class 18
language of mental health 108–9
mental health first aid (MHFA) training 38, 99, 103, 114–15
nurture training and provision 118–19
play therapy 117
Richard Branson philosophy of training staff 122
thinking about 119–20
value of talking and listening 110
whole-staff training 111
staffroom gossip 56, 57–8, 62, 65, 160, 163
staff–student relationships 74, 90
Start with Why (Sinek) 13
STEM subjects 143
stigma 3, 8, 20, 78, 104, 107, 109, 111–12, 133, 162, 170, 180, 197
language and challenging 36, 65, 120, 138, 196–7
mental health stigma 36–7, 45, 130–1, 169
proactive approach to challenging 37–9
reducing 111–12, 113
storytelling 116, 117
strategic thinking 13–15, 16
Street Child (Doherty) 191–2
strengths and difficulties questionnaires (SDQs) 44, 99
stress 11, 12, 54, 98, 103, 189, 196 *see also* post-traumatic stress disorder (PTSD)
academic stress 126–7, 169
and anxiety 39, 64, 139, 197
chronic 66, 68
cortisol, stress hormone 67
distress 2, 40, 41, 152, 160
impacts 16
on staffs 55, 56, 58–61, 65, 69, 112
student agency and wellbeing 144–5
student voice, enabling 47, 112, 122
Altrincham Grammar School for Girls (case study) 143–6
contributing on whole-school ethos 135–9

empowering pupil through communication 139–41
issues specific to needs of boys 131–3
power of voice 125–6
pupil's emotional wellbeing, impacts on 126–31
thinking about 141–2
substance abuse 22, 76, 78, 129, 131
disorders 114
local substance misuse services 172
suicide 5, 52, 67–8, 74, 80, 89, 128–9, 190, 192, 194 *see also Fight for Young Lives, The* (Kemp); Molly Rose Foundation; self-harm
supervision 69, 116, 123, 145–6, 160
surveys 43, 45, 52, 99, 142, 152, 156, 157 *see also* Teacher Wellbeing Index (TWIX)
anonymity in 59
mental health and wellbeing survey 12, 58–60, 144–5
parental survey 34, 44, 148
staff survey 33–4, 58–60

talking, value of 38, 85, 88, 90, 95, 110 *see also* communication; talking therapy
talking therapy 116–17, 170
targeted support and provisions 87
intensive provision 7, 82, 100, 165
managing transitions 48, 51, 87, 96–8, 118, 146, 188
offered by school to pupils 93–6
protective factors in school environment 2, 47, 74, 78, 88, 90–3, 100, 145, 153
risk factors in school environment 2, 74, 76, 88–90, 98, 101
selective provision 98–100, 165
Stratford School Academy (case study) 102–5
thinking about 101–2
universal provision 88, 101, 120, 144, 165, 167, 187, 199
teacher subject knowledge 179

teaching assistants 12, 31, 33, 51, 54–5, 61, 69, 79, 90, 99, 108, 193 *see also* higher-level teaching assistants (HLTAs)
tender organisation, for healthy relationships 171–2
therapies 37, 46
   cognitive behaviour therapy (CBT) 113, 169
   drawing and talking therapy 116–17
   family therapy 167
   individual therapy 157, 166
   play therapy 117–18
Thrive (software) 43
Thriving Schools programme 170
toxic masculinity 132
transition in education 48, 51, 87, 96–8, 118, 146, 188
   breaktime and inter-classroom transitions 98
   in-year transitions 97
   transition between lessons 97–8
   transition between schools 97
trauma 22, 41, 77, 78, 94, 100, 116–18, 123, 159
triage system of assessment 81
triangle of community 10, 32, 147, 157
trusted support for children 94–5
tutor programme 32

unconscious bias 38, 107, 111–12
United Nations Convention of the Rights of the Child (UNICEF, 1990) 136

universal provision, mental health support 88, 101, 120, 144, 165, 167, 187, 199
upper pay scale (UPS) 54

values statement, at school 15–16, 27, 42
verbal insults 36, 98
Vision for Luton 2040 122–3

wellbeing ambassadors 137–8, 144
Wellbeing Curriculum, The (2021) 6, 42, 92
Wellbeing Toolkit, The (2019) 3, 6, 57–8, 148
wellbeing Wednesdays 11–13, 145
whole-school approach 7, 29–30, 88–9, 110–12, 118–19, 168–9, 180, 196
whole-school ethos 119
   intent statement 16, 21, 111, 136, 137
   mental health champions, role of 138
   school council or pupil parliament 92, 122, 136–7
   wellbeing ambassadors role 137–8, 144
Wind in the Willows, The (Grahame) 193
Women's Aid organisation 171–2
World Health Organisation 1–2, 37
   definition of mental health 1, 17
   mental disorder, report on 5
World Kindness Day 187
worry boxes provision 35

young carers support 172
YoungMinds 133, 135, 170
young violence reduction services 172

Zephaniah, Benjamin 195

Praise for
The School Mental Health Toolkit

The School Mental Health Toolkit not only provides you with the knowledge but the practical next steps to improving provision in your school. A must for any school leader. **Ben Hobbis, Primary School Middle Leader and Founder of the Step Up Network CIC, @MrBHobbis**

The School Mental Health Toolkit provides practical support for school leaders and teachers to prioritise wellbeing and embed it in their practice through the helpful 'THINK' (Time, Holistic, Inclusive, Non-judgmental, Knowledgeable) acronym. **Ben Levinson OBE, Director of School and Trust Improvement and Executive Headteacher, @mrlev**

Andrew Cowley does it again! This is another excellent resource for schools that want to embed an effective whole school approach to mental health and wellbeing. Not only does Andrew's wisdom shine through but the wide range of school case studies bring the ideas to life and show other schools a way forward. **Adrian Bethune, Founder of Teachappy, @AdrianBethune**

The breadth and depth of diverse perspectives in this new book makes it an invaluable guide for Mental Health First Aiders looking to create strategic and operational impact within their educational setting. **Bukky Yusuf, Senior Leader and Educational Consultant, @bukkyyusufofficial**

Andrew Cowley doesn't just walk the walk, he does it with compassion, kindness and authority. A must read for anyone involved with Mental Health in education! **Kerry Bridges, Mental Health and Wellbeing Lead, @CSandL**

As a leader of wellbeing in international schools, I found this book affirming and motivating, emphasising compassion, cultural understanding, and practical strategies to create inclusive wellbeing initiatives for school communities. **Rhiannon Phillips-Bianco, Head of Wellbeing, Globeducate.**

This book is a must have. Andrew's expertise is evident, and up to date research is presented in an accessible way. Andrew understands the context that busy practitioners are working in and offers practical strategies, engaging case studies and carefully thought out opportunities to reflect. **Sarah Watkins, Lecturer and author, @mini_lebowski**

From staffroom to classroom, this treasure chest of golden nuggets transforms mental health support from theory to action. The practical handbook that every modern school needs! **Aimee Presnall, Founder of Well-Nest**